Seen in
the Mirror

Seen in
the Mirror

Things from the Cartin Collection

David Zwirner Books

Acknowledgments

David Zwirner wishes to thank Mickey Cartin, without whom this exhibition
and publication would not have been possible, as well as Steven Holmes and
David Leiber for their close collaboration and support. We would also like to
thank Luke Syson for his engaging text.

For their work on the exhibition, we are grateful to Cy Amundson, Stephen
Arnold, Kristina Berger, Susan Cernek, Stacy Cerullo, Allison Chipak, David
Kennedy Cutler, Kit Fretz, Collin Hatton, Maris Hutchinson, Octavia Knox,
Paula Kroll, Vida Lercari, Julia Lukacher, Ryan Markgraf, Kerry McFate,
Ellis Edwards Reese, Kelly Reynolds, Bronwyn Roe, Max Rosenberg, Elsa
Smith, Virginia Stroh, Jessica Zegans, and Lucas Zwirner.

For their work on the publication, thanks are due to Sergio Brunelli, Luke Chase,
Fabio Ferrandini, Zeno Ferrandini, Doro Globus, James Goggin, Elizabeth
Gordon, Amy Hordes, Daniela Ioan, Jessica Palinski, Mari Perina, Molly Stein,
Jules Thomson, and Joey Young.

I want to acknowledge here the many people who have enriched my life in so many and varied ways. Many of those named here have had a direct and profound influence on me, shaped my views of the world and my reaction to it, and shared with me their joy, humor, love, pain, and wisdom. Others have influenced me in extraordinary ways without even a single meeting. By that I mean that our lives took place at different moments in time, and instead I was able to meet them and feel their pulse through what they left behind: their paintings, words, sounds, and triumphs. All of those named here have given me hope and, to the extent that I possess it, the courage to keep finding my way.

They are: Anne Aaron, Hank Aaron, Josef Albers, Francis Alÿs, Carlos Basualdo, Nicholas Baume, Wallace Berman, Forrest Bess, Till-Holger Borchert, James Brown, Miller Brown, Lloyd H. Bugbee, Alaina Cartin, Andy Cartin, Arnold Cartin, Dylan Cartin, Edith Cartin, Ella Cartin, Fanchon Cartin, Greg Cartin, Henry Cartin, Janice Cartin, Morris Cartin, James Cohan, Joe Coleman, Bob Compagna, Gene Conley, James Corcoran, Joseph Cornell, Dennis Coscina, Walter Cronkite, R. Crumb, Bob Dylan, Jim Eacott, Ralph Erickson, Richard Feigen, Spencer Finch, Edward Fisher, Paul Edward Fitzpatrick, Tony Fitzpatrick, Walton Ford, Nicholas Fox Weber, Gregory Gillespie, Edith Goldberg, Mark Greenwold, Jörn Günther, Jeffrey Hatten, Linda Cartin Hatten, Mark Hatten, Richie Havens, Jonathan Hill, Megumi Hill, Paul Hilli, Morris Hirshfield, Steven Holmes, Sam Hyman, Alfred Jensen, John Kane, Danny Katz, On Kawara, Phyllis Kind, Martin Luther King Jr., Harvey Knowles, Paul Laffoley, Charles LeDray, David Leiber, Steven Leiber, Carol LeWitt, Sol LeWitt, Mark Lombardi, Rachel Maddow, Marcus Marschall, Agnes Martin, Tony Meier, Sam Messer, Andrea Miller-Keller, Wes Mills, Donald Moffett, Giorgio Morandi, Fabrizio Moretti, Larry Muzroll, Hugo Nathan, Carter Nelson, John Ollman, Roman Opałka, Katie Parfenoff, Peter Pasciucco, Giacomo Pozzi, Martin Puryear, Joel Quenneville, Martín Ramírez, Tom Regan, James Rondeau, Henri Rousseau, Bertrand Russell, Bill Russell, Tom Sachs, Adam Schiff, Elmar Seibel, Andrew Sendor, Linda Sherby, Cary Smith, Gian Enzo Sperone, Myron Stout, Jack Tilton, Fred Tomaselli, Ben van Berkel, Maurice Wade, Whitney Ward, H. C. Westermann, Martin Wilner, Allan Lundie Wise, Ludwig Wittgenstein, Adolf Wölfli, Albert York, and David Zwirner.

Mickey Cartin

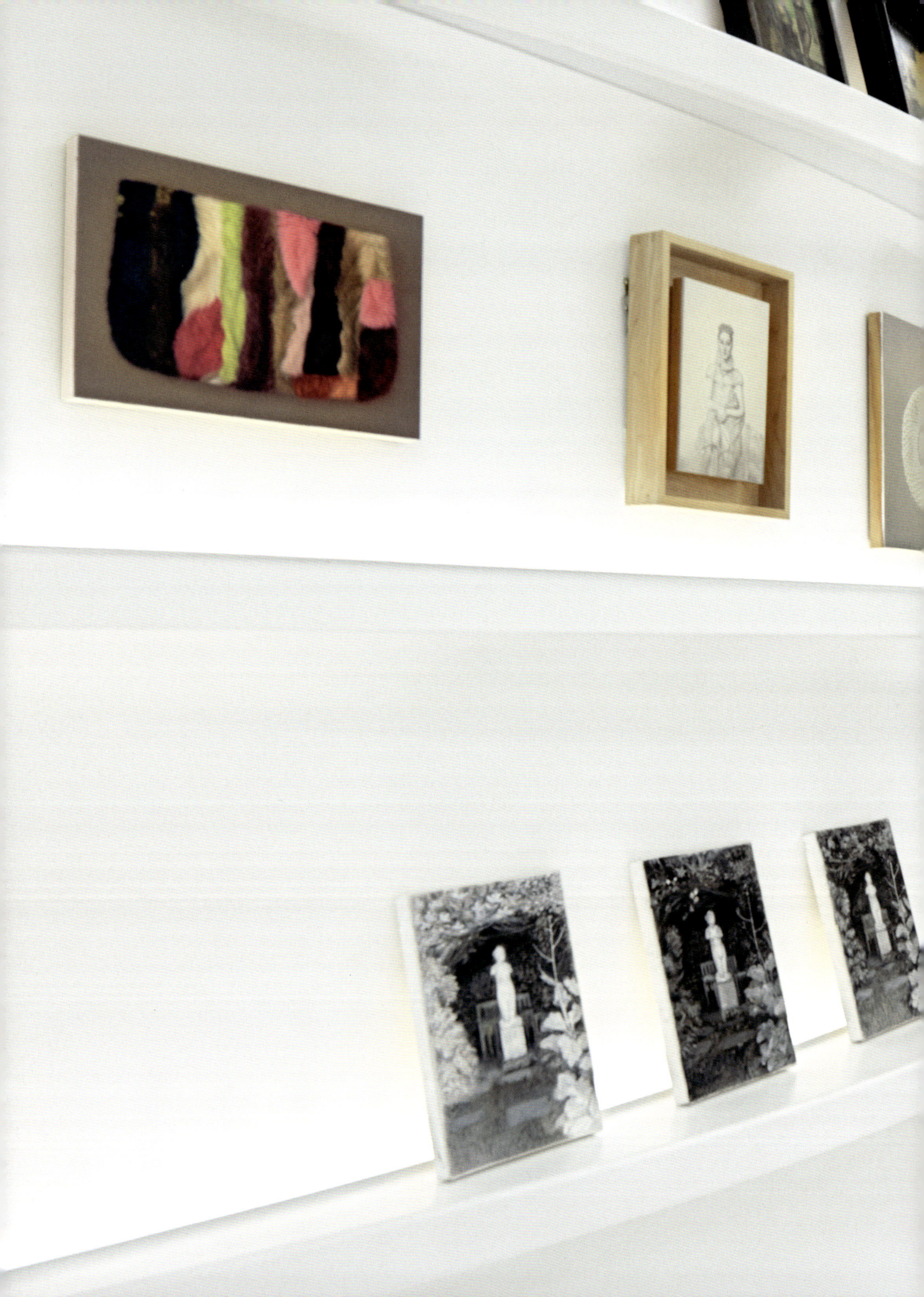

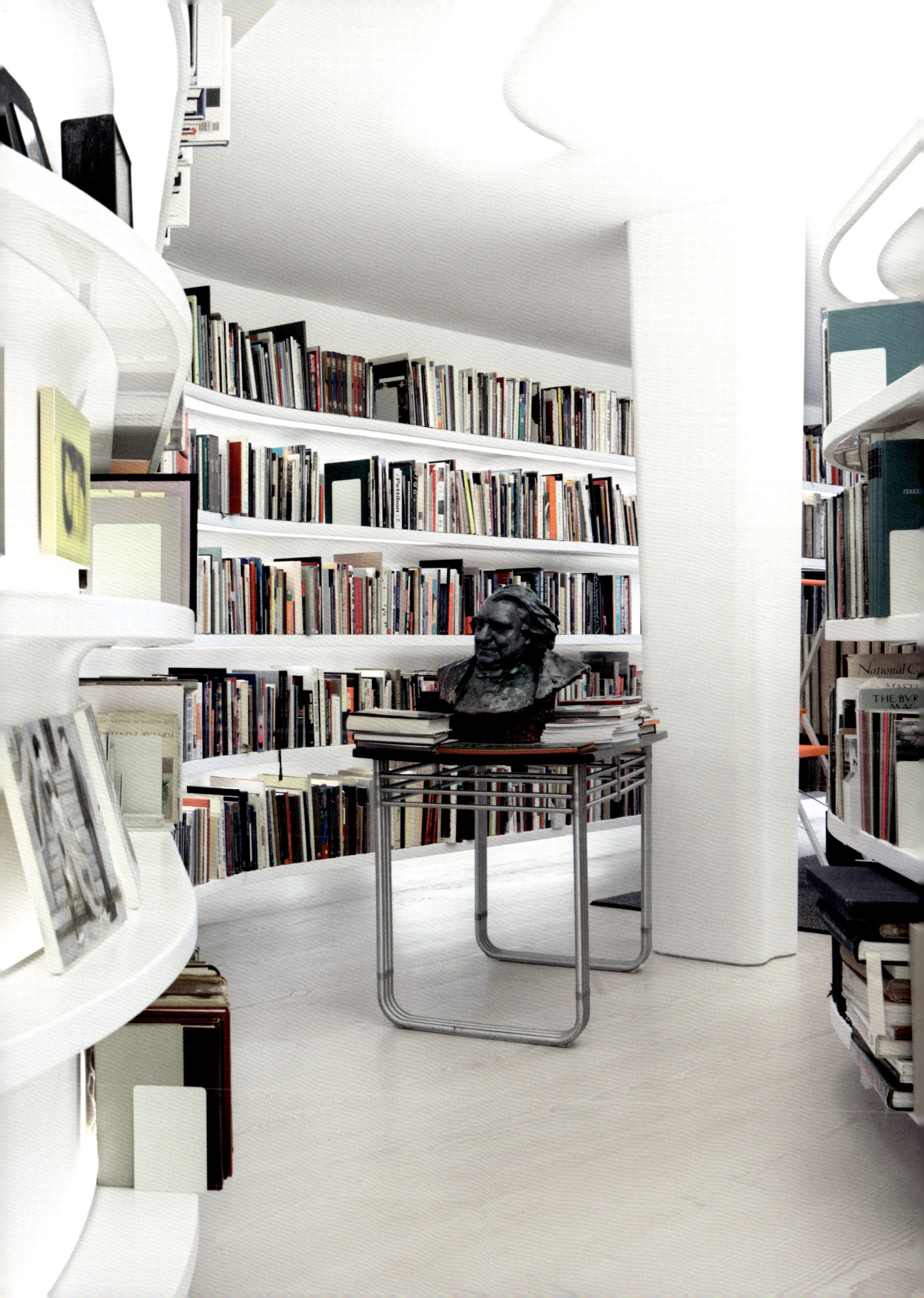

Luke Syson

An Intensity of Vision

Mickey Cartin is par excellence a collector.

Collectors are solitary. They sit alone at the center of the universe of the things they have gathered, coolly, logically . . . instinctively . . . compulsively, obsessively. A collection radiates from that one person, with every object or work of art now relating individually to the woman or man who has chosen it, who has perceived its particular meaning within the mass.

Collectors are connected. Their acts of acquisition are collaborative, networked within a community of experts and dealers and agents, advisers, official and unofficial, and—friendly or competitive—fellow collectors. And, if the collection is of modern art, of artists.

Collectors are connective. They make links. The works they own are joined up and arranged into groups and sequences: histories, families, series, schools, species, patterns, categories, hierarchies. That mapping might still be highly intuitive, the processes destined always to remain open-ended, or it can help us determine order in the chaos of existence, and to understand the governing principles of common structures, of resemblances. That kind of sequence and grouping might even, on accession, be completable, and it can provide the spaces and logics, the taxonomies, in which to insert the things that are as yet unknown.

In other words, collections almost always provide methods by which we can better understand the collector and, simultaneously, the universe (however that is defined) and our place in it. Sixteenth- and seventeenth-century European cabinets of curiosities—those omnium-gatherums of the natural and the man-made—valued the rare, the precious, the unusual and the exotic, the exquisite masterpiece and the freak of nature. The cabinet absorbed the spirit of the princely treasury, the protected place for precious stones and metals worked by great artisans into marvelous jewels. So it was in the cabinet that the unicorn's horn and the made-up mermaid might jostle for space with textiles and carvings from Africa and the Americas; where the nautilus shell could be honored with an elaborate silver mount; where a tiny masterpiece, a painting on copper or parchment, for example, could be celebrated as a work of exemplary genius.

Specialist Enlightenment collections of the kind that gave rise to modern museums and the separated departments within them imposed discipline. Indeed, they created disciplines: paleontology, numismatics, botany, the history of art itself. Stones, butterflies, prints, miniatures, medals. These series usually posit forms of progress, processes of one thing begetting another as complex and sequential as any Old Testament genealogy. They measure evolutions. They define. They insist upon system. And, above all, they reflect our world back to us in ways that find—or even impose—order.

And collections are also acts of autobiography. They chart collectors' encounters and flowing enthusiasms, their crazes perhaps, their passions always, whether permanent or fleeting. Thus they're cabinets of a person's own curiosities, in the metaphorical sense of the word. They're both private and revealing, mirrors of the self.

Mickey Cartin's collection does all these things and it does them together, in ways that are deliberate and instinctive. Certainly, it has its sequences and groups, its things staged in cases, some of them made or made up by artists, for example, by the twentieth-century artists Alighiero Boetti, Joseph Cornell, or Ed Ruscha. Or by the mid-sixteenth-century painter of the amazing *Wunderzeichenbuch*—the Augsburg *Book of Miracles*. And Cartin extracts works from sequences artists have envisaged. One thing can still beget another, and he is the Linnaeus, the Bernard Berenson, of the human creative interior made visible. His collection charts the places from which our creativity emerges: the visionary and the insane, the idiosyncratic and perceptive, the illusory, from moments of chance, intensity, imitation, and insight. He wants to know artists (he feels compelled to talk to them, a lot, and perhaps even when they're dead), insiders and outsiders, in the academy or in the studio, working at the kitchen table, in a field, or in an asylum. He wants to see beneath their surfaces and to see how they see beneath surfaces, to analyze their subjectivity and their obsessiveness, perceived here as complementary opposites. Cartin's pattern making is consequently wonderfully unstable and unsettling. It breaks down hierarchies and it makes discoveries, not least of artists themselves. His chains of being are often dreamlike; his mirrors can be misty.

Let us think then about the artists whose works are represented in Cartin's collection, what kinds of things they have made, and what their individual outputs put together might—just might—tell all of us, rather than just Cartin himself. What, I should ask more simply, have they told me?

Mickey Cartin's organized, disorganizing self-portrait contains many self-portraits, images of *Selbst*. I find in these works a useful starting point, a kind of center to the collection. Josef Albers, Giorgio de Chirico, Otto Dix, Vilhelm Hammershøi, Peder Krøyer, and Max Liebermann are all giants of late nineteenth- and twentieth-century art, but not necessarily figures who fit into the too-easy sequence of modernism, the traditional tracking of art's *translatio imperii* from Paris to New York. John Kane is, as the artist himself explains in his title, "Seen in the Mirror" (p. 146). But these are all pictures that are about much more than mirroring mere physical appearance. They are self-analyses, acts of significant self-revelation. A painting of an artist is not just a surface image; it can be an opening up, *A Doorway* (for example) *to Joe* (Coleman) (p. 66). These pictures reflect, but they penetrate, too.

They can also distort. Cartin seems also to be interested in partial or unreliable witnessing, in object making that leads us somewhere but also misleads. Tom Sachs, for example, makes a Mondrian from gaffer tape and plywood (p. 158). Victoria Gitman creates a series of Beauties, painstakingly rendering in oils the effects of graphite in the drawings of women by Ingres and the other old masters she copies. Cartin has extracted just one of this series for his collection, putting it into a new set of sequences. So our expected realities disintegrate almost as quickly as they are established. Series can be broken up, we are reminded. Meanings change. This is a collection that is profoundly uninterested in quotidian experience. It rejects the impersonal, the rule-bound. As an aim for painting, observing or recording isn't nearly enough.

     Luke Syson

Artists' self-portraits extend, of course, far beyond the painting of themselves in mirrors. If an artist chooses, he can reveal himself as much or as little as he wants in works of all kinds. These are the artists whom Cartin wants to get to know. And sometimes his choices are less than obvious. Albrecht Dürer, for example, was a Renaissance rationalist seeking rules that would lead to the depiction of ideal human proportion and investigating the microscopic details of plants or an animal's fur. But the two prints that have caught Cartin's eye show a more mystical Dürer. Or rather an artist whose scientific looking was at the service of something larger, as he envisaged the ways in which the miraculous can be interwoven, contained within, or sit alongside the apparently workaday. In one print (p. 74), the appearance of a crucifix between the antlers of a stag, encountered while out hunting, seems mythical. In the other work (p. 75), the birth of Christ happens in a corner, tucked away under peeling paint and crumbling plaster, while someone draws water from a well outside.

Josef Albers, at first sight, might seem to be another coolheaded analyst. But his theory of color actually critiques or transcends the scientific. "In visual perception," he wrote, "a color is almost never seen as it really is—as it physically is. This fact makes color the most relative medium in art. In order to use color effectively it is necessary to recognize that color deceives continually."[1] More deceit. More mysticism. More transcendence. And a system provided for all three.

"This is not a seascape" is inscribed on a work by the performer, philosopher, and painter Thierry De Cordier, labeling what seems to us exactly that, an image of the seas—albeit a grandly turbulent and chillingly empty one. He means, I think, that he is setting out to paint something much bigger than simply what waves, water, and sea-foam look like—that this is an emotional and imaginative representation of the great forces of nature, swirling, powerful, more enormous than even the sublime. He is imaging Mer-mère. Lucas Arruda paints, he says, states of mind rather than landscapes as such. And for Joseph Yoakum, once a circus runaway, providing multiple unreliable origin stories, and only working intensively toward the end of his life in the late 1960s, Nature and God were the same thing. He had traveled, or at least that's what he said, and his landscapes are identified with real places. But they are fantastic, conjured, the names taken from his atlas and his *Encyclopedia Britannica*. His own art-historical classification is—rather drearily I think—as an outsider artist. I don't think Cartin is particularly interested in that taxonomy—one that excludes what it pretends to embrace.

Cartin's collection instead reveals all three artists as players within a continuum, successors to painters such as the extraordinary nineteenth-century German artist Carl Gustav Carus, or Peder Balke, a Norwegian urban idealist and creator of intensely worked panels of sea and cliffs, of moonlight bursting through clouds, of Scandinavian Sturm und Drang. Carus is another particularly fascinating figure from the past who transcended his own rationalism to take great imaginative leaps into the unknown. Carl Jung stated that it was Carus who originated the idea of the unconscious as an essential part of the human psyche. He was a precise scientist—an obstetrician and the first

1   Josef Albers, "Introduction," in *Interaction of Color* (New Haven, Connecticut: Yale University Press, 1963), p. 1.

observer of the vertebrate archetype, so important for the theory of evolution. But he also invented the concept of *Erdlebenbildkunst*—the pictorial art of the life of the earth—in which the inner workings of geology were to be expressed as a more than Romantic vision. The results are thrilling.

Cartin's painters are uncanonical. In a way, they, too, have been overlooked, and this is a collection that makes the less noticed precious. Some indeed may perform as artistic curiosities, as freaks and one-offs—the bezoar stones and bearded ladies of the history of art—but our task is to see their larger significance. Charles LeDray makes collections—and he makes the objects in them—of the pointlessly little, as exhibited in his huge ceramic miniatures installation (p. 63), or by replicating the displayed detritus of the homeless. Ed Ruscha, in 1969, classified a series of stains (pp. 94–95). They both remind us of the power of the apparently trivial, or the disregarded.

And, in parallel, indeed as a kind of counterbalance or corollary, Cartin's collection proposes taxonomies of the visionary, the illusory, the prophetic, the dreamt, the monstrous, and the miraculous. Joachim di Fiore was an early medieval interpreter of prophecy and a great and influential apocalyptic thinker. Though his writings were roundly condemned—by Thomas Aquinas no less—they went on being copied and imitated for centuries after his death, as in Cartin's mid-Quattrocento manuscript by a pseudo-Joachim, which is illustrated with the impossible made real (pp. 174–175). And the presence in the collection of a *Resurrection of Christ* by the anonymous Master of the Virgo inter Virgines (p. 153) reminds us of the enormous miracle inherent in this much-painted, taken-for-granted scene. They're the historical preface to all kinds of vision in the collection.

This is a collection that is therefore carefully calibrated to bring out the marvelous, the exceptional, and the portentous in works that in more ordinary contexts might be seen as small acts of artistic peculiarity. Michele Pace del Campidoglio's monumental hound becomes odder, larger in our memory and imagination. Carl Dahl's ships become monstrous foreshortened hulks, vast and weirdly unfamiliar (see pp. 122, 123). Fernand Khnopff's portrait of a sweet little girl turns out to be Comte Roger van der Straeten-Ponthoz (p. 141). This is a way of looking, of understanding otherwise mundane things as all separately extraordinary. It's a way of responding to art that, in Cartin's collection, can even incorporate the printmaking of Rembrandt (see pp. 135, 148, 150). In these prints, Rembrandt's elderly sitters are imbued with such an intensity that they become more than themselves. Cecilia Edefalk's sequence of statuary paintings floats into our consciousness like a recurring dream (see p. 70).

A dream? Or an Elysium? The context of this collection restores the visionary to the use of a gold ground in a medieval Italian painting by Giovenale da Orvieto. The *Mystical Marriage of Saint Catherine* becomes mystical indeed. We are in no doubt as to the heavenly setting, and it is fascinating and provocative to see Christian legend treated as the equivalent of the more personal belief systems that spur artists. It's enormously stimulating, too, to trace a thread between primitive panel painting to Albert York (see pp. 124, 125)—another hidden-away, overlooked artist. He is a wonderful discovery within Cartin's collection, set on making an earthly paradise. And he is another artist

      Luke Syson

whose pictures have the strange, extra reality of the dream. Even Giorgio Morandi's potentially solidly grounded still lifes become transcendent and indeterminate (see pp. 90, 91). The unreality of painting itself is heightened here.

Begets. This collection begets ideas, reveries, and it goes into unexpected territory, makes unexpected leaps. I would not have expected to reencounter Algernon Newton here. And yet his description of strong shadows in a wide street is revealed as beautiful and strange (p. 78). There is beauty to be found everywhere, even in a gasometer, he thought, depending on the artist's vision. Vision again—and still used in a way that can contain the visionary.

Newton seems, at first sight, the absolute artistic antithesis of Adolf Wölfli, who, sexually abused as a child, became an abuser of children and was confined to a psychiatric hospital, where he had hallucinations and where he drew intensively, minutely, insanely. The lunatic as artist. The artist as lunatic. Is there always real space between them? In Cartin's example (p. 109), Wölfli describes a ladder to heaven—as intricate as any medieval jewel, and perhaps containing another self-portrait in place of the expected Jacob.

Forrest Bess is a key protagonist here. He also had visions, which he turned into paintings, images with symbols that could, he believed, transport the viewer to different states of consciousness (see pp. 100, 101). A convinced disciple of Jung, a believer in the power of Australian Aboriginal rituals (as he understood them), he underwent self-performed surgery to turn himself into a pseudohermaphrodite, to arrive at what he believed was a perfect state. Another lunatic? Or a kind of prophet? These artists appear the antithesis, as I say, of Newton, but actually they share with him an intensity of vision. All of Cartin's artists have that.

This is a collection of works concerned with the psychological, the metaphysical, the pathological. And it ventures, I'd venture, into the adventurous realm of pataphysics, the parodic neo-science of imaginary solutions invented by Alfred Jarry. There's a clue in Cartin's painting of Wittgenstein by Thomas Chimes, one of a series of forty-eight panel portraits that Chimes began with Jarry himself, which grew rationally at first in depicting members of Jarry's cultural circle and then pseudoscientifically through the artist's own associations. This is a pseudophilosophy that goes beyond the metaphysical to explore (unsystematically? logically? both?) the virtual or imaginary nature of things as revealed by heightened vision of poetry or love or science, which can be grasped and lived as real.

Mickey Cartin is a collector. This is his collection. But this feels different from other, more standard collections of things or images. "Roll up! Roll up!" he seems to cry. "Welcome to my imaginarium, to my cabinet-circus of artists and visionaries and lunatics! Watch, relax, while they take you to my brilliantly constructed universe of the spirit!" So we are tempted to ask: Is that how he lives his life, by the ungraspable laws of pataphysics? Or has he provided the means whereby we might find our own inspiration in this body of work to leave behind the ordinary, the dully real, if only for a spell.

Pages 16–17
View of the Cartin residence,
New York, 2022

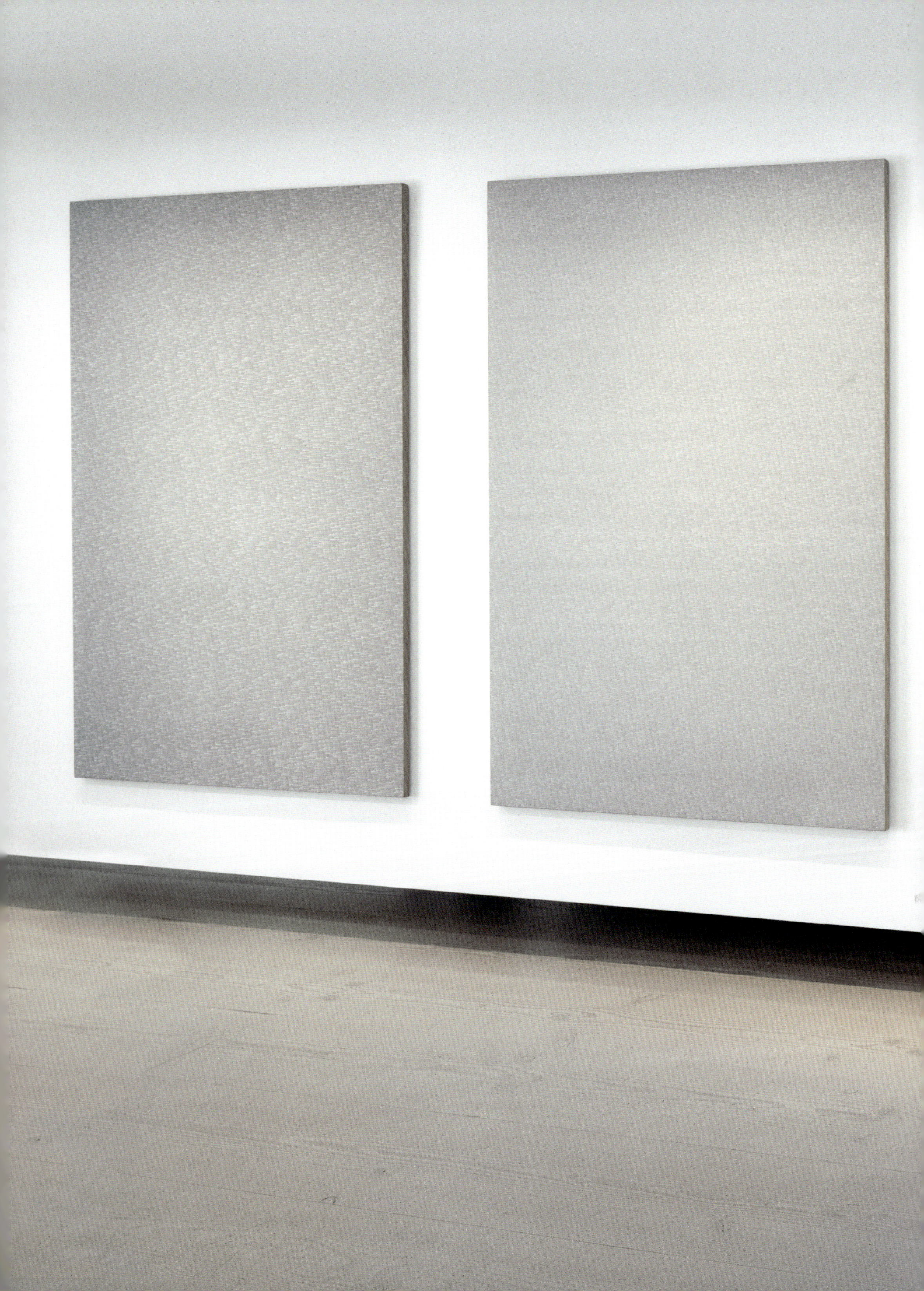

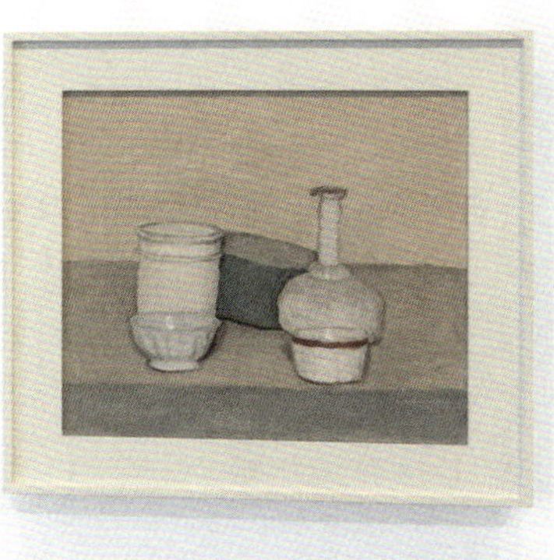

Steven Holmes

Ceci n'est pas une collection

When I first became aware of Mickey Cartin's collection, I thought I understood it. To me, a new curator at the time, it was clearly a collection of contemporary art, centered mostly on conceptualism and minimalism. Works by Sol LeWitt, Agnes Martin, and Roman Opałka, as well as Jean-Michel Basquiat, Spencer Finch, Wolfgang Laib, Charles LeDray, Glenn Ligon, and Tom Sachs, were installed throughout Cartin's home. I can still remember the exhilaration of thinking about how these artists were all together in one place, how they differ in some ways but how as a group they made sense. Nearly twenty years later, the collection is baffling to me. As time has gone by, my ability to answer basic questions about what the collection is *of* has dissipated. The questions are perfectly reasonable. Obvious even.

What happened?

Two things.

First, as I came to know the collection more thoroughly, the less I could say it was one thing or another, focused on this or that kind of art. Agnes Martin and Sol LeWitt made sense together, as did Carl Andre and John McCracken; Glenn Ligon and William Anastasi; Christopher Orr and Michaël Borremans. They still do. But what did Paul Laffoley or Joe Coleman have in common with them? Or with each other for that matter? Why was Martín Ramírez here with Fred Sandback? Spencer Finch with Adolf Wölfli? Myron Stout with Morris Hirshfield? Early on I thought I could identify certain broad groups, loosely gathered around makeshift categories of, say, the strange, the psychoanalytic, the outsider, the visionary, philosophy and thought, time, objects of frisson. But these groups, which are sometimes contradictory and at best tentative, represented only a small part of a rapidly growing collection. The collection was like a hydra sprouting heads, with each new work acquired resulting in new categories.

Secondly, and this took time, I realized that despite appearances to the contrary, Cartin had no interest in building a collection that made sense. Acquiring artwork in order to tell a story (art-historical or otherwise), or to unite works that theoretically "belonged" together, or to display wealth, or to create wealth, or to impress people, was never his goal. It still isn't. Instead, I was learning, he was acquiring work because each individual object, in some way or another, captured his imagination, his curiosity. Each work was here because it thrilled him. It didn't matter to him that curators or other observers might struggle to recognize an order or structure to this group of things.[1] All that mattered was how each object made Cartin feel, how it moved him in some primal way, how it prompted him to think. This was a collection devoid of any intentional organizing principles. There were no art advisers, because there was nothing for them to do.

Today Joe Coleman shares walls with Josef Albers, Alfred Jensen, Giorgio Morandi, and Fred Tomaselli in a Greenwich Village loft designed by UNStudio's Ben van Berkel. In a living space that animates the collector just as much as it houses the collection, fifteenth-century illuminated manuscripts rest on midcentury modern furniture; a LeWitt wall drawing looks across the space at a stalk of wheat carved from human bone, a work by Charles LeDray; Albrecht Dürer prints hang with a drawing by R. Crumb. There is poetry in

1   At different moments, Cartin has been (erroneously) thought of as a collector focused only on conceptualism, or outsider art, or, more recently, old masters and rare books.

these pairings, not prose, since there is no grammar and there are no rules. Just two thousand objects brought together by an omnivorous curiosity.

Yet the word "curiosity" feels too soft here. It lacks the sense of urgency within Cartin to gain total knowledge of the art and artists who interest him. The drive to know is so fundamental that it afflicts Cartin in areas beyond art: he is drawn to subjects as diverse as the moral status of animals, Wittgenstein's writings, moral philosophy, human nature, and baseball. Cartin's lifelong obsession with baseball is expansive, encompassing players' stories, the game's historical moments, its statistical history, its complex and nuanced strategies, and a vast reserve of personal reflections and anecdotes regarding players. This is the way he is with artists as well, seeking to understand all aspects of artists' lives—the way they think, how they see, what they make, and how they are connected to one another in complex social, intellectual, and historical webs.

It began in childhood, with coins, stamps, books, and, of course, baseball cards. The distinction between accumulating and collecting is an important one. For a young Cartin, the accumulation of baseball cards was simply a byproduct of an imagination that brought the world of baseball into his own backyard, as he played the roles of pitcher, batter, fielder, and roaring fan all at once. An accumulation of coins represented history; stamps, places. Like talismans, these things allowed him to *become*.

Around the same time Cartin began collecting art, in the mid-eighties, he was becoming involved with the Wadsworth Atheneum Museum of Art, in Hartford, his hometown. As a child and adolescent, he would visit the museum and ask many of the questions a kid would ask of any art museum. Questions about individual objects (such as the mummified human remains in a sarcophagus or a Joseph Cornell box he came to identify decades later) led to wondering what a museum was. Why were these things here? As an adult, trips back to this museum brought not just moments of pleasure but a growing comprehension as well.

Historically, the Wadsworth has been at the forefront of several avant-garde movements of the early twentieth century, with the legendary director Chick Austin bringing some of the most challenging work of the time to the galleries and to the permanent collection.[2] As Cartin became more involved in the museum, serving as a trustee from 1995 to 2005, he became more familiar with the collection and its history under Austin. He still recalls the moment he learned of a series of acquisitions Austin made in quick succession: Piet Mondrian's *Composition in Blue and White* (1935), the first Mondrian acquired by a museum in the United States, in 1936; Joseph Cornell's first soap bubble box, the first Cornell acquired by a museum, in 1938; and Caravaggio's *Saint Francis of Assisi in Ecstasy* (c. 1595–1596), the first Caravaggio acquired by a museum in the United States, in 1943. An early abstract work, a surrealist work, and a baroque masterpiece: these works share no evident taxonomy or taste. They were united by virtue of each having an energy, vitality, prescience, and urgency within their individual moments and places. Each is, in its own way, exceptional.

2   Austin served as director from 1927 through 1944.

    Steven Holmes

This was a lightbulb moment for Cartin. It meant anything that stimulated the imagination and took you places could function in a way similar to art. A collection—including Cartin's own small but growing collection—could be this.

The Cartin Collection now includes early printed books and manuscripts, and paintings, sculptures, and works on paper from the fourteenth century through the current moment. Many objects represent close personal relationships Cartin has formed with artists. Others are first of their kind, seeds of future revolutions in art and thought, from Josef Albers's first homage to the square, *Homage to the Square (A)* (1950; p. 49), to early printed books and manuscripts as well as first editions of books containing the origin of ideas in philosophy and science.

When historical artists first catch his attention, Cartin immediately starts adding to the reference library everything written about them: biographies, exhibition catalogues, monographs, catalogues raisonnés. This process of building up a reserve of information can take place either before or after an acquisition, and hours spent eagerly reading give rise to the kind of understanding a rabbi achieves in mastering the interconnectedness of the Talmud and Midrash. Not quite systems, these intricate textual webs can include an artist's biography, education, social world, influences, teachers, students, exhibitions, and commissions, all in service of complete knowledge of an artist's domain and place in history.

Cartin's curiosity takes a similar but expanded form in connection to artists who are still living and working. A bibliography is built and conversations rapidly flourish with a variety of people inside and outside the art world. In many cases, Cartin will develop personal and lasting relationships with them. These relationships might in other times and places appear to be a form of patronage, since artists and patrons, or collectors, are so historically intertwined as to be a trope. We have an image of the patron as a beneficent figure offering generosity as part of a complex arrangement that produces culture in exchange for social capital. But this image, of course, does not capture what these relationships are like in the absence of exchange: collectors and artists who are simply friends, for whom art and exchange is but one (often minor) aspect of the way they spend time together.

Sol LeWitt, who was born in Hartford, was a friend and mentor to Cartin, introducing him to the works of Carl Andre, Alighiero Boetti, Stanley Brouwn, Hanne Darboven, and many others. For nearly forty years, Cartin has spent long hours in studios, in galleries, and at the dinner table with Joe Coleman, Cecilia Edefalk, Spencer Finch, Tony Fitzpatrick, Walton Ford, Gregory Gillespie, Mark Greenwold, Wes Mills, Fred Tomaselli, Tom Sachs, Andrew Sendor, and Martin Wilner, among many other artists. Sometimes he bought work, but usually he did not.

Cartin also has made good friends and tutors among museum directors, gallerists, and curators. In Hartford, Cartin spent much time with the curators Nicholas Baume and James Rondeau when each was at the

Wadsworth Atheneum in the early stages of their careers, and these friendships continue today. James Corcoran, David Leiber, Steven Leiber, Marcus Marschall, Fabrizio Moretti, Hugo Nathan, Gian Enzo Sperone, Jack Tilton, and David Zwirner, among other gallerists, showed an eager Cartin new corners of the art world, while book dealers including Jörn Günther, Jonathan Hill, and Giacomo Pozzi brought him into the realm of early printed books and illuminated manuscripts.

The first acquisition of a work of art, John Kane's self-portrait *Seen in the Mirror* (c. 1928; p. 146), came at the end of a long process of inquiry, research, and interrogation. Cartin began with simple questions. John Kane was an immigrant from Scotland who came to the United States and found work in the steel mills, railroads, and mines in and around Pittsburgh, but who was he otherwise? What moved Kane to come home at the end of long days of grueling labor and paint? What possessed him to make art, as opposed to doing something else? And what was the relationship between the impulse to create and this self-portrait in particular, where Kane looks at himself in a mirror? How did he see himself, the world around him? How do any of us? Are all works of art, ultimately, self-portraits? As the questions piled up, Cartin went in search of answers, sending letters to anyone who might tell him something about this obscure painter.[3]

In time, he acquired a second Kane work (see p. 147). Like the talismanic power of the baseball cards, stamps, and coins of his childhood, these paintings took him places. With each subsequent moment of questioning and probing, a group of objects slowly came together, like a celestial body formed through a process of collision and accretion, rather than from a desire to create a collection.

Other works to first arrive in the collection were by artists Madge Gill, Nikifor, Martín Ramírez, Bill Traylor, Adolf Wölfli, Joseph Yoakum, and others who are still referred to as outsider artists. While Cartin vigorously rejects the term "outsider," which was coined by Roger Cardinal barely a decade before these works entered the collection, he did subscribe to Cardinal's notion of "a culture of one," a description of artists who live and work within completely unique worlds of their own discovery or creation.[4] Unconstrained by academic categories or any conventional taxonomies, these works make particular sense in terms of the curiosity that continues to power the collection.

Like Wölfli, artists such as Forrest Bess, Alfred Jensen, or Paul Laffoley make work, in part, from a compulsion to understand and externalize, or articulate, inner and sometimes mystical epistemological systems. Though these systems can be opaque to others, they are just as complex and speculative as any other aesthetic or formal structure. Alfred Jensen's *Ionic Order* (1979; pp. 126–127) is a type of mathematical chart that combines color theory with the orbital patterns of Jupiter's moon Io. It is a hermetic system of Jensen's creation alone. Wölfli's *Die Himmels Leiter* (1915; p. 109) is part of an expansive system that combines idiosyncratic musical notations, inscrutable biography, and depictions of the artist as various heroic figures, such as Saint Adolf.

3   Cartin eventually met with the Kane scholar and Carnegie Museum of Art director Leon Arkus during a research trip to Pittsburgh.

4   See Roger Cardinal, *Outsider Art* (London: Praeger, 1972). For Cartin, market and academic politics have encouraged a notion of "otherness" that distracts from seeing these artists in relation to others whose work may be concerned with fundamentally similar themes, ideas, or processes.

5   In 1965, Opałka embarked on a series of paintings that he referred to as "details" of a singular conceptual work: the recording in paint and recitation of all numbers from one to infinity. Each detail is a canvas measuring seventy-seven by fifty-three inches. The first in the series features a black background on which he painted numerals in white, with the number one in the top left corner. Subsequent backgrounds became more gray, and the later details are almost monochromatic, as the backgrounds are lighter while the numbers remain white. Opałka continued the project for forty-six years, until his death in 2011. The last detail in the series ends with the number 5,607,249.

The architect Paul Laffoley's body of work brings together explorations in philosophy, architecture, and the origin of mankind, as well as his own invented iconography, in drawings that blend architectural style with visionary themes. The bespoke symbology of Forrest Bess continues to mystify art historians and artists alike who look for meaning in a puzzle that is easily solved by remembering that Bess described to Betty Parsons over many years that his work is primarily just the representation of what appeared to him in visions.

Other artists in the collection are likewise occupied by unique and singular projects. Roman Opałka undertook a single work of art to paint all the numbers from one to infinity.[5] Giorgio Morandi (who made landscapes and portraits earlier in his career) is best known for a group of still lifes: paintings of vessels on a table, which he endlessly rearranged, as he revised and refined the series. Agnes Martin said that her life was committed to a singular quest for beauty in color and line. And, of course, there is Josef Albers.

Albers's first *Homage to the Square*, executed in 1950, was acquired in 2009 and has come to occupy a primacy of place in the collection. This unassuming thirty-by-thirty-inch painting in hues of gray would germinate to become one of the most important projects of twentieth-century art. Its standing in the collection is not for its market or art-historical value but for its status as the clearest example of the collection's apparent interest in incunables, a term that refers to books printed before 1501 and applied here by analogy. The *Homage* constitutes the inception of an idea with revolutionary potential. A quiet gray painting conceals its status as an inflection point in the history of art.

A collection within a collection, Cartin's library contains numerous incunables, such as the *Μέγα Ἐτυμολογικόν* (in Latin, *Etymologicon magnum*), printed in 1499,[6] and the comedies of Aristophanes, printed in 1498. Books that were printed after 1501 from manuscript sources, called editiones principes, are also here.[7] Key texts in the history of philosophy and science have at various times been found in the collection, including first editions of Immanuel Kant's *Critique of Pure Reason* (copies of both the "A Text" of 1781 and the "B Text" of 1787) and a copy of the first printing of the complete works of Plato in Greek (1513) (which once belonged to Thomas Jefferson's son-in-law who lived with Jefferson at Monticello). The second edition[8] of Copernicus's inflammatory but revolutionary *Concerning the Revolutions of the Heavenly Orbs* (*De revolutionibus orbium coelestium*) has shared a shelf in the library with first editions of the works of Descartes, including the *Discours* (1637) and its explosive "Cogito, ergo sum"—the ground zero of rationalism. Wittgenstein's *The Blue Book* and *The Brown Book*[9] are here with the first appearance of his major work the *Logisch-Philosophische Abhandlung* (1921) and the final *Tractatus Logico-Philosophicus* (1922).[10] The first appearance of continuous Greek print is found in the *Noctes Atticae of Aulus Gellius* (1469), while beside it sits Agostino Giustiniani's text containing the Psalms printed in Arabic, Greek, Latin, Hebrew, and Chaldean, the so-called Polyglot Bible or Genoa Psalter (1516).[11] First editions of the moral philosophy of George Berkeley, David Hume, John Locke, and John Stuart Mill are at home here, as are copies of the Nuremberg Chronicle (1493; see

6   The *Etymologicon magnum* is a Greek lexicon, the first printed in Greek, and is both an incunable and an editio princeps. This particular copy was once owned by Agostino Giustiniani, the editor of the Polyglot Bible.

7   An editio princeps is a book that marks the movement of a text (and the ideas conveyed in the text) from the limited world of the manuscript to a book printed with movable type, marking a shift to a profoundly different kind of social literacy both in kind and degree.

8   The second edition was the corrected, authoritative, and influential 1566 edition.

9   Lecture notes compiled by Wittgenstein's students are two separate books bound in a single volume.

10   Cartin has copies of the first appearance in text of the only two books published in Wittgenstein's lifetime.

11   Giustiniani's *Psalterium Hebraeum, Graecum, Arabicum et Chaldaeum cum tribus Latinis interpretationibus et glossis* is the first instance of Arabic set in type.

p. 179), Koberger's Ninth German Bible (1483), Maximilian's *Theuerdank* (1517), and a book that revolutionized printed book illustration, Stephan Fridolin's *Schatzbehalter* (1491). Luca Pacioli, the inventor of modern accounting and the designer of the first proportional typeface, is represented by his *De divina proportione* (1509), illustrated by Leonardo da Vinci, who worked alongside Pacioli in Milan.

This grouping of early printed texts is joined by several manuscripts, including the illuminated manuscript the *Pontifical of Ferry de Clugny* (pp. 176–177) and the phantasmagorical *Wunderzeichenbuch* (*Book of Miracles*) (c. 1552; see pp. 106–107), the latter discovered in a small castle near Augsburg in 2006. The pontifical[12] was illuminated by Loyset Liédet and Lieven van Lathem between 1475 and 1476 and contains ninety-six miniatures and illuminated capital letters throughout. Its provenance runs from Cardinal Ferry de Clugny of Tournai (c. 1430–1483) to Pope Sixtus IV (1414–1484)[13] and was later in the collection of one of the greatest bibliophiles and patrons of philosophy in history, Queen Christina of Sweden (1626–1689).[14] The *Book of Miracles* contains 167 illustrations of strange, mysterious, miraculous events in European and biblical history. This obscure book captured Cartin's attention instantly, and he bought it on the spot. Within several years of acquisition, a project to identify the origin and meaning of this book was organized with the art historians Till-Holger Borchert and Joshua Waterman.[15]

The *Book of Miracles* is but one example of work in the collection concerned with different systems of knowledge—scientific, religious, singular, or hermetic. On Kawara's Date Paintings (see pp. 59–61) and details from Roman Opałka's *1965/1–∞* project (see p. 52) may suggest a cool conceptualism, but these works are highly meditative, religious in their strict observance of practice and devotion to time. Morandi's faithful practice in his *natura morta* works, Agnes Martin's singular search for beauty, and Albers's *Homage* project are all instances of fidelity to an idea through a rigorous and almost ritualistic practice. More explicitly sacred works have included Hans Memling's Madonna and Child rondel (c. 1487–1490; p. 145) and devotional panels by the Master of the Tiburtine Sibyl (see p. 143), Jan Provost (see p. 142), Lorenzo Monaco (see p. 132), Taddeo Gaddi (see p. 133), and Giovenale da Orvieto, which all evoke the theologically miraculous. *The Resurrection of Christ* (c. 1483–1498; p. 153), a visually strange early Dutch painting with a haunting provenance, by the anonymous Master of the Virgo inter Virgines, is a tautological marvel—an oneiric depiction of the central Christian miracle. Dürer's *Saint Eustace* (c. 1501; p. 74) and his *Nativity* (1504; p. 75) depict, respectively, the miraculous vision of a cross between a stag's antlers and the virgin birth. Frédéric Bruly Bouabré, Alfred Jensen, Joseph Yoakum, and others have made work based in highly developed but exclusive and hermetic knowledge systems.

Self-portraits and portraits have always been part of the collection, going back to the beginning, of course, with Kane's, and including works by Joe Coleman (see p. 66), Mark Greenwold (see p. 166), Sam Messer, Jim Torok, and Wölfli. But over the past ten or more years, this group has grown,

12 A pontifical is a manuscript commissioned for the use of a bishop in the execution of the sacraments, ceremonies and rites unique to a bishop.

13 Sixtus IV added it to the Vatican's Apostolic Library by 1481.

14 Descartes, for instance, went to Stockholm in 1649 to become Christina's tutor and to help her establish the Royal Swedish Academy of Sciences. The pontifical passed through several noted English collections before it was acquired by Cartin in 2009.

15 A facsimile with commentary by Borchert and Waterman was published by Taschen in 2013.

     Steven Holmes

with the addition of self-portraits by Josef Albers (p. 51), Carlo Bugatti
(p. 117), Giorgio de Chirico (p. 69), Vilhelm Hammershøi (p. 113), Augustus
John, Peder Krøyer (p. 68), and Max Liebermann (p. 151), among others.
Interestingly, however, most of these portraits and self-portraits have
something that is just a little off. Fernand Khnopff's portrait of the young
Count Straeten-Ponthoz (1894; p. 141) shows him dressed as a girl, which
wasn't unusual at the time, then was for a period, and now no longer is
again—a historical merry-go-round of notions of gender. Or Willem Key's
A Portrait of Margret Halseber of Basel – The Lady with Two Beards
(c. 1550; p. 140). Albers's Cézanne-inspired self-portrait shows the master
side-eyed, gazing out as inquisitive as Cartin is looking back. Hammershøi,
a magician of the interior, paints himself oblivious and ambivalent, preoc-
cupied by a space outside the frame that only he can see. Lotte Laserstein
lurks in the murky background of her grandmother's portrait (1924; p. 103).
Coleman's self-portraits materialize from often gruesome pathologies.
In Friedrich von Amerling's portrait of Franz I of Austria (1832; p. 115), the
emperor's head is a marvel of phrenology. Rembrandt's mother is diminu-
tive, disembodied (1628; p. 150). These portraits are strange.

The collection as a whole is itself strange. Some people might suggest
the word "eclectic" to describe it, but that word misses something
important. I prefer the word "surreal." The surreal is a place of illogic, of
the unexpected, a place of collision and surprise—a place where ordinary things come together in extraordinary ways. Meaning is palpable,
but furtive. Cartin's collection is, likewise, an alchemy of ideas, thoughts,
impulses, and epistemologies that lacks the coherence we look for in
what we typically think of when we use the word "collection." His is an
accumulation of discrete things, held together only by curiosity, taken
into possession without regard for categories or classifications, all arriv-
ing independently and eventually coming to rest in powerful but only
accidental adjacencies. There are none of the basic elements that ground
most collections here. There are no organizing principles, no intention-
ality in its coming together, and no overarching categorical engine driving
it. And so, by most definitions of the word, as most people use the term,
this isn't a collection at all.

Cartin Residence
New York

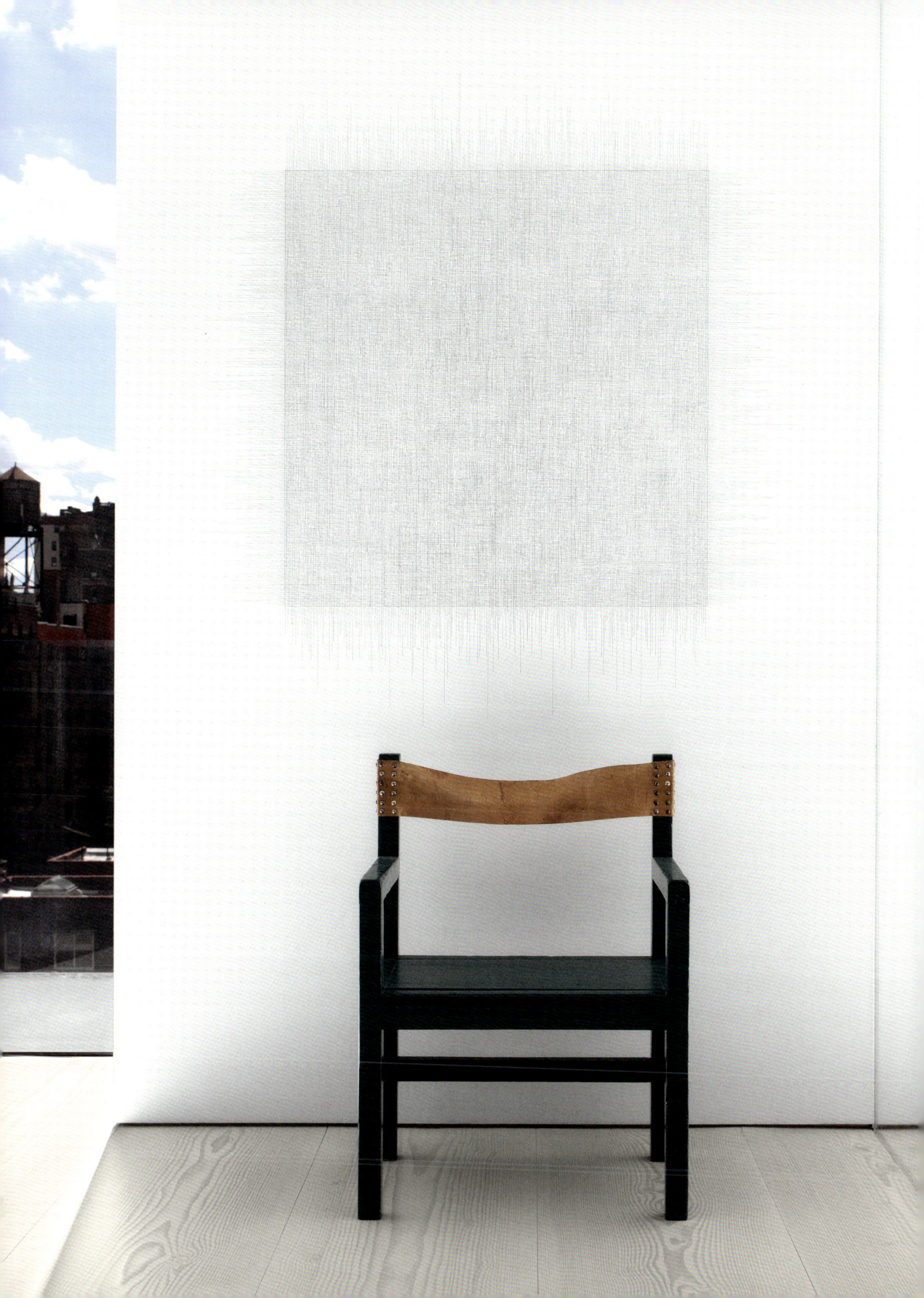

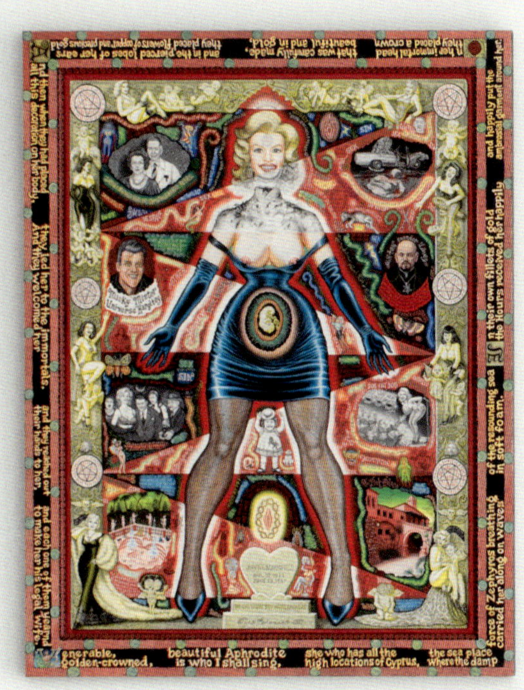
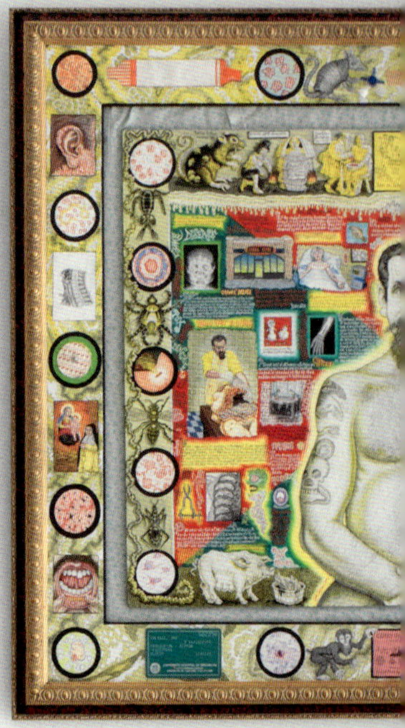
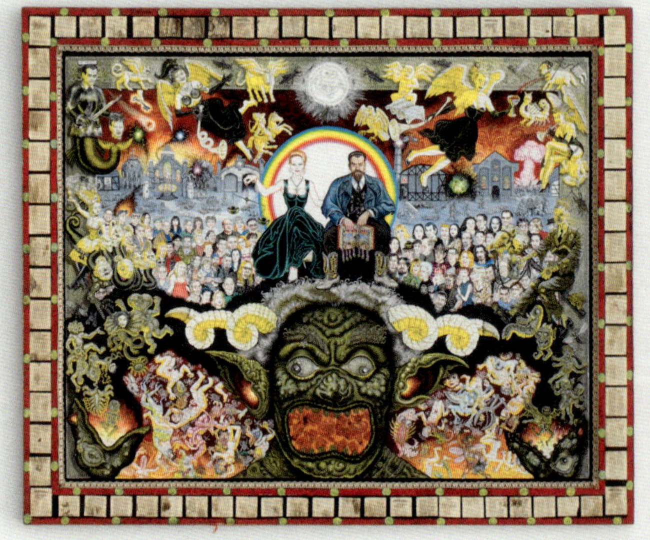

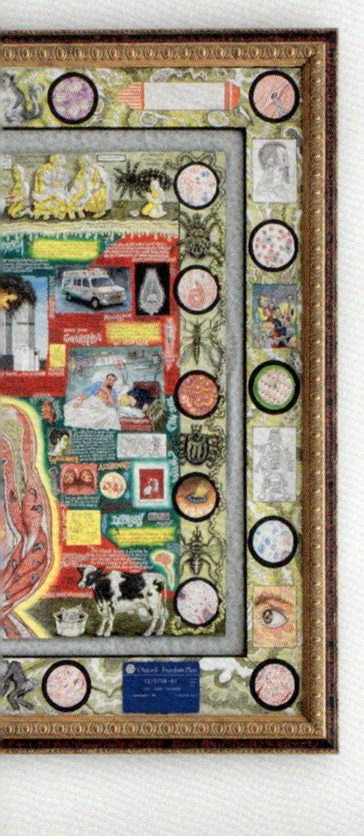
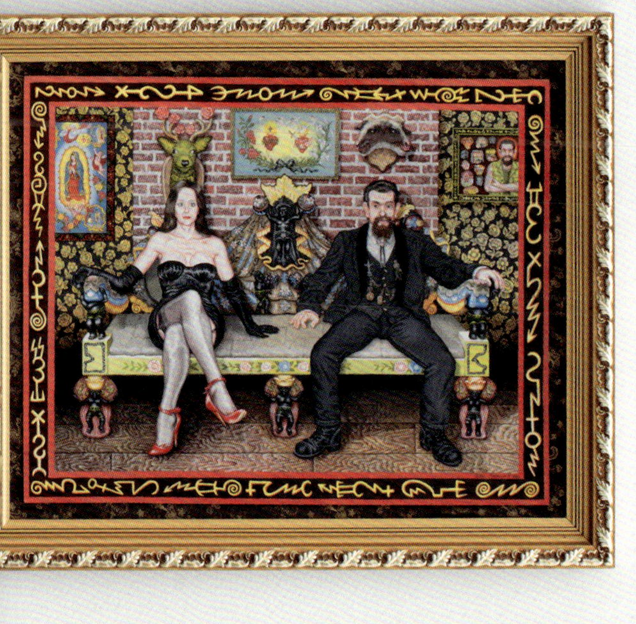
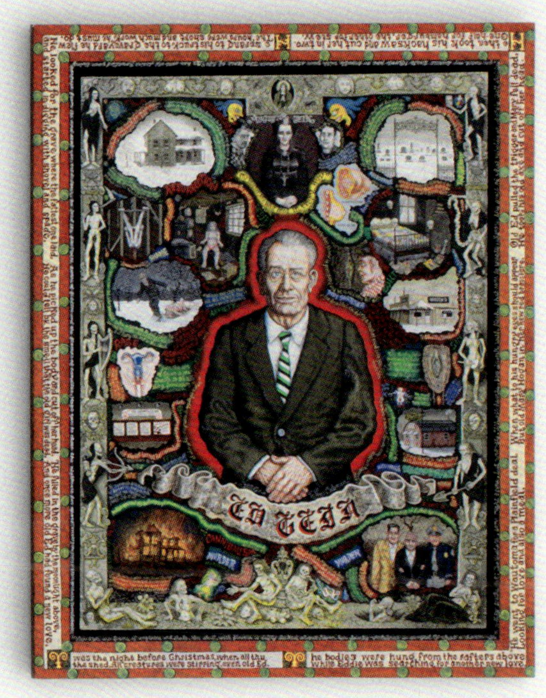

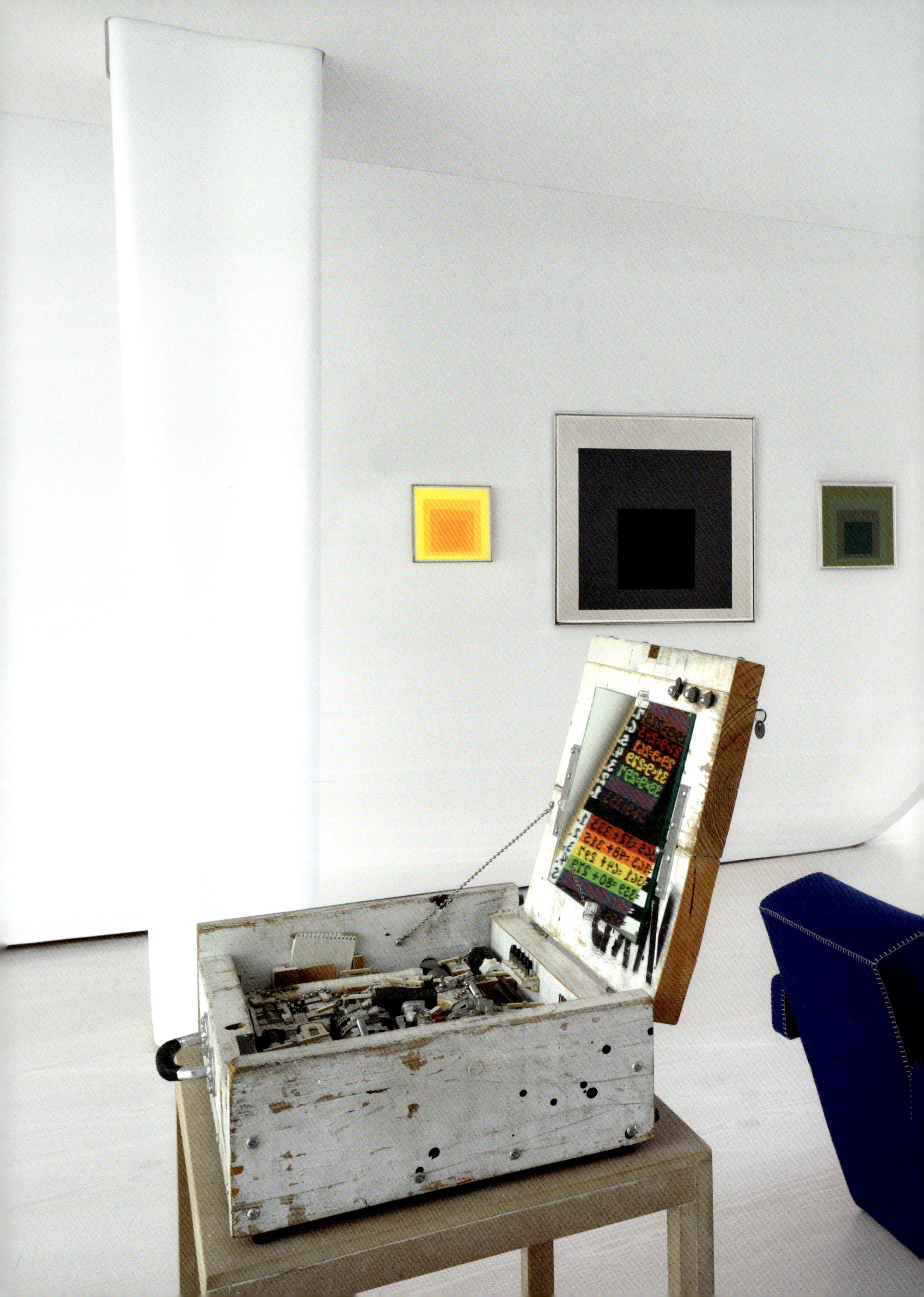

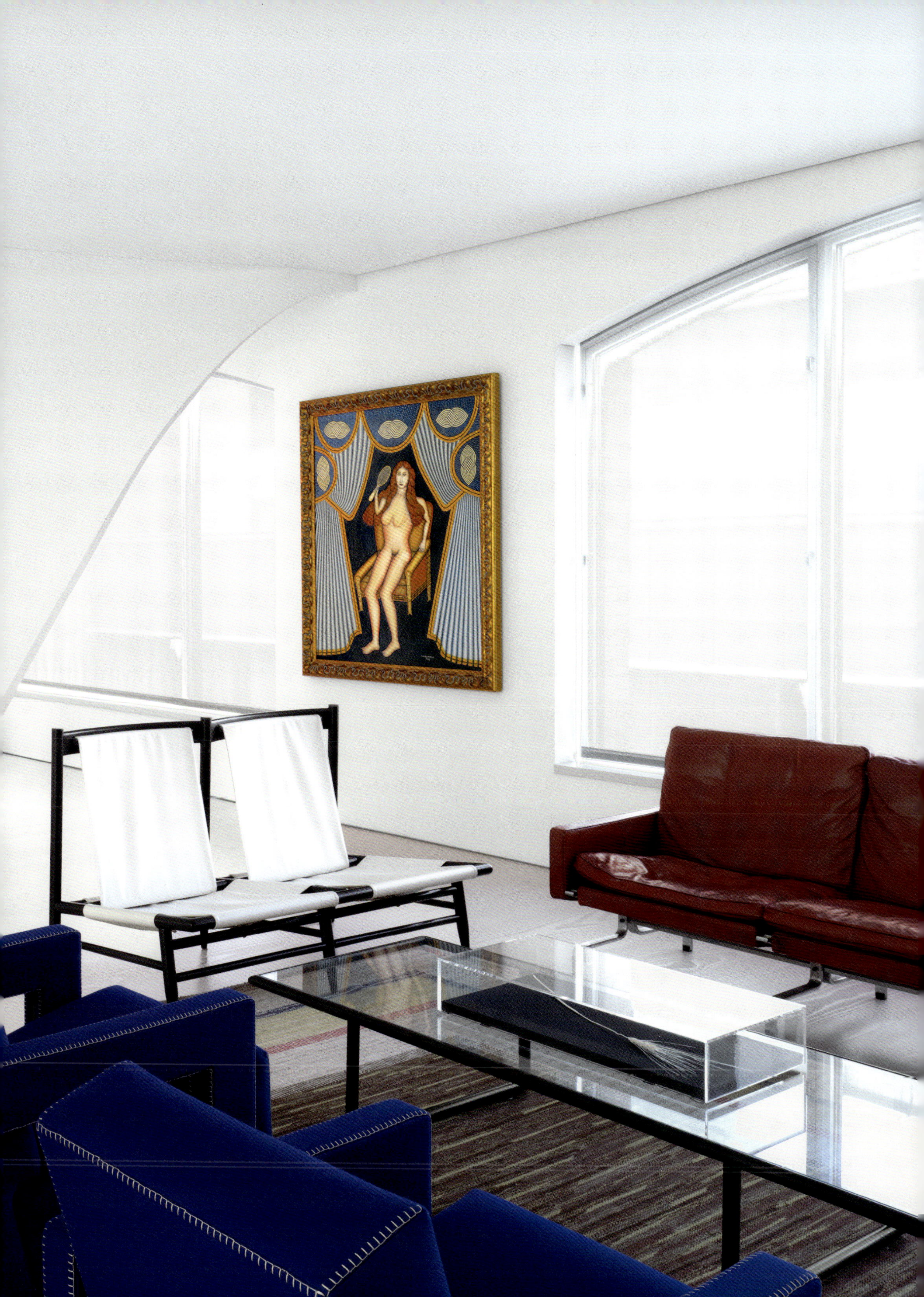

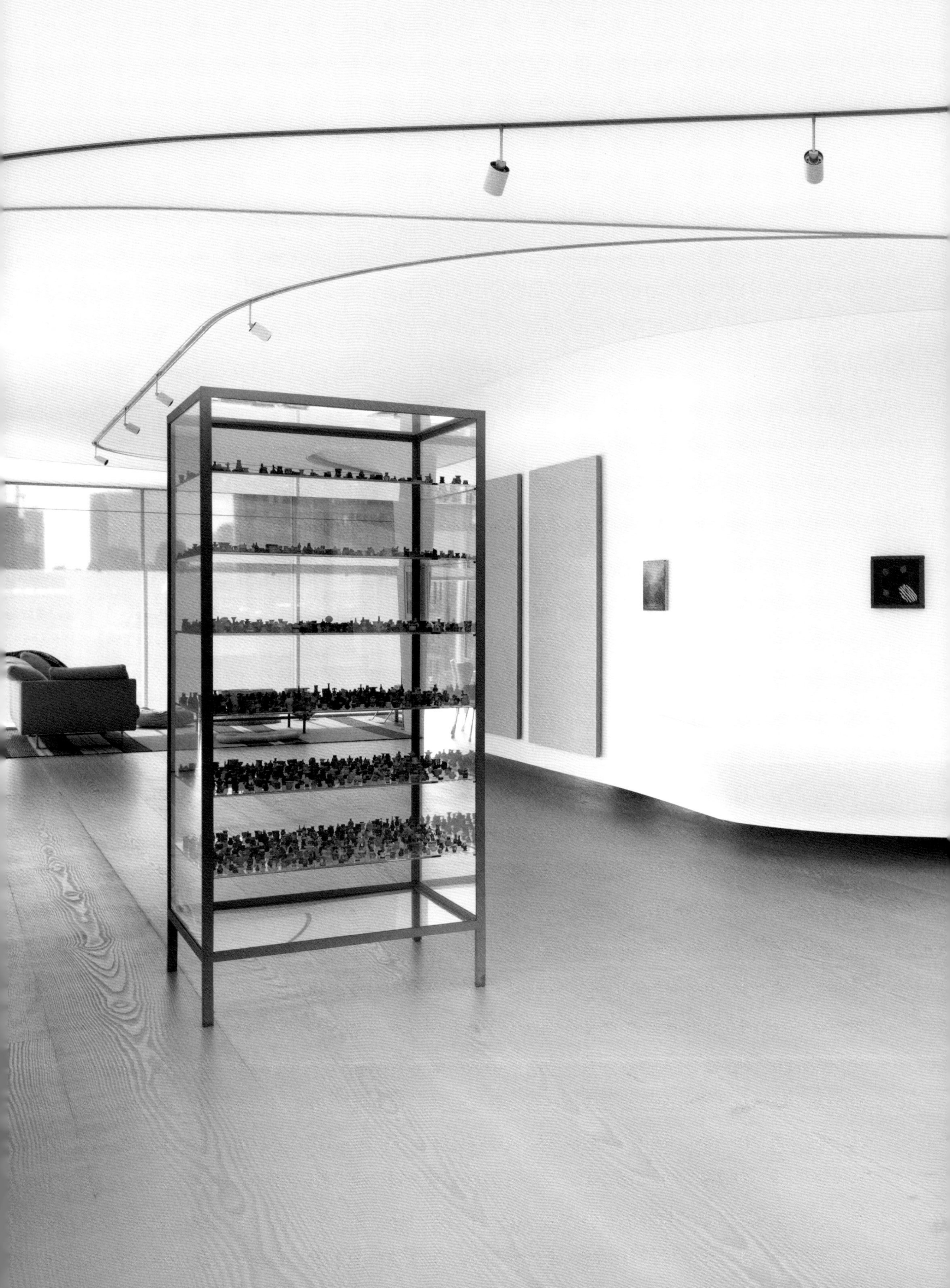

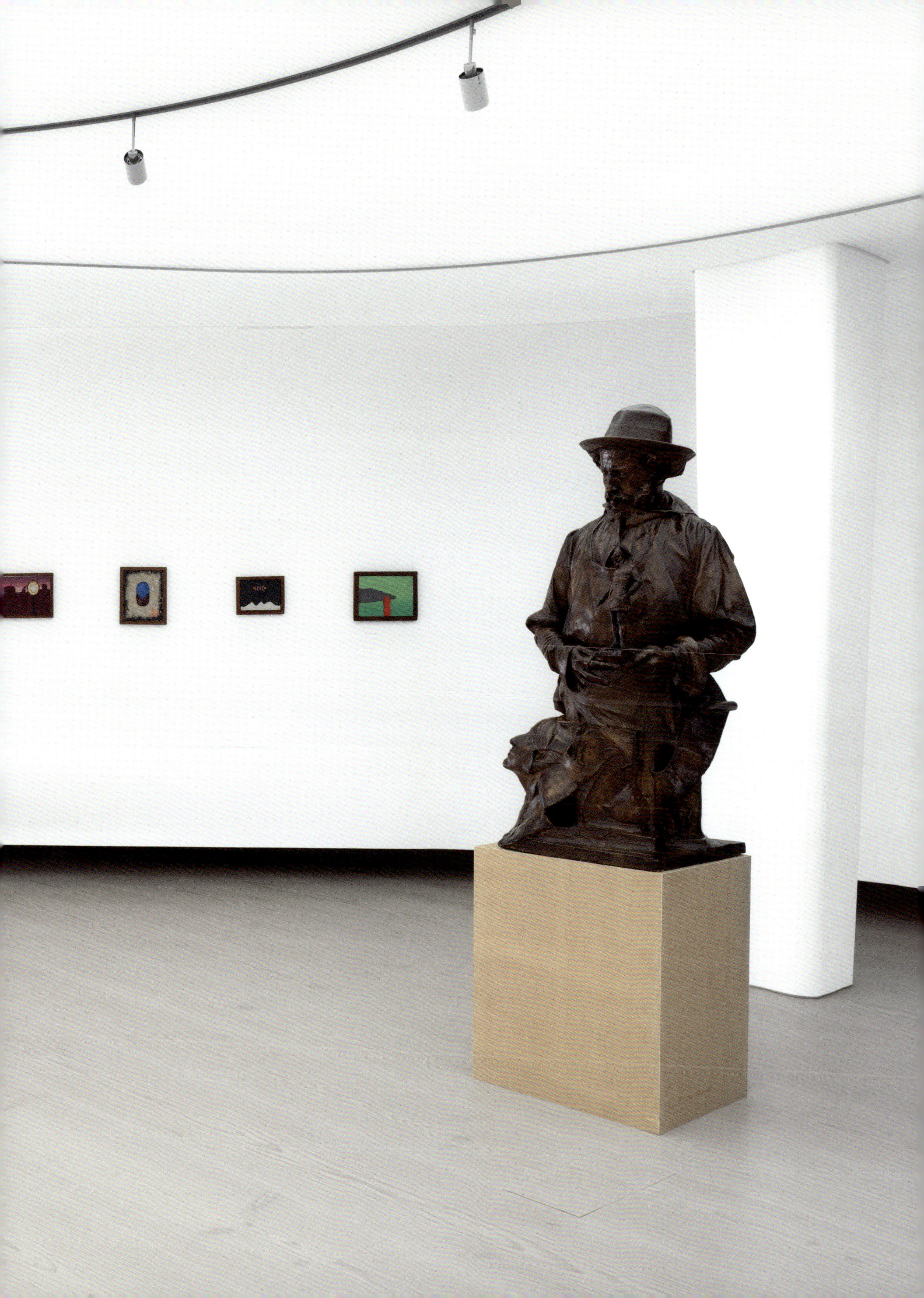

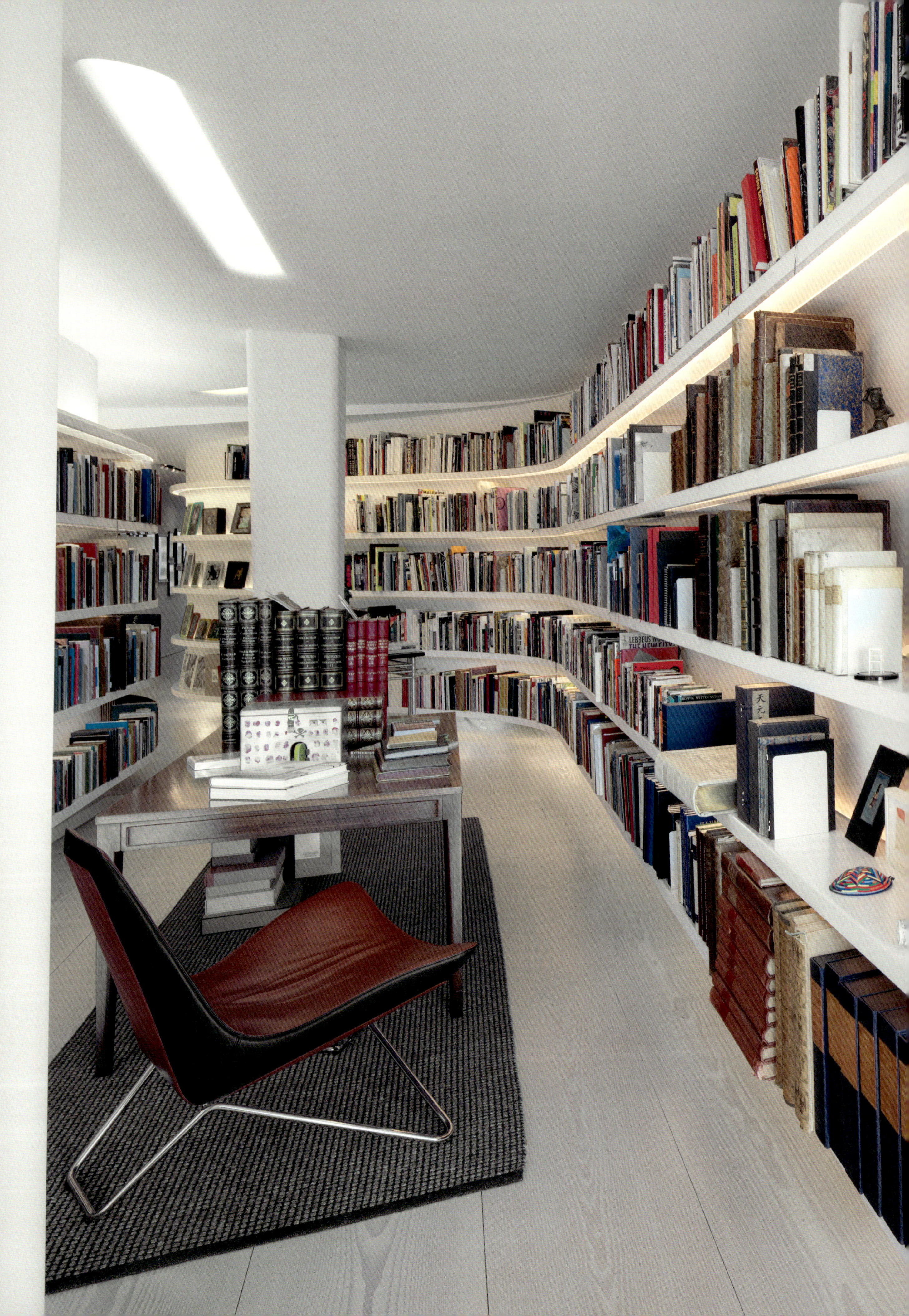

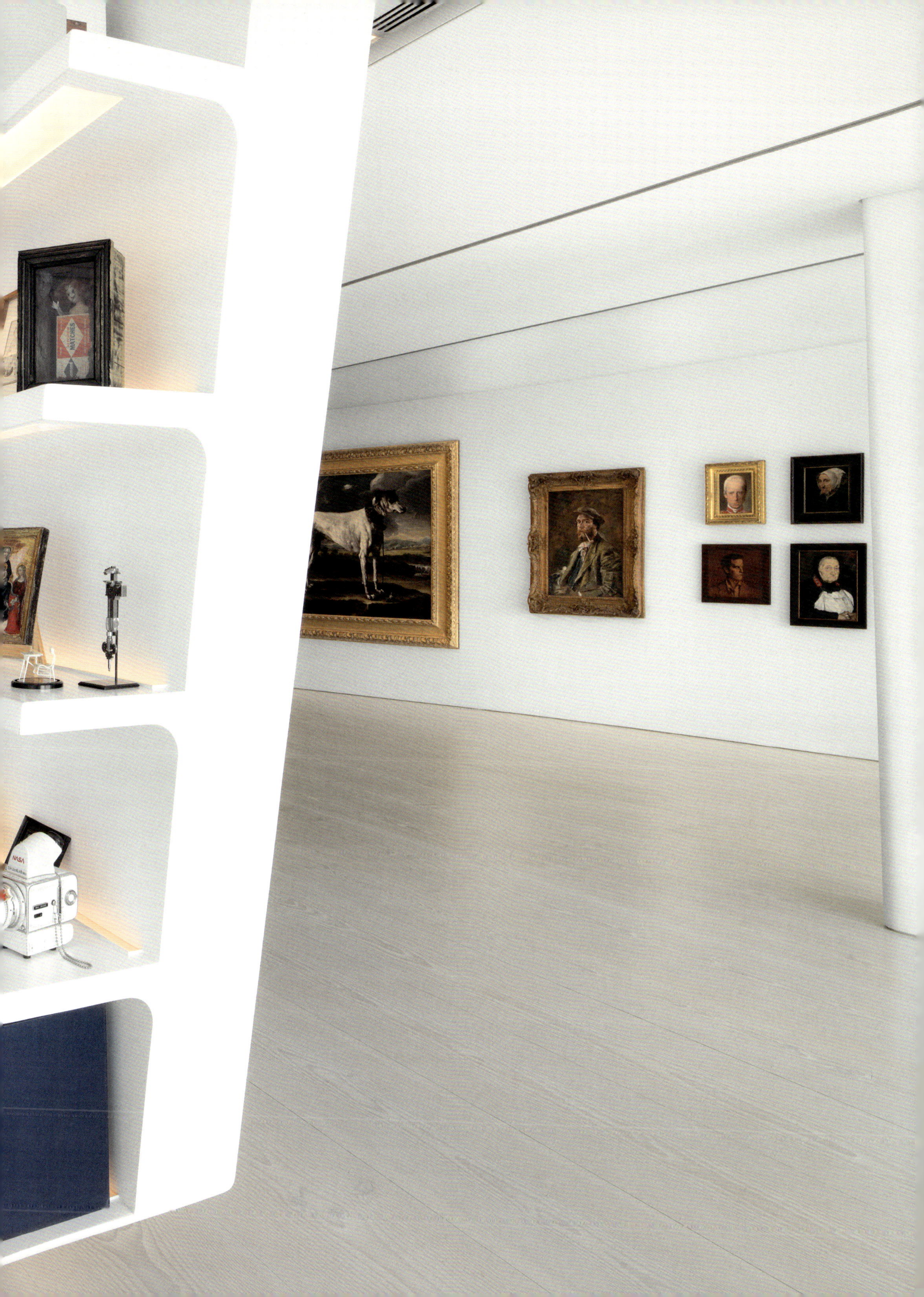

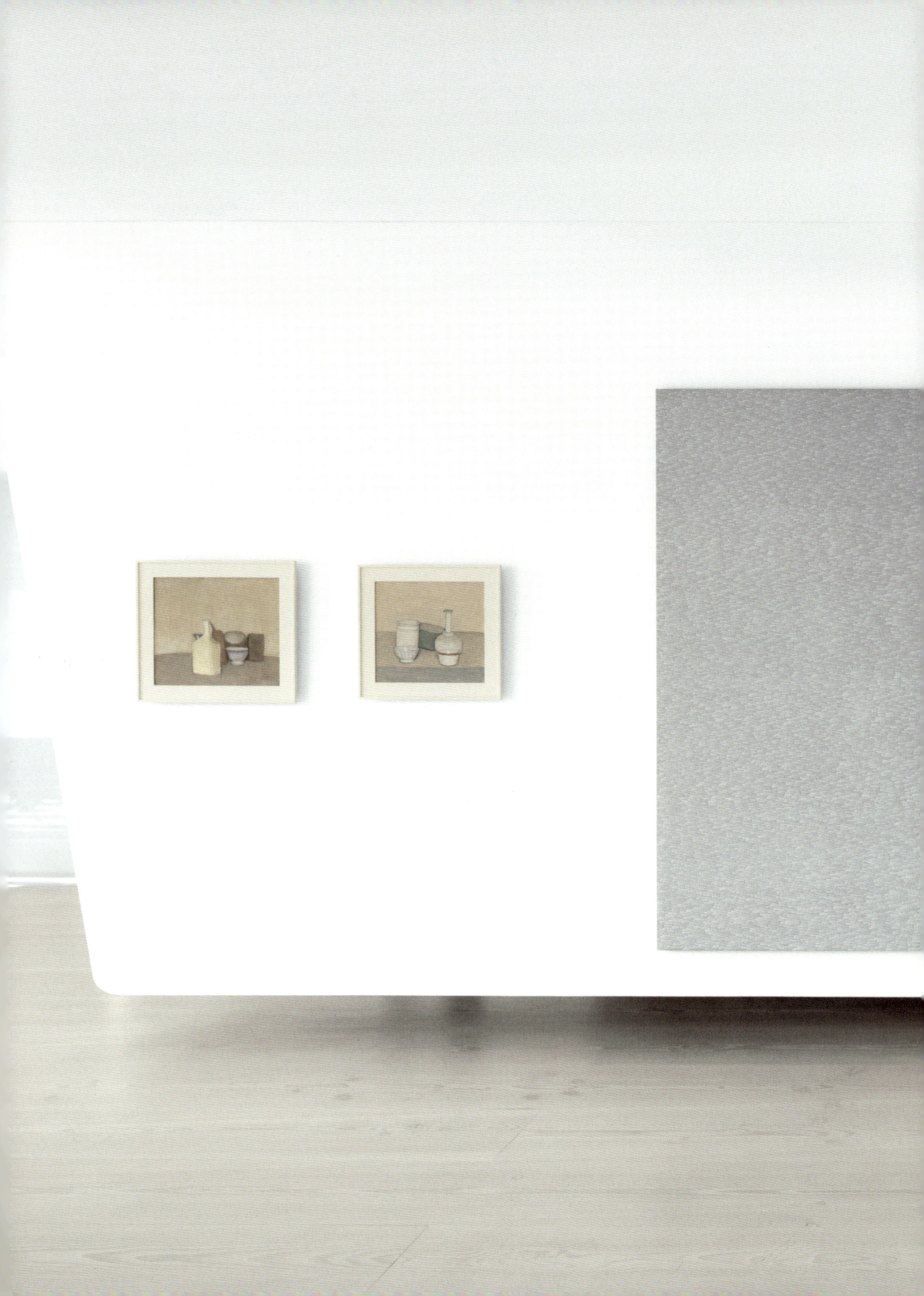

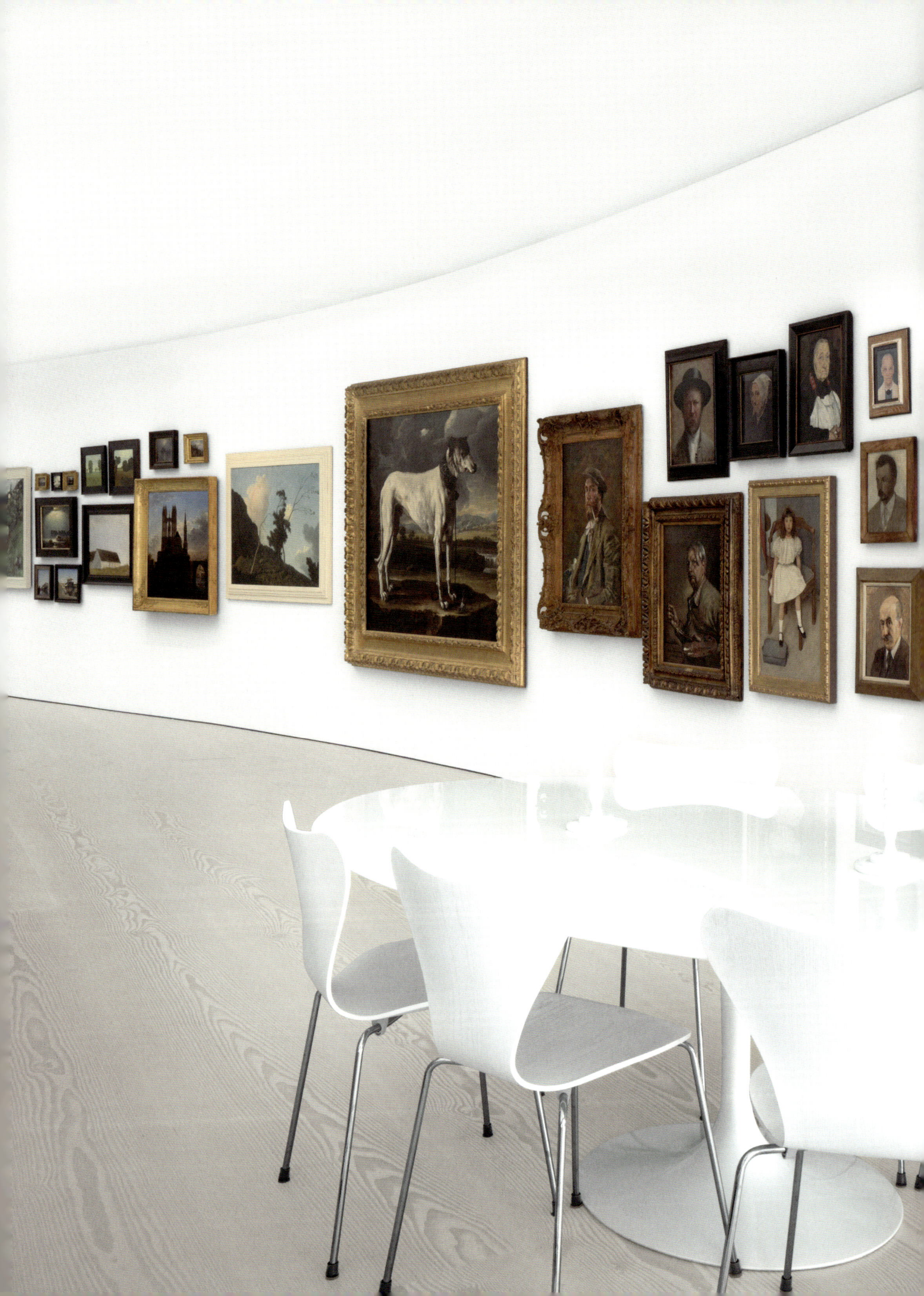

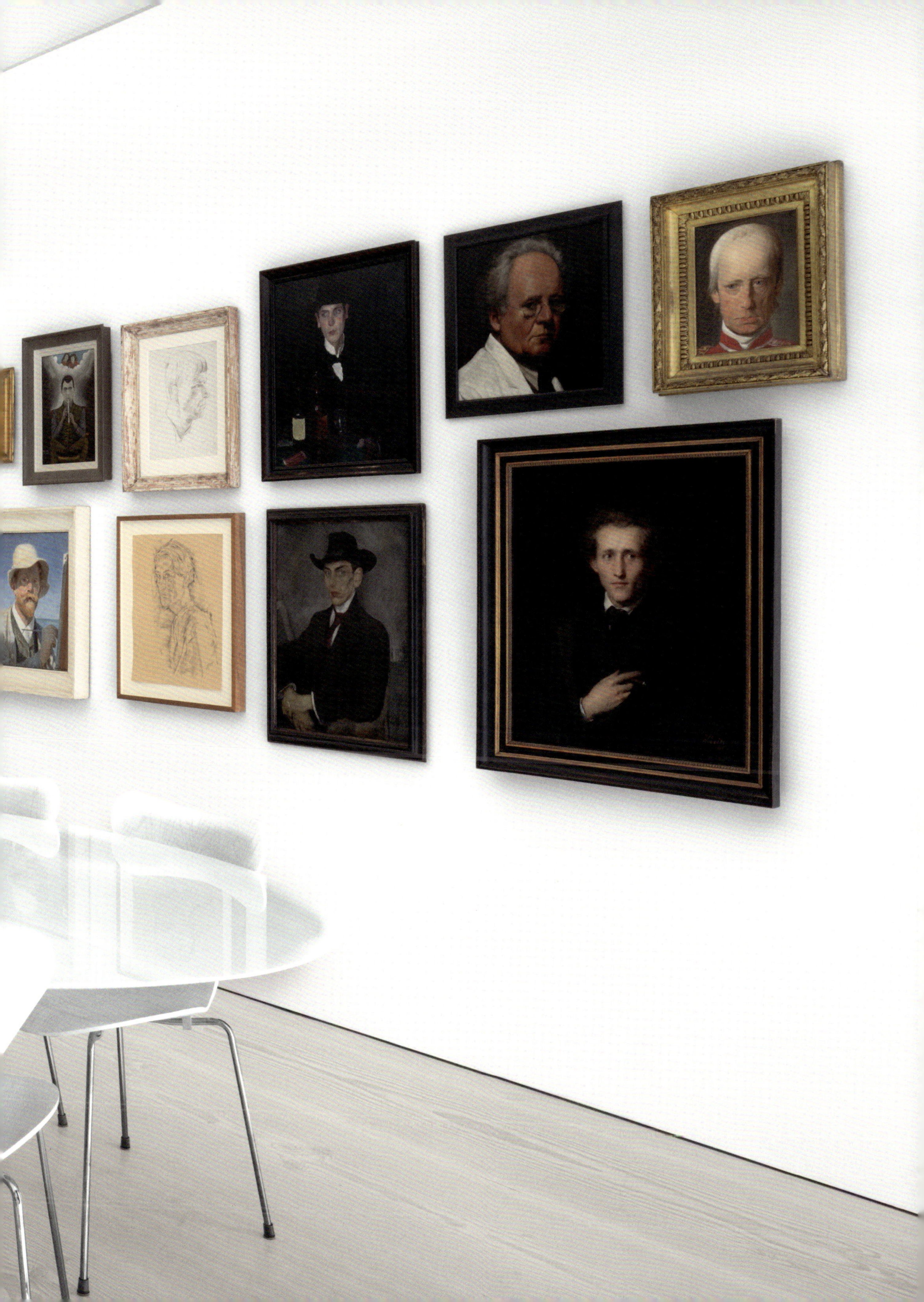

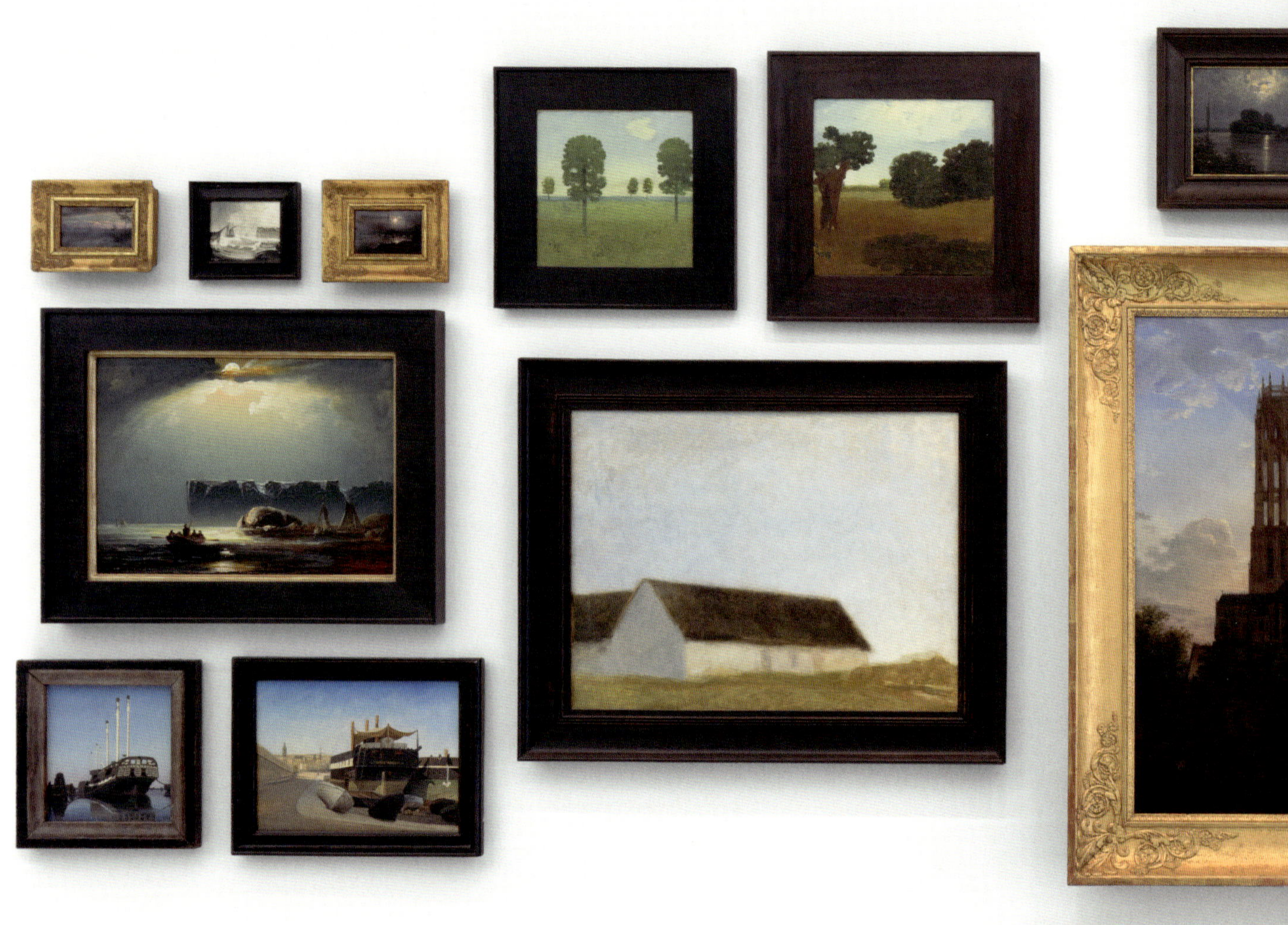

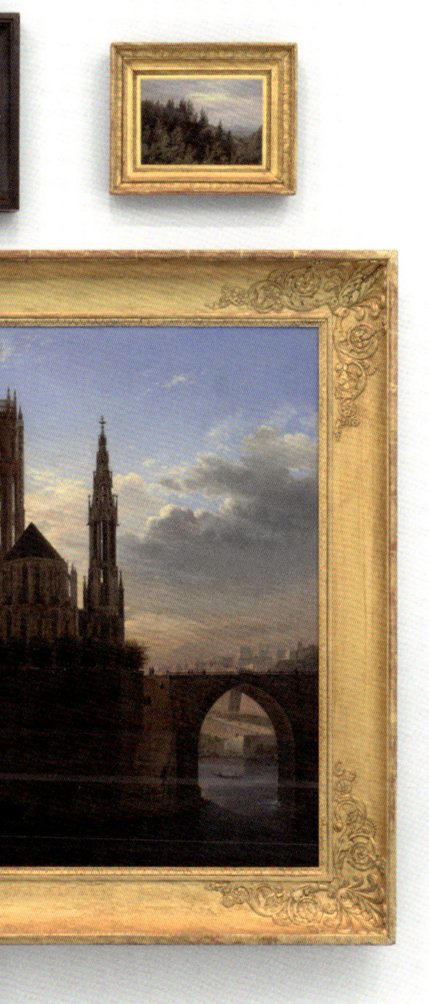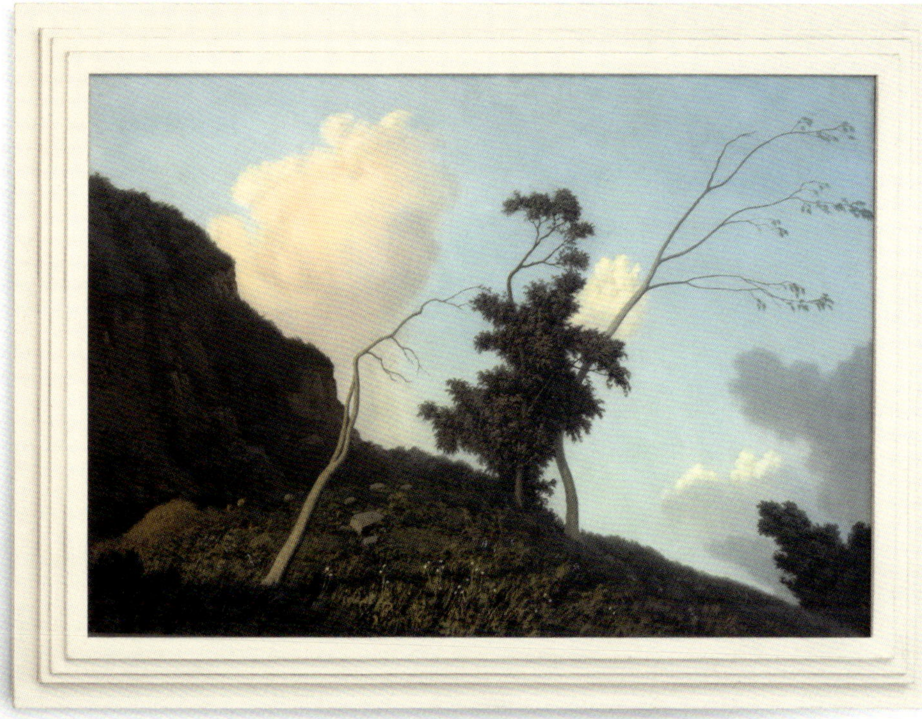

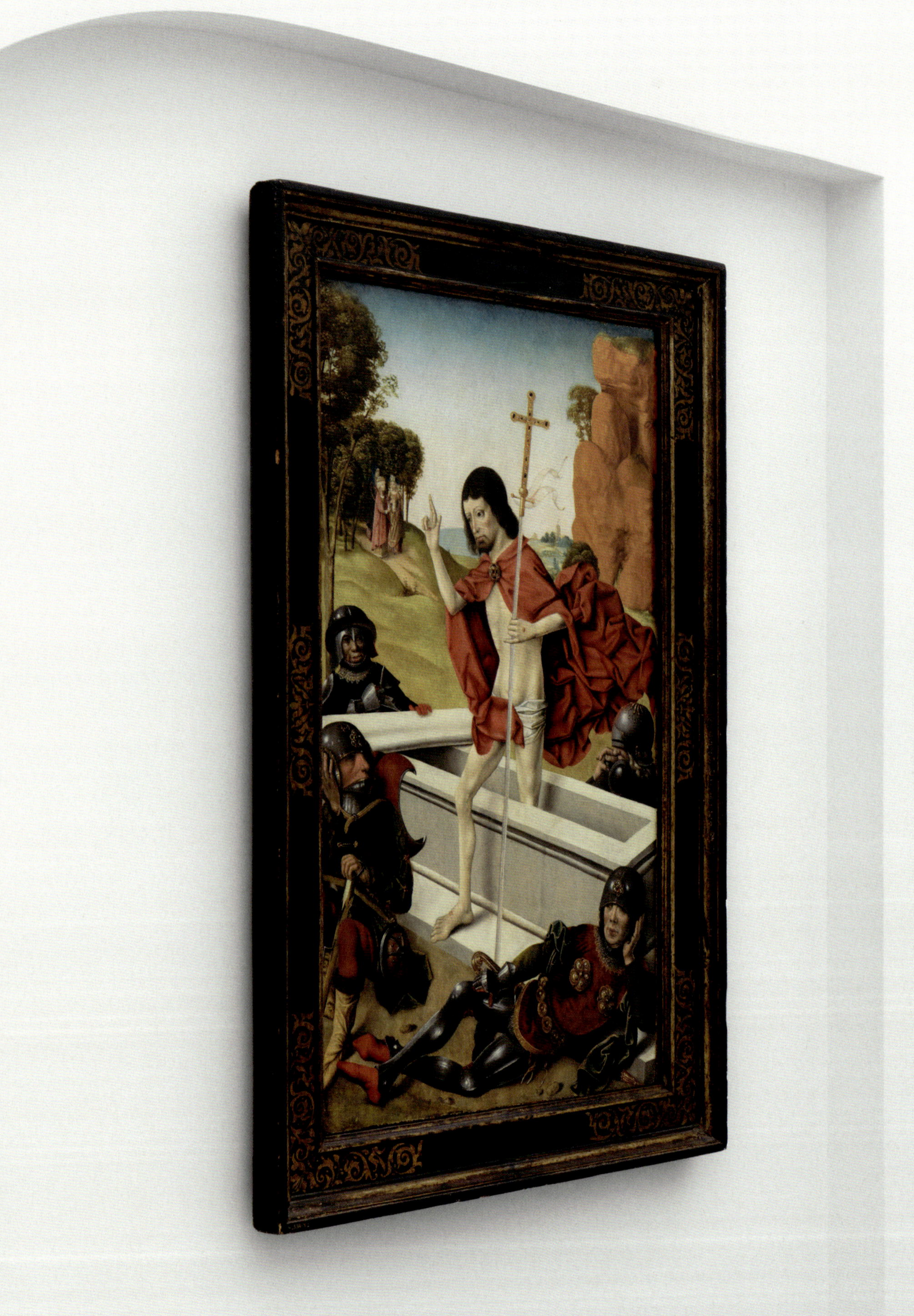

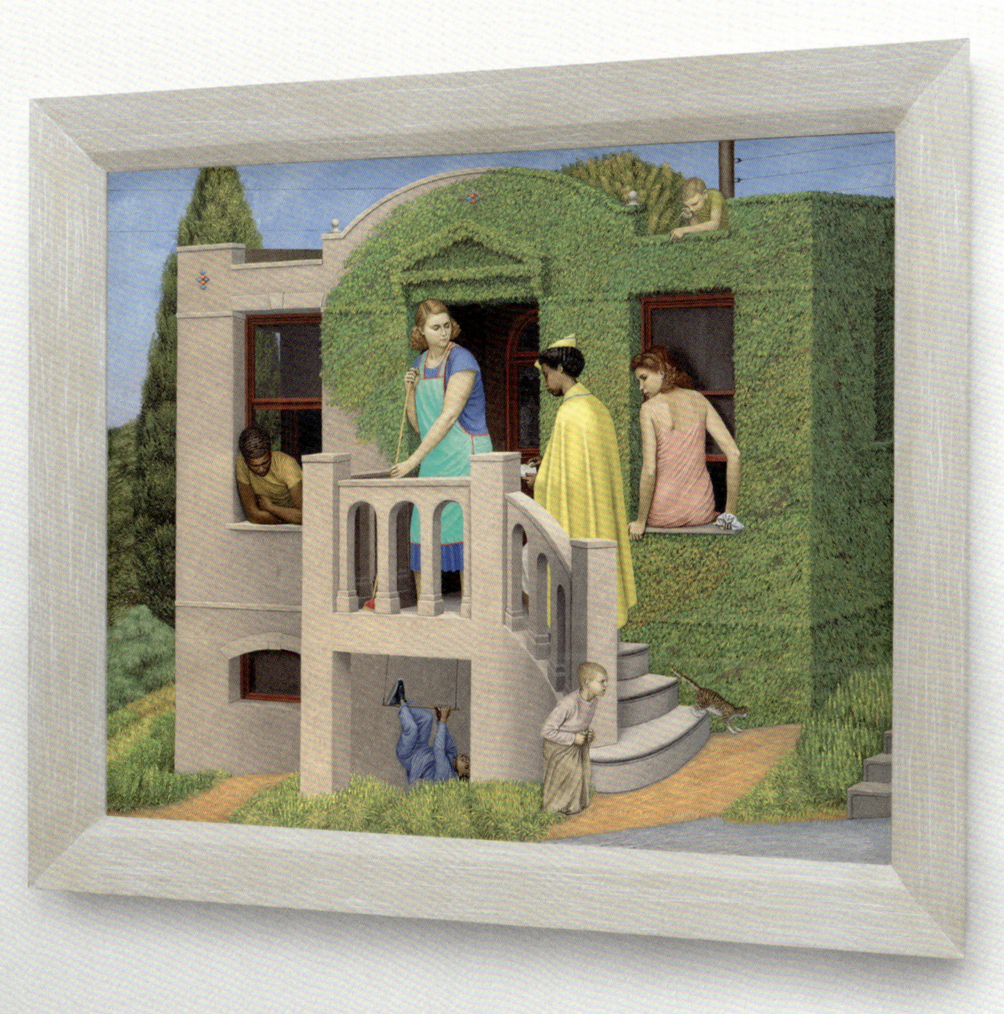

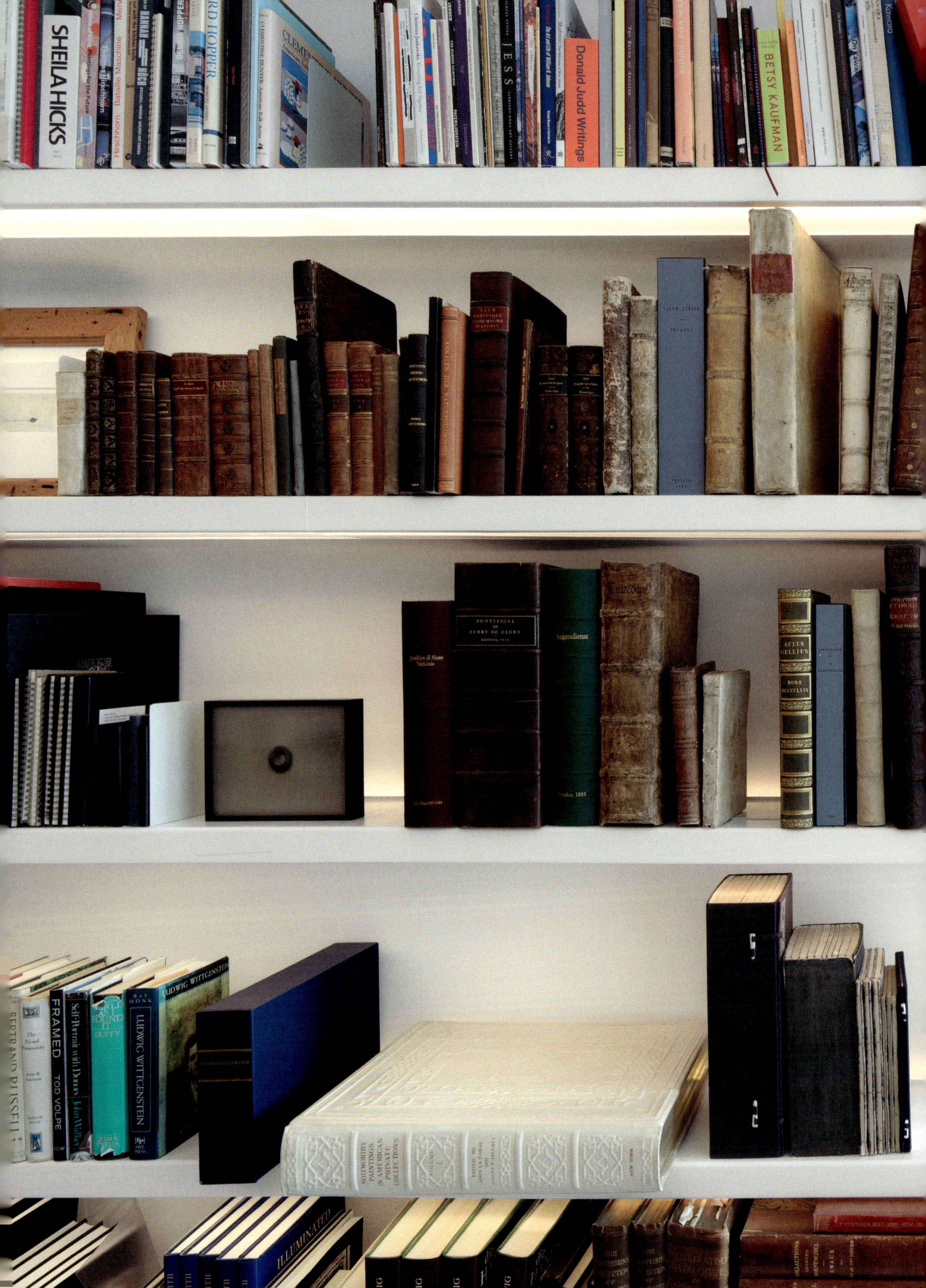

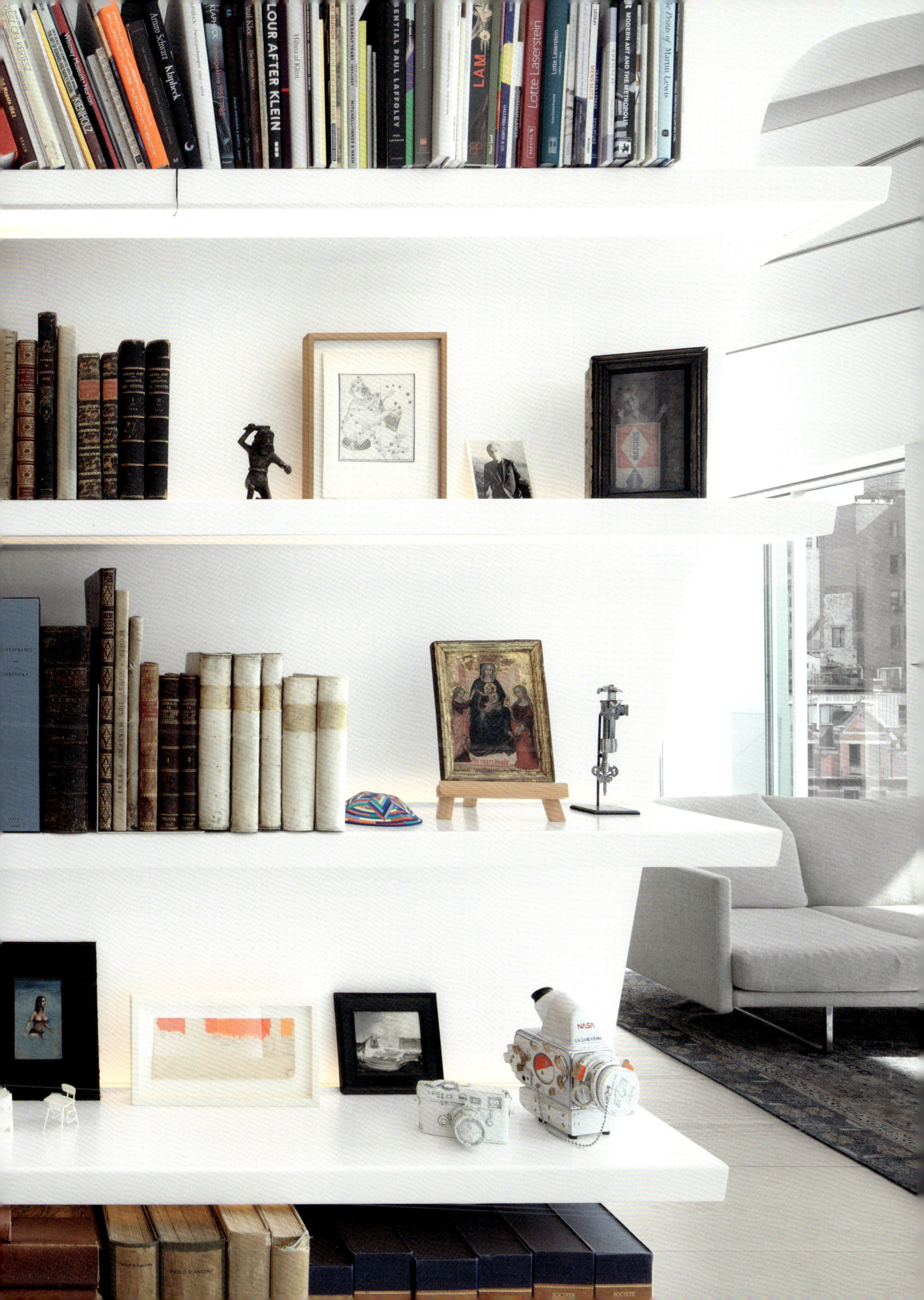

With works from the exhibition
*Seen in the Mirror: Things from the Cartin
Collection*, David Zwirner, New York

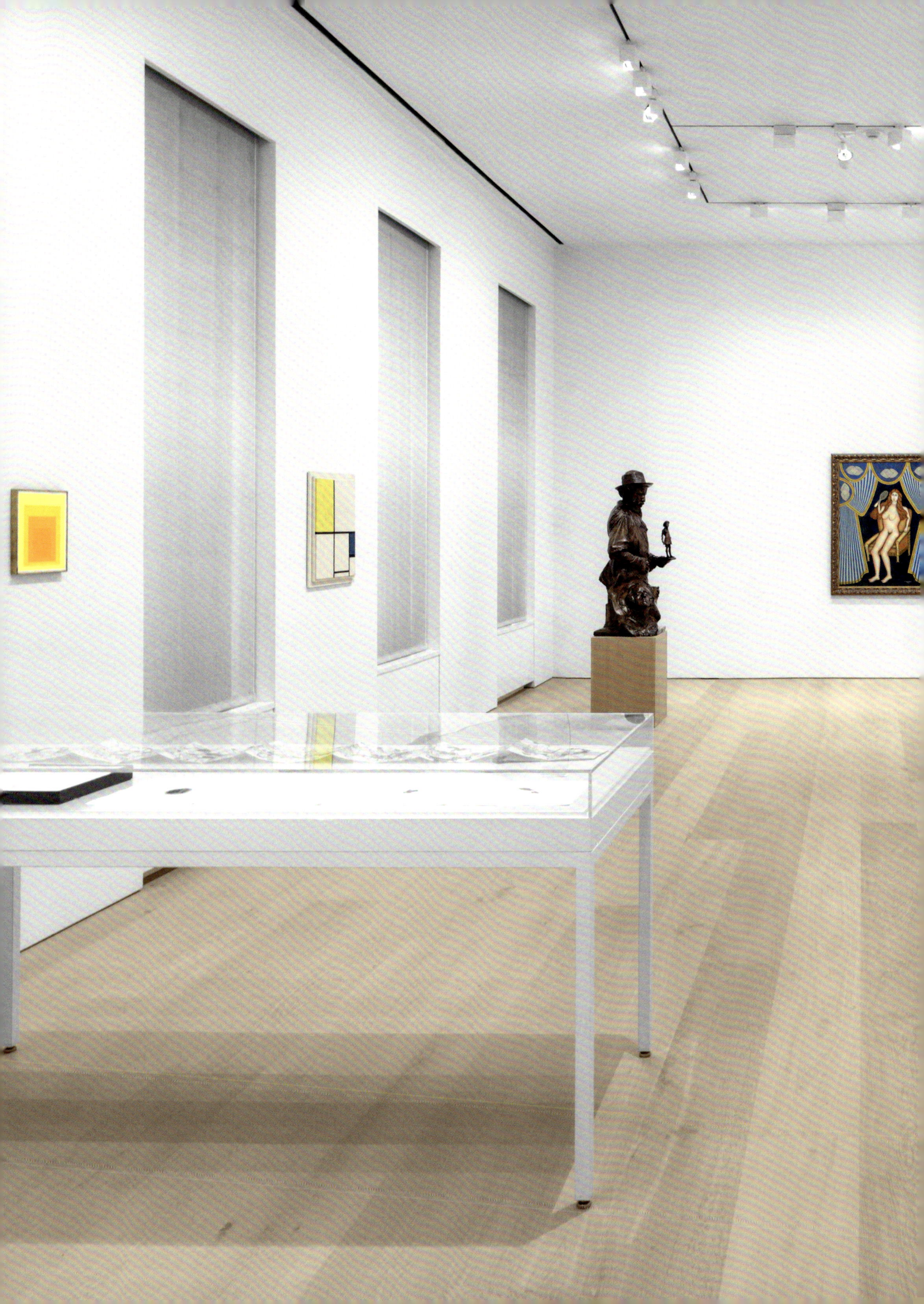

Josef Albers
Homage to the Square (A), 1950
Oil on Masonite
30 ½ × 30 ½ inches | 77.5 × 77.5 cm

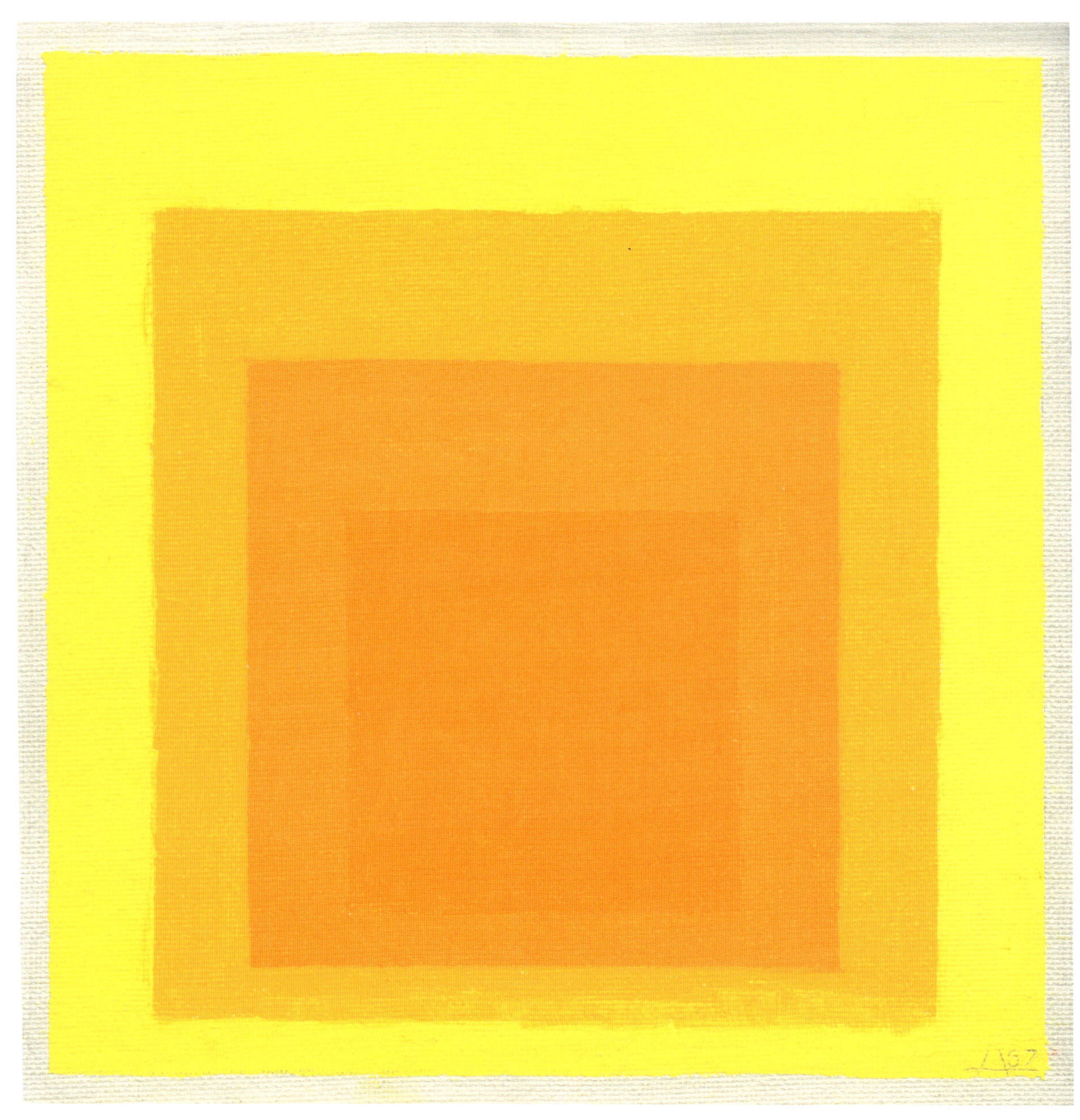

Josef Albers
Study for Homage to the Square, 1967
Oil on Masonite
12 × 12 inches | 30.5 × 30.5 cm

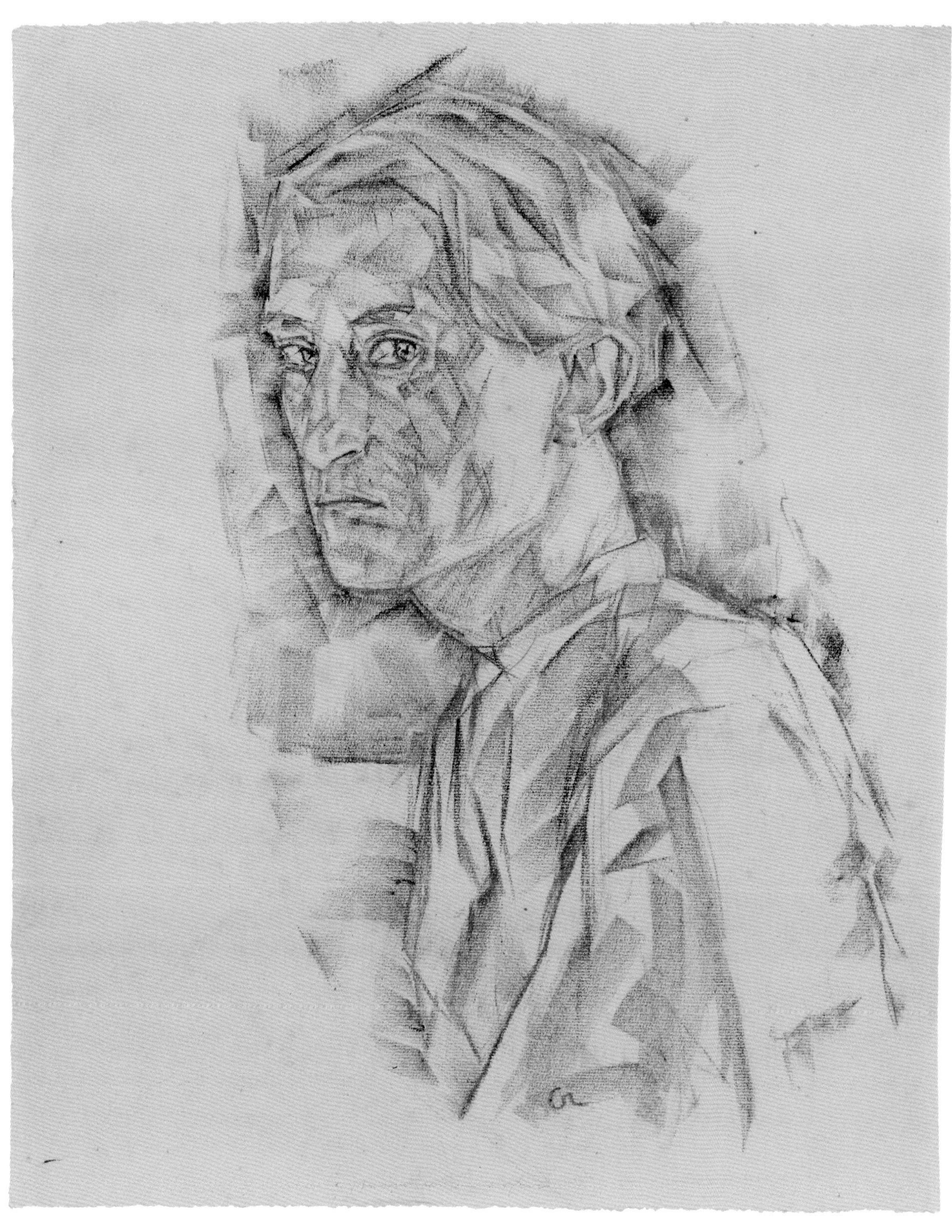

Josef Albers
Self-Portrait III, 1917
Lithographic crayon on paper
18 ⅞ × 15 ¼ inches | 47.9 × 38.7 cm

Roman Opałka
1965/1 – Infinity Detail 3,820,343–3,843,981, 1965
Acrylic on canvas
77 ¼ × 53 ¼ inches | 196.2 × 135.3 cm

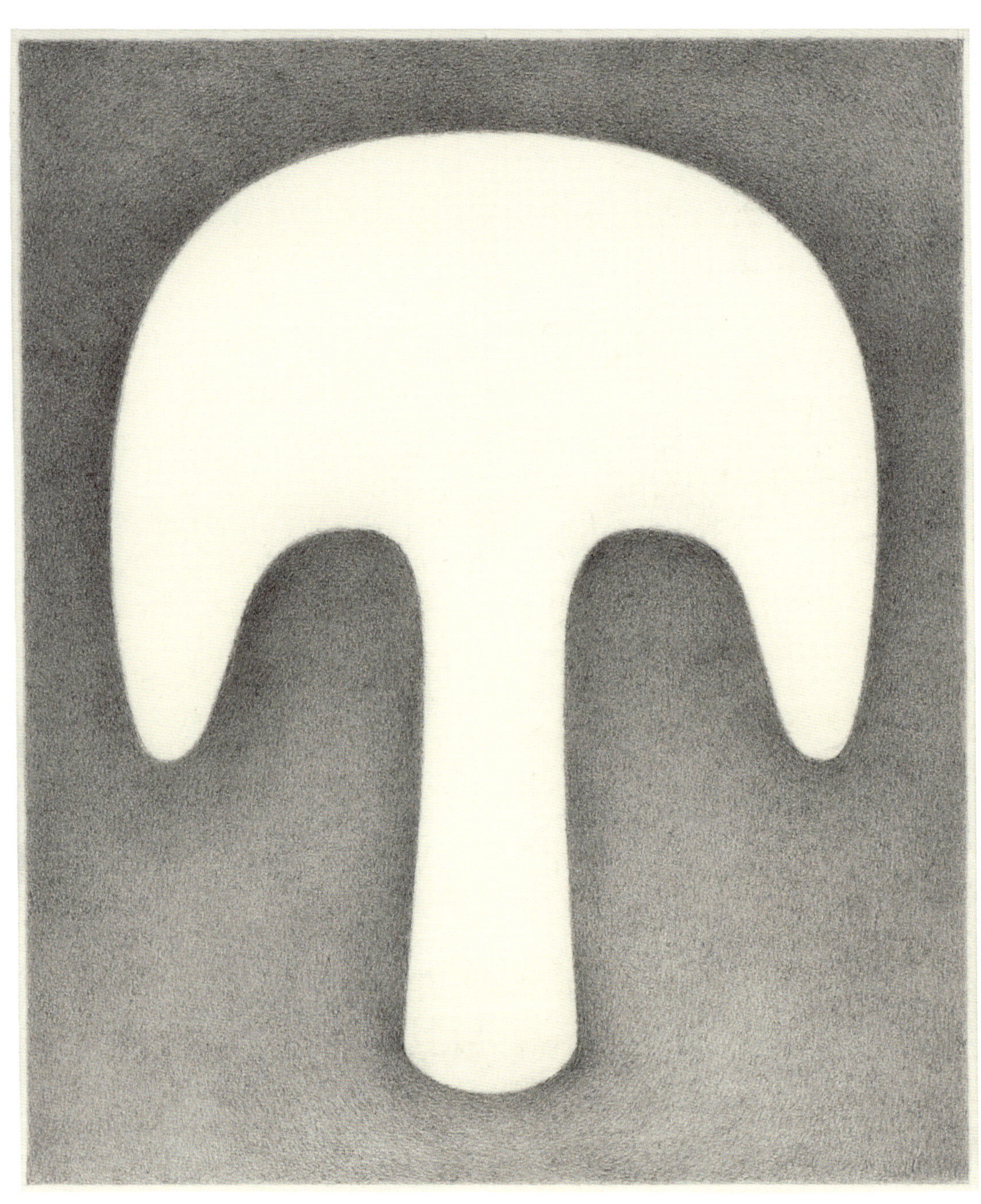

Myron Stout
Tiresias II, 1965
Graphite on paper
6 × 5 inches | 15.2 × 12.7 cm

Myron Stout
Untitled, 1979
Graphite on paper
2 ⅝ × 3 ⅜ inches | 6.7 × 8.6 cm

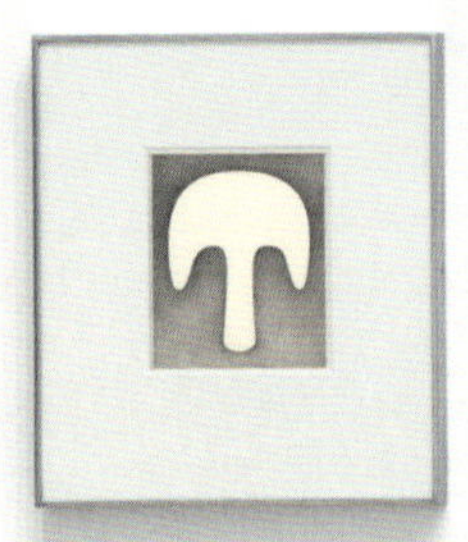

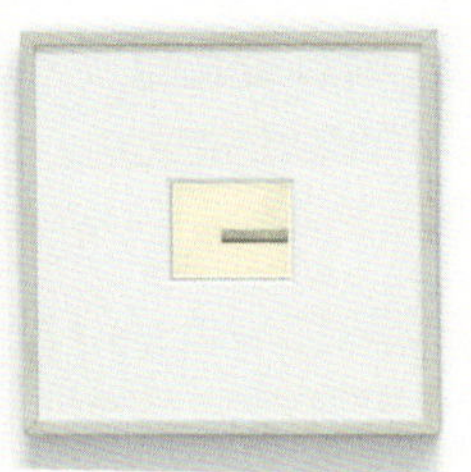

Myron Stout, 1965

Myron Stout, 1979

Roman Opałka, 1965

On Kawara
18 JUN. 1989–24 JUN. 1989, 1989
From *Today*, 1966–2013
Acrylic on canvas; seven paintings
Each: 10 × 13 inches | 25.4 × 33 cm

18JUN.1989

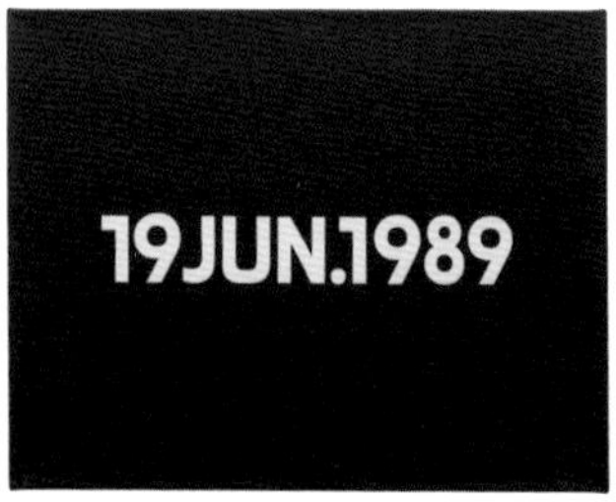

19JUN.1989

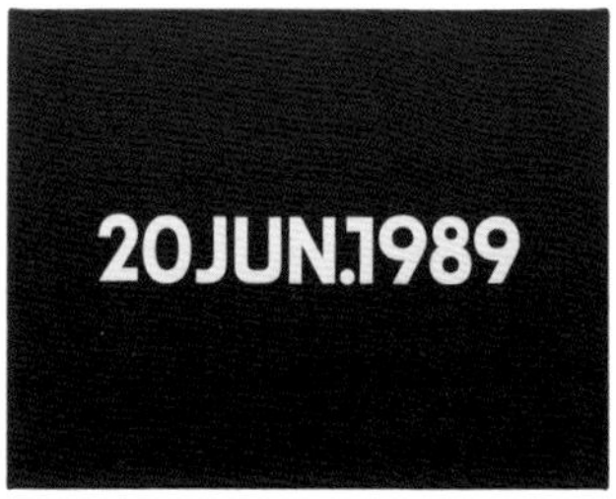

20JUN.1989

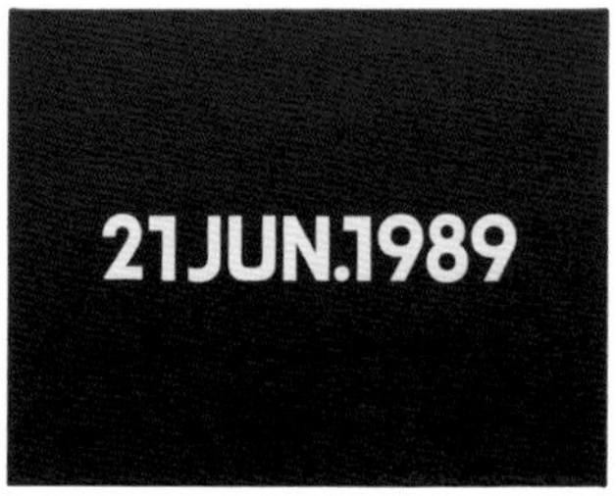

21JUN.1989

22JUN.1989   23JUN.1989   24JUN.1989

Charles LeDray
Untitled, 1996–2003
Glazed ceramic, glass, and steel
80 × 36 × 36 inches | 203.2 × 91.4 × 91.4 cm

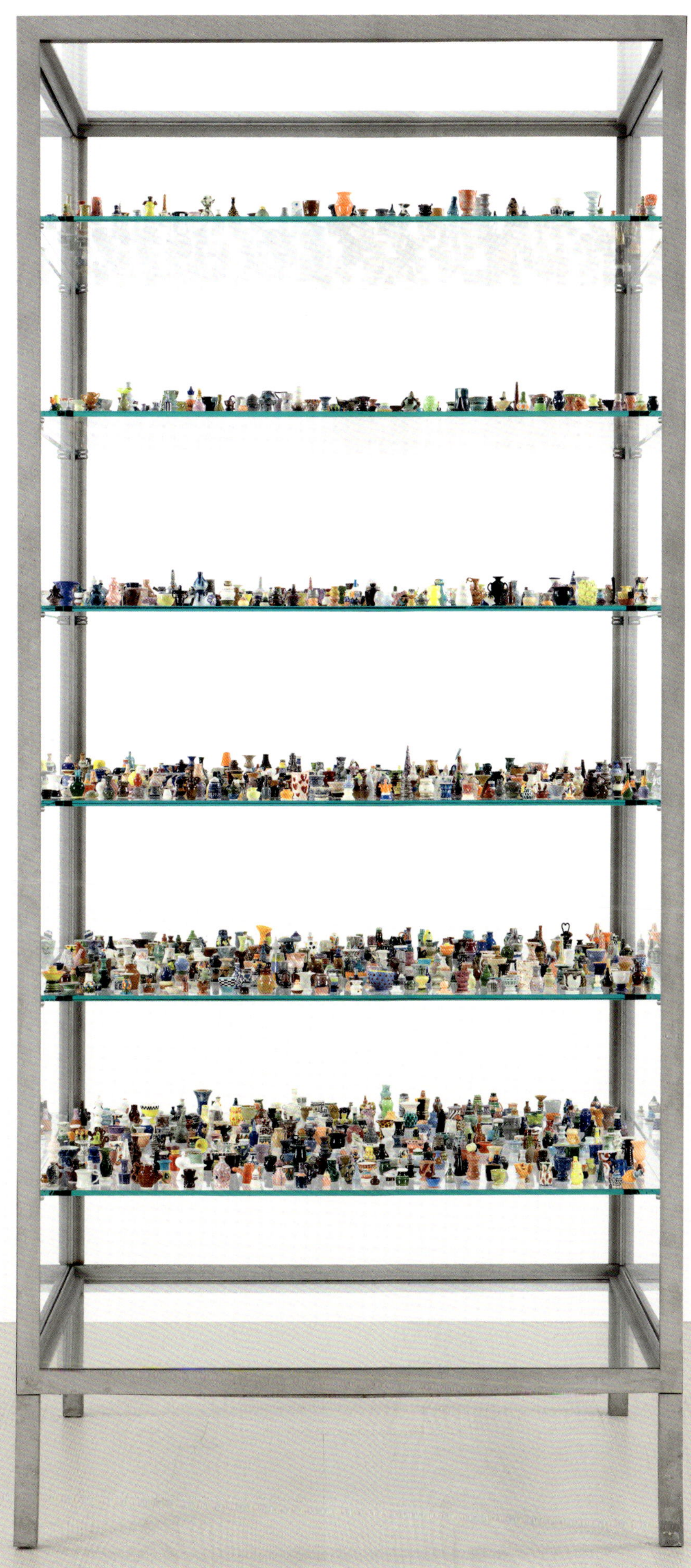

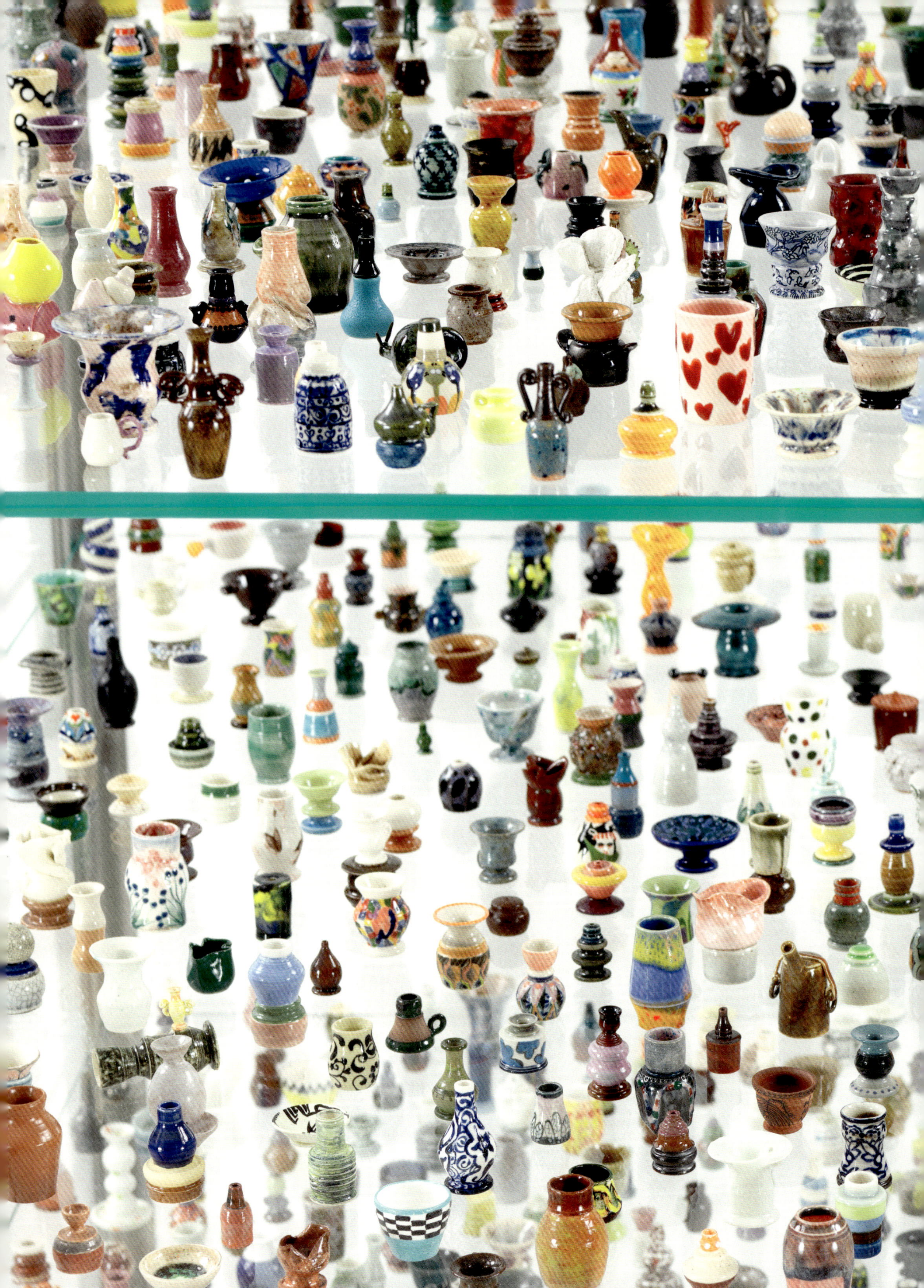

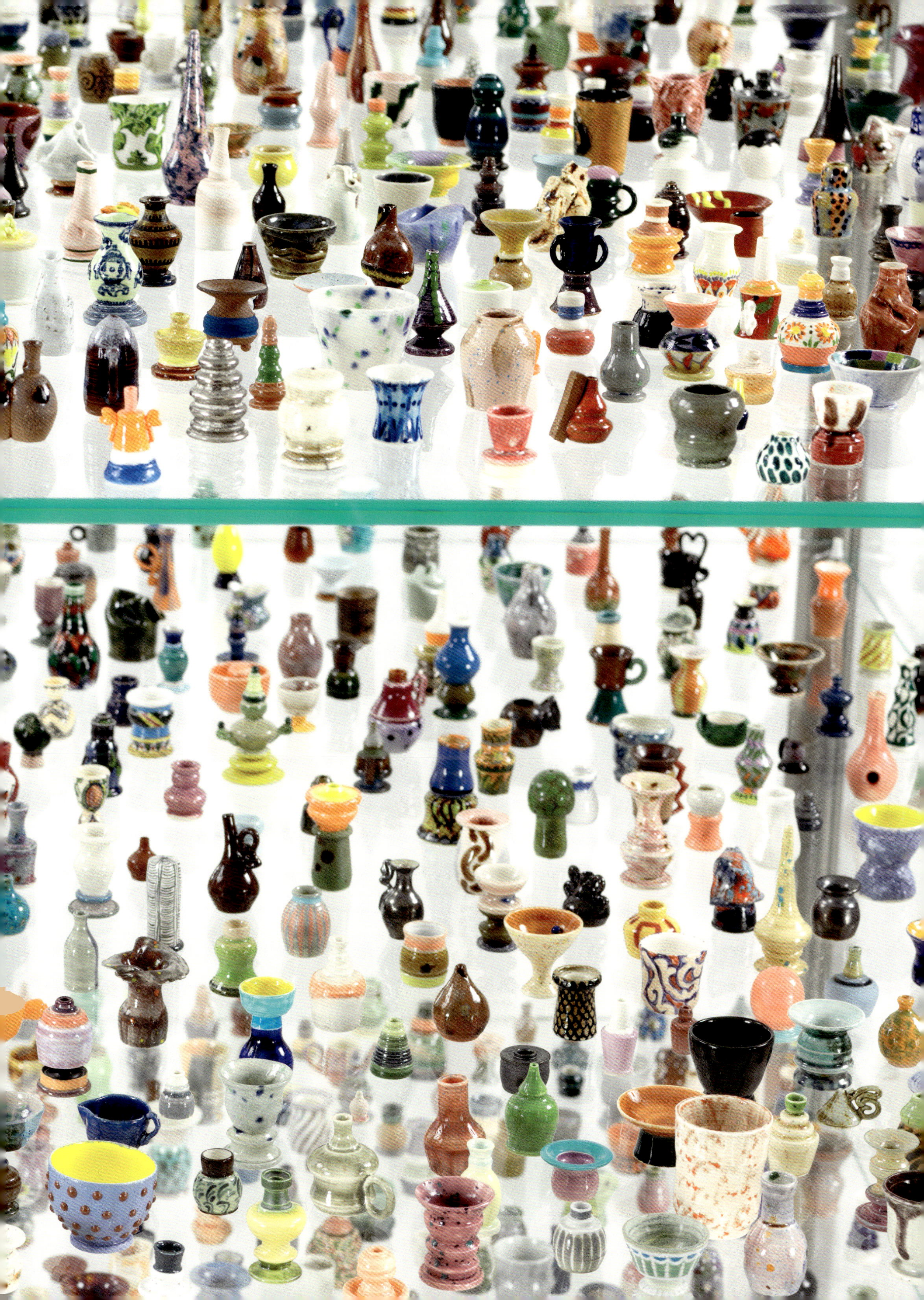

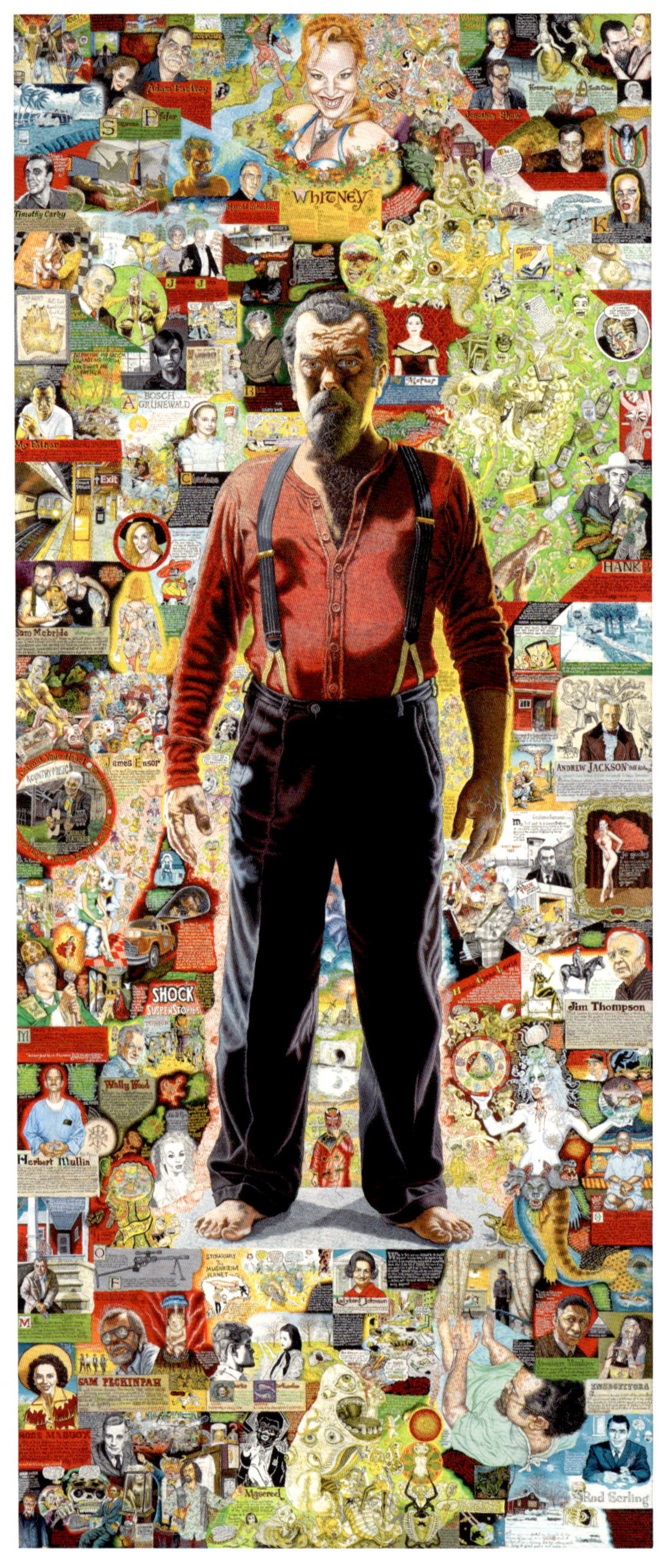

Joe Coleman
A Doorway to Joe, 2007–2009
Acrylic on wood panel
77 × 33 inches | 195.6 × 83.8 cm

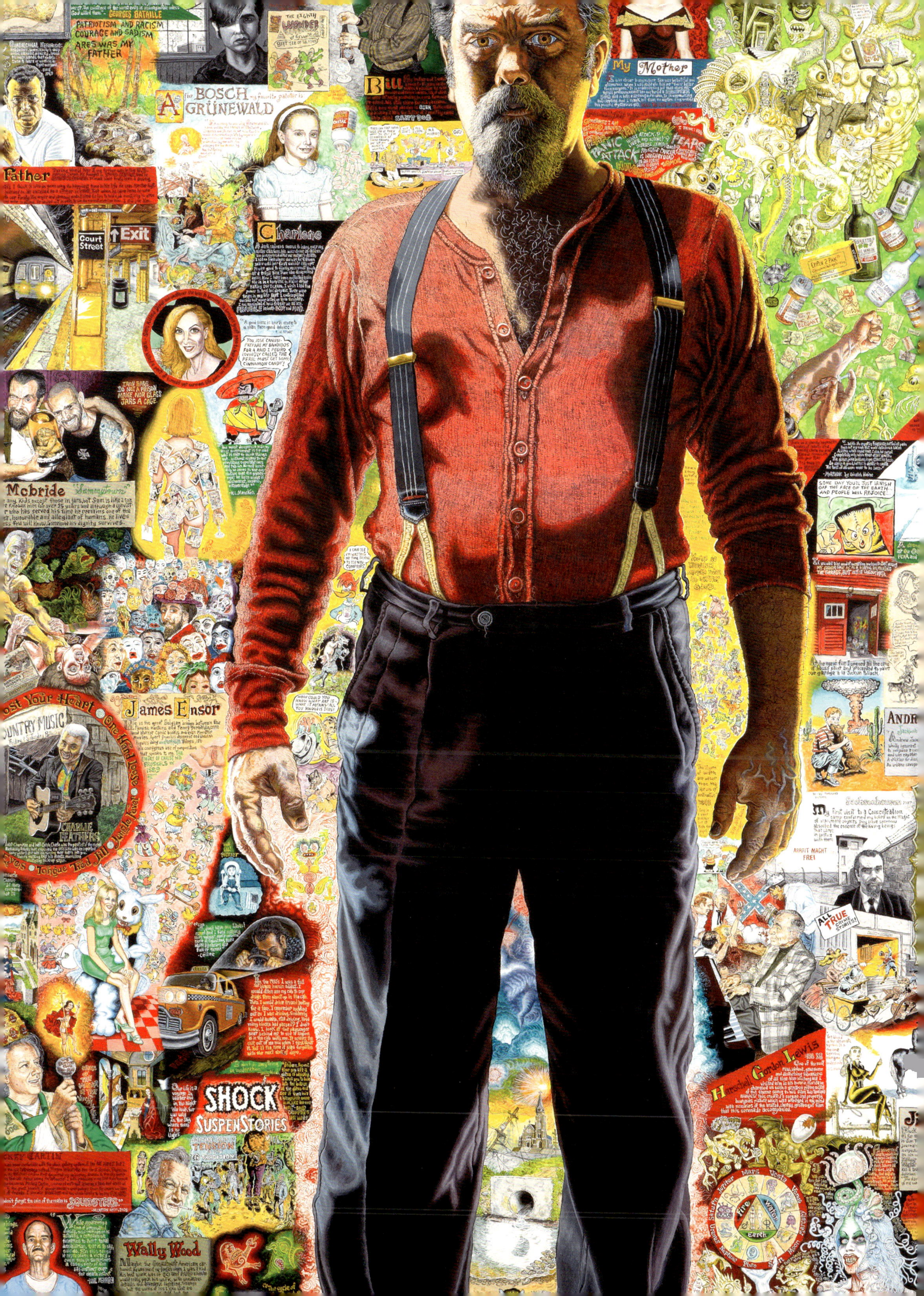

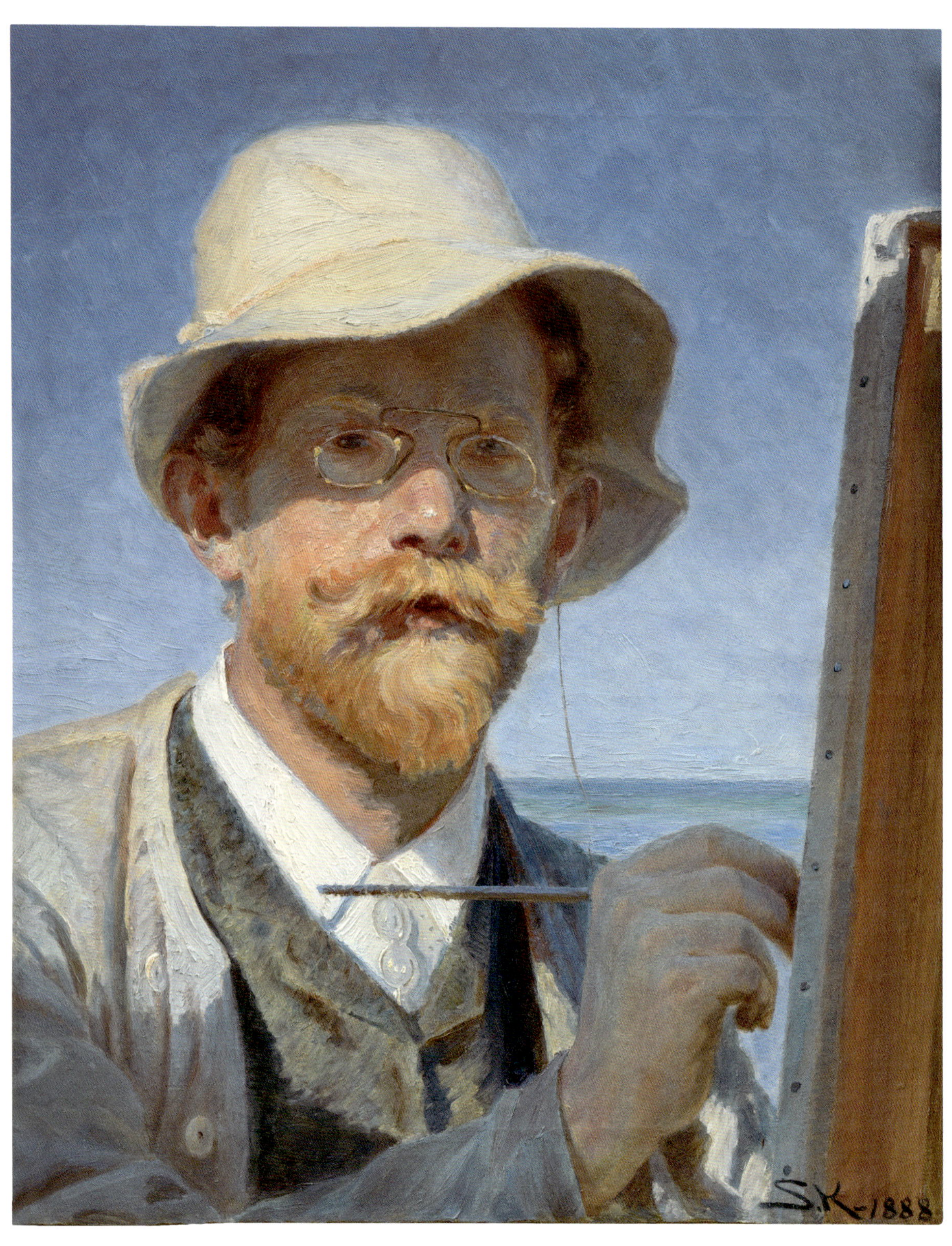

Peder Krøyer
Self-Portrait on the Beach of Skagen, 1888
Oil on canvas
19 ⅝ × 16 ¼ inches | 49.9 × 41.3 cm

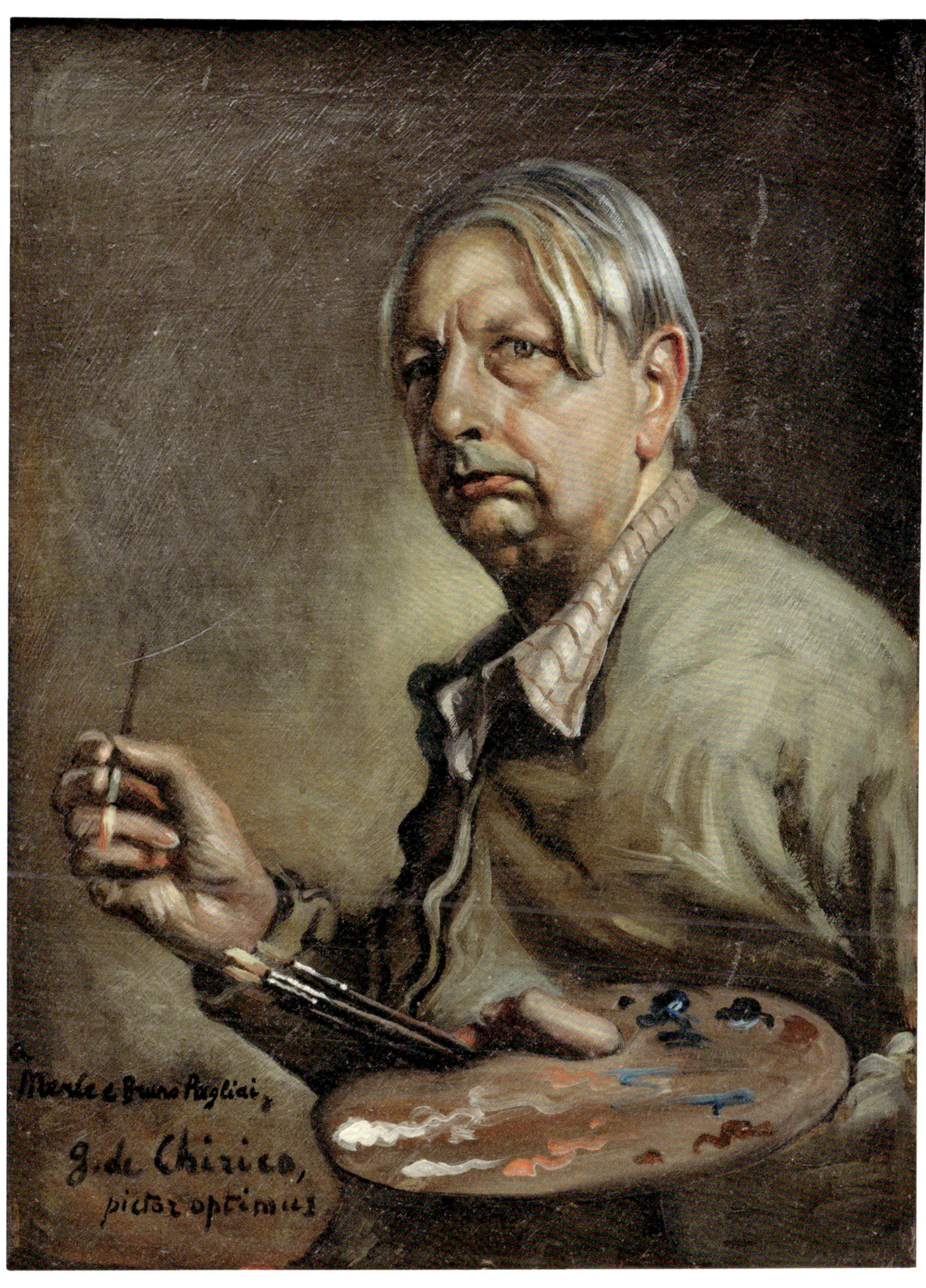

Giorgio de Chirico
Autoritratto (Self-Portrait), 1948
Oil on Masonite
26 ¾ × 20 ¼ inches | 68 × 51.4 cm

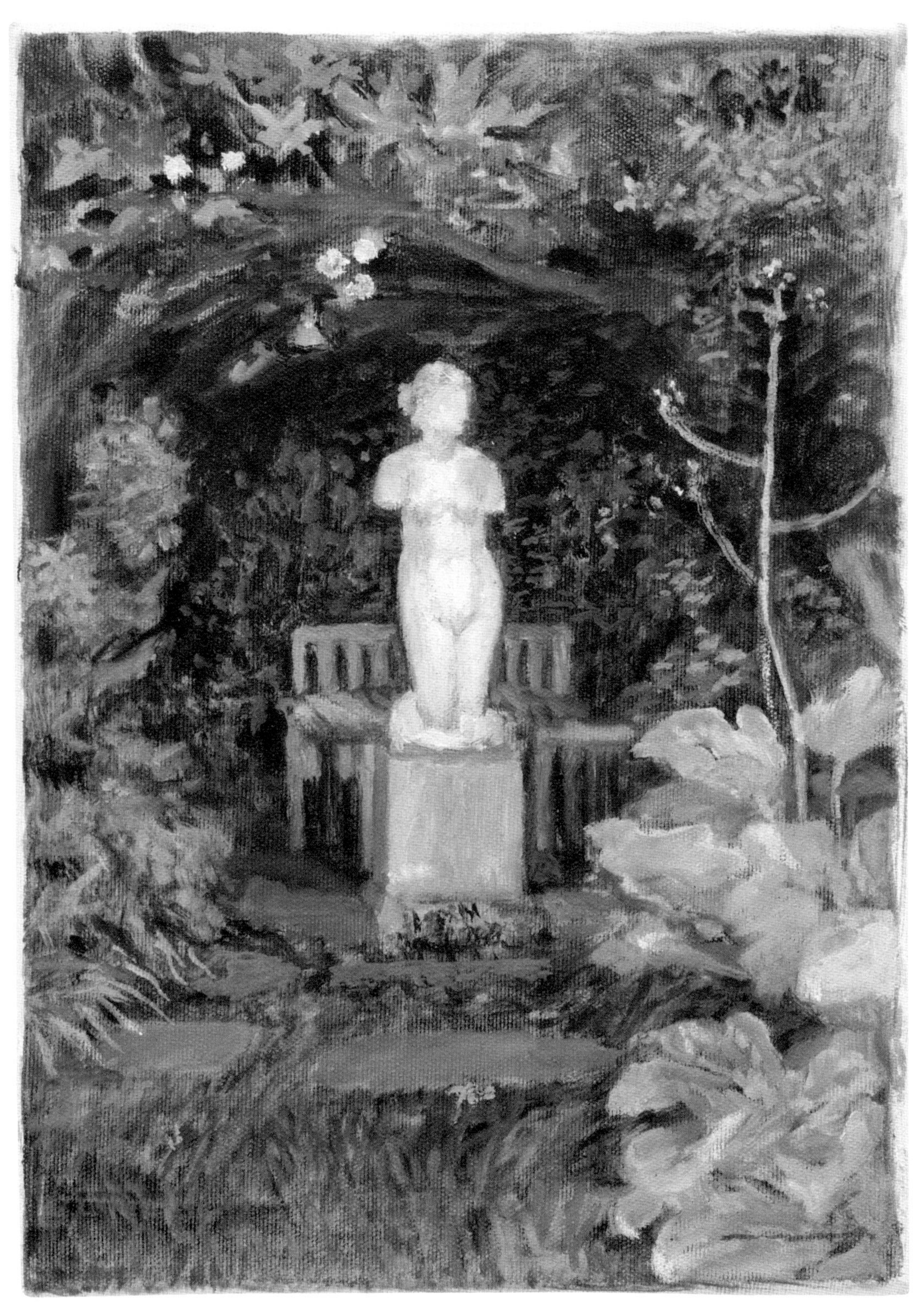

Cecilia Edefalk
Double White Venus, 2000
Oil on canvas
8 ¾ × 6 ⅜ inches | 22.2 × 16 cm

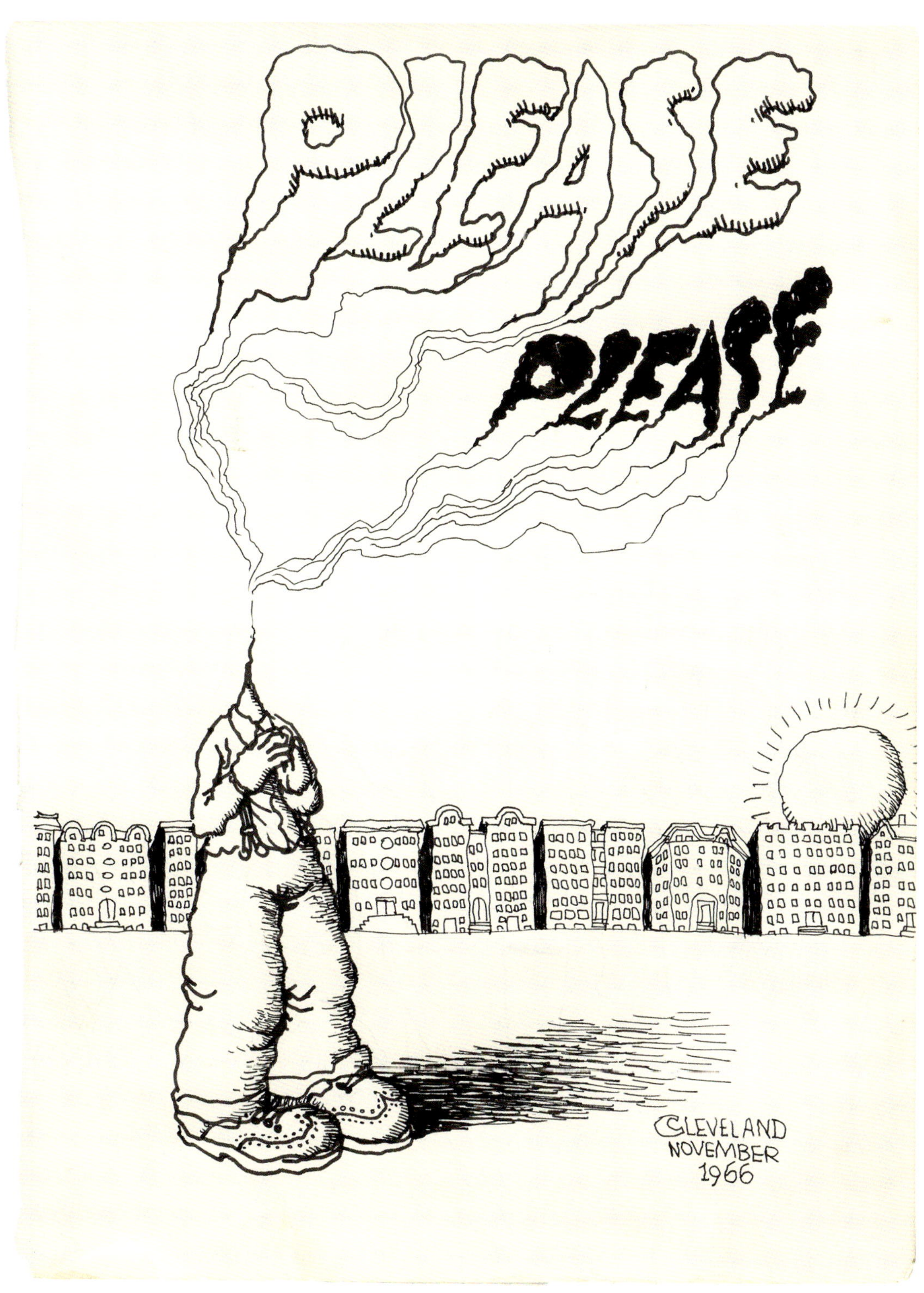

R. Crumb
Please Please, 1966
Ink on paper
10 × 7 ¼ inches | 25.4 × 18.4 cm

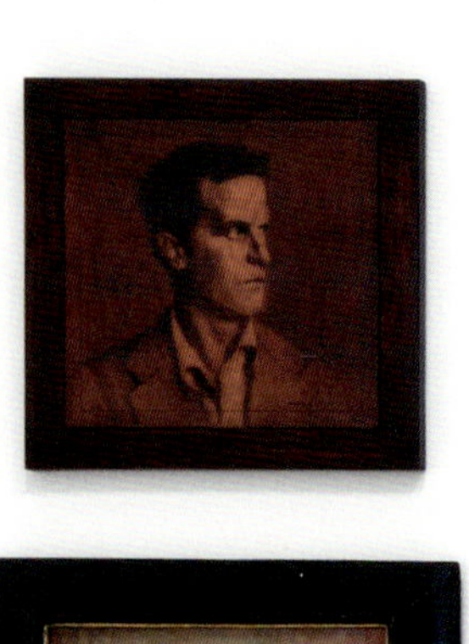
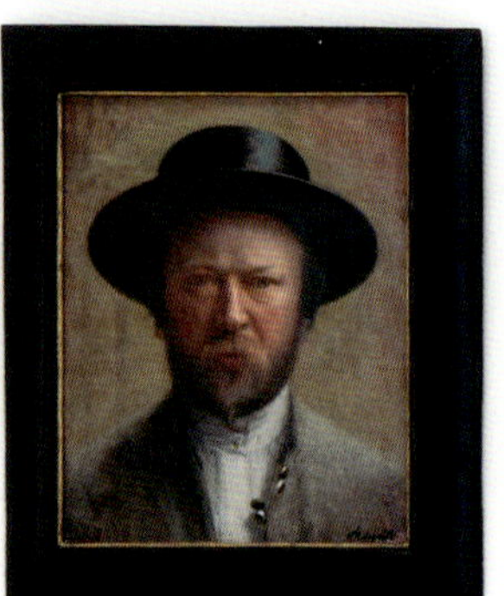
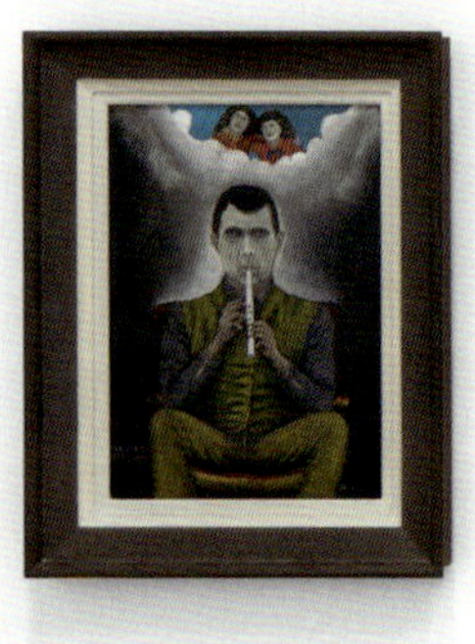
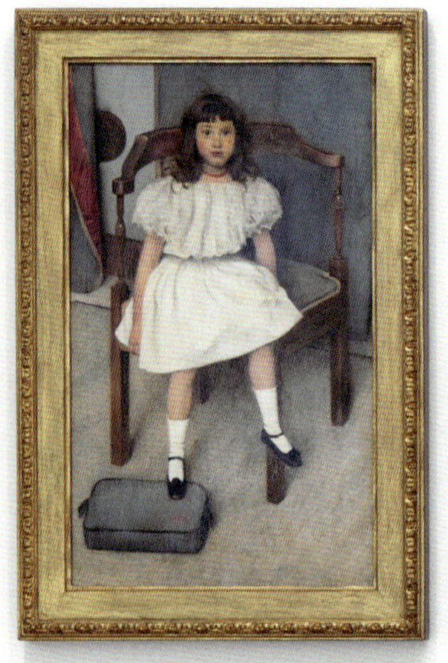
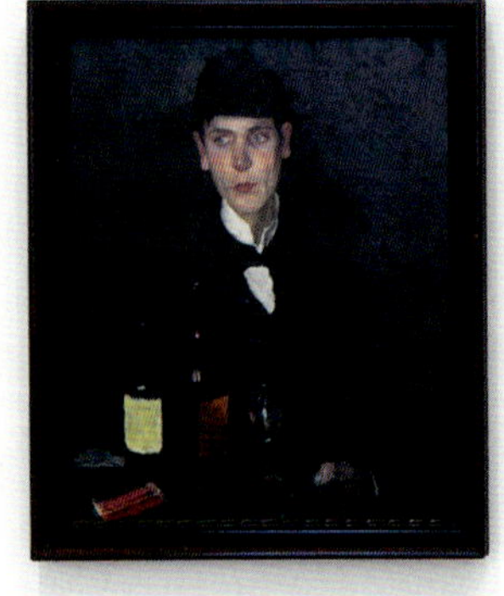
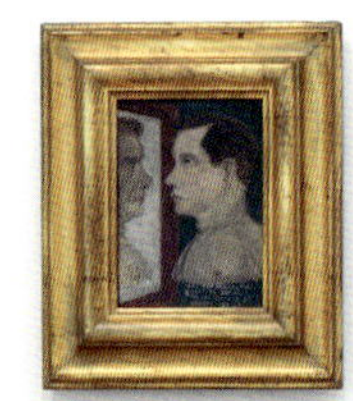
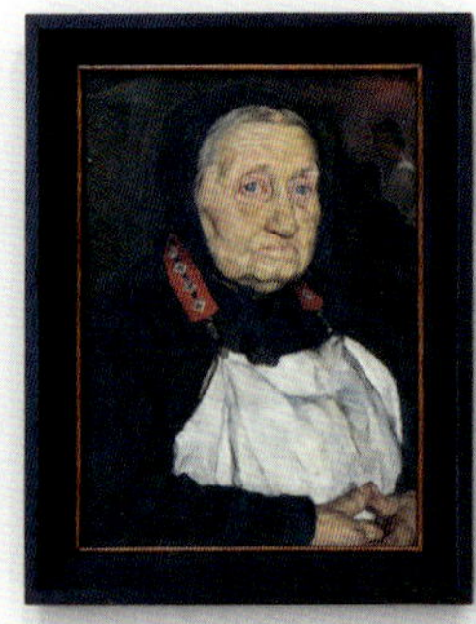
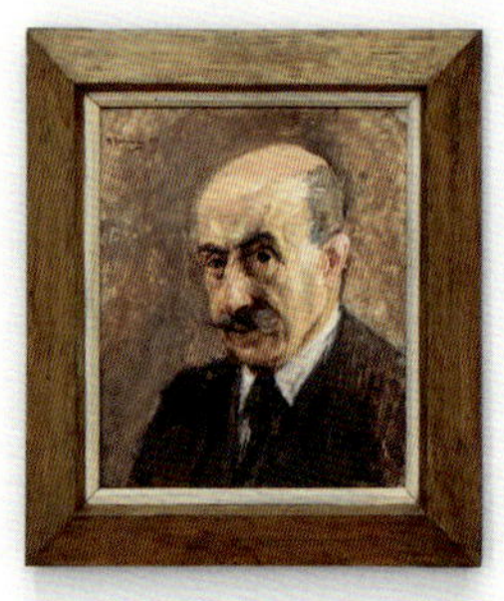
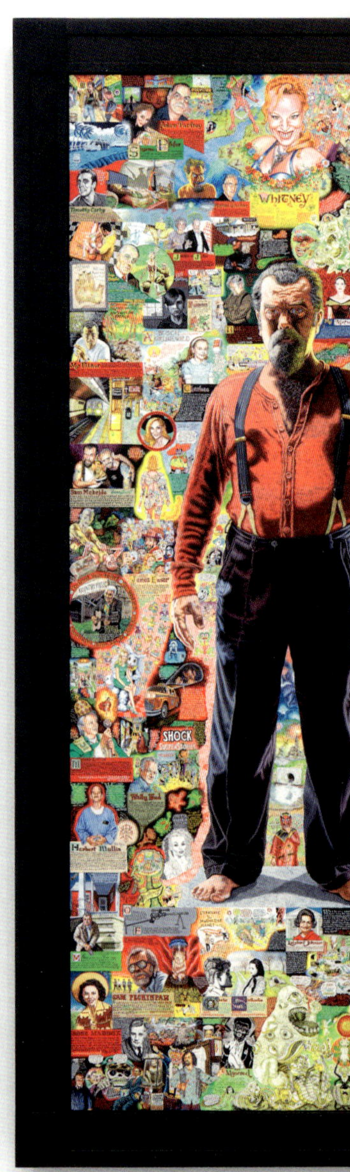

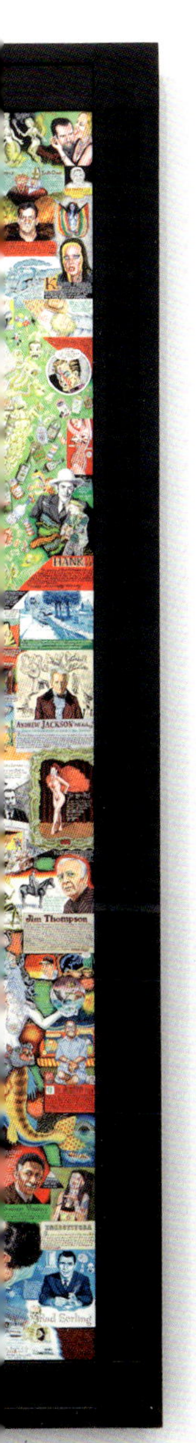
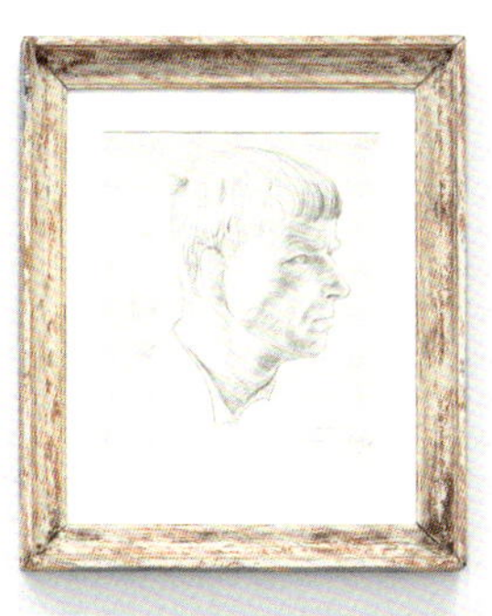
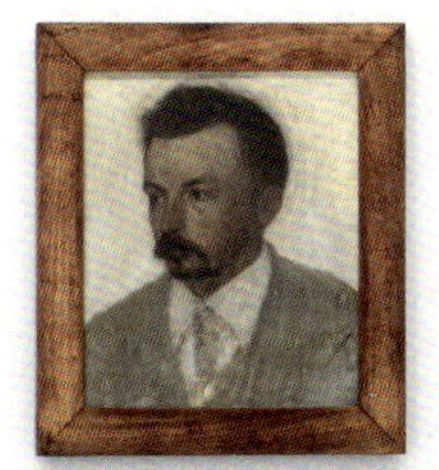
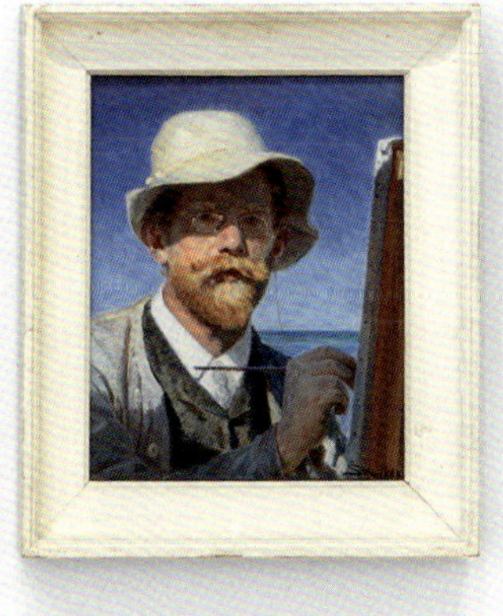
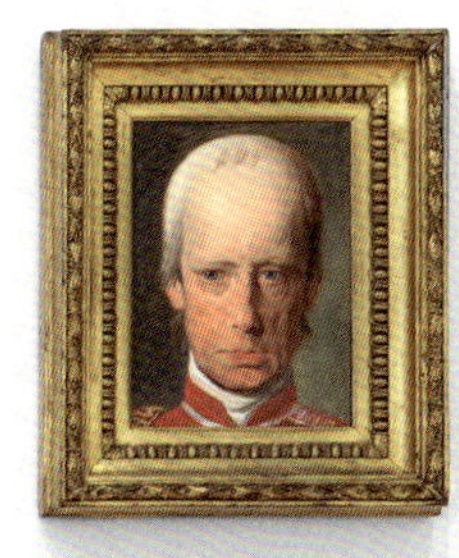
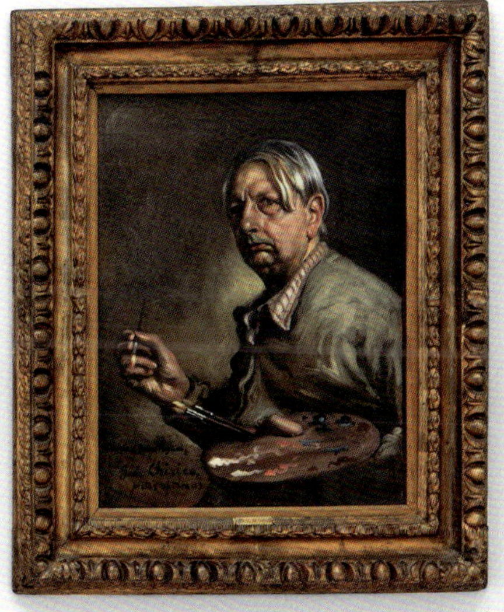
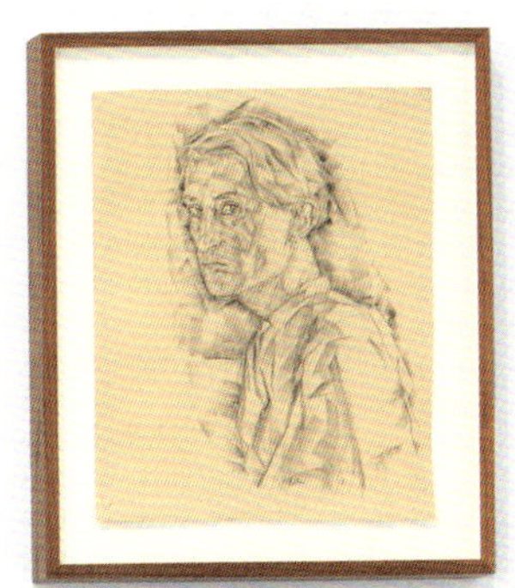
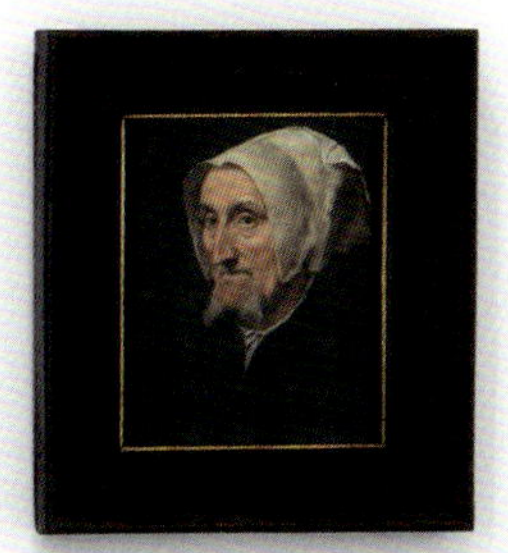
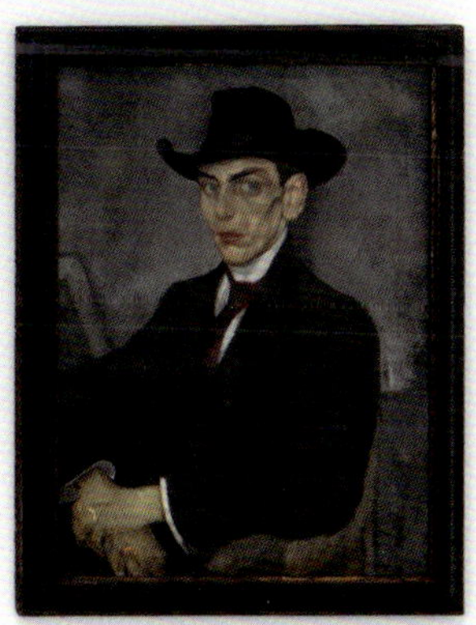

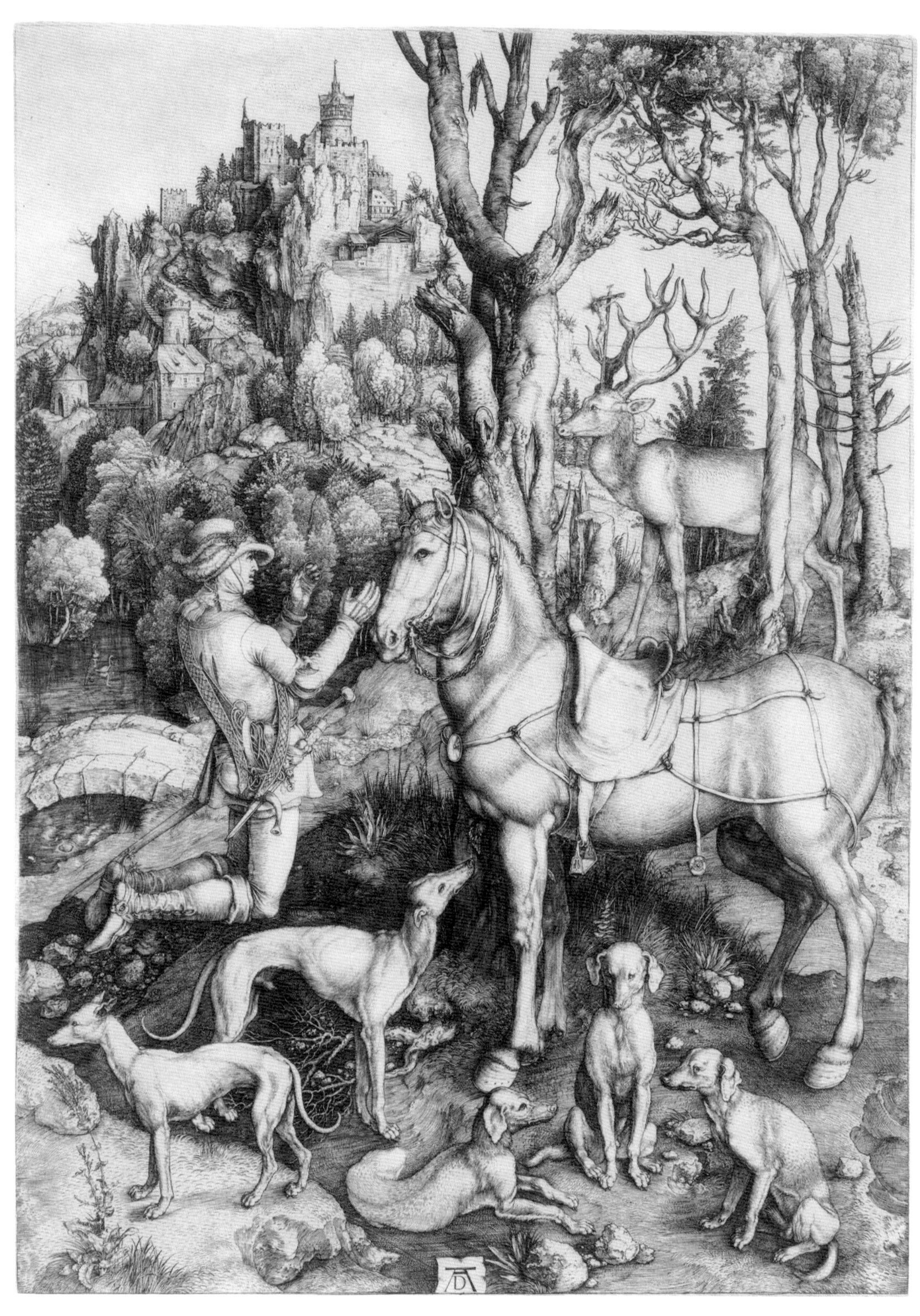

Albrecht Dürer
Saint Eustace, c. 1501
Engraving
13 ¾ × 10 ⅛ inches | 34.9 × 25.7 cm

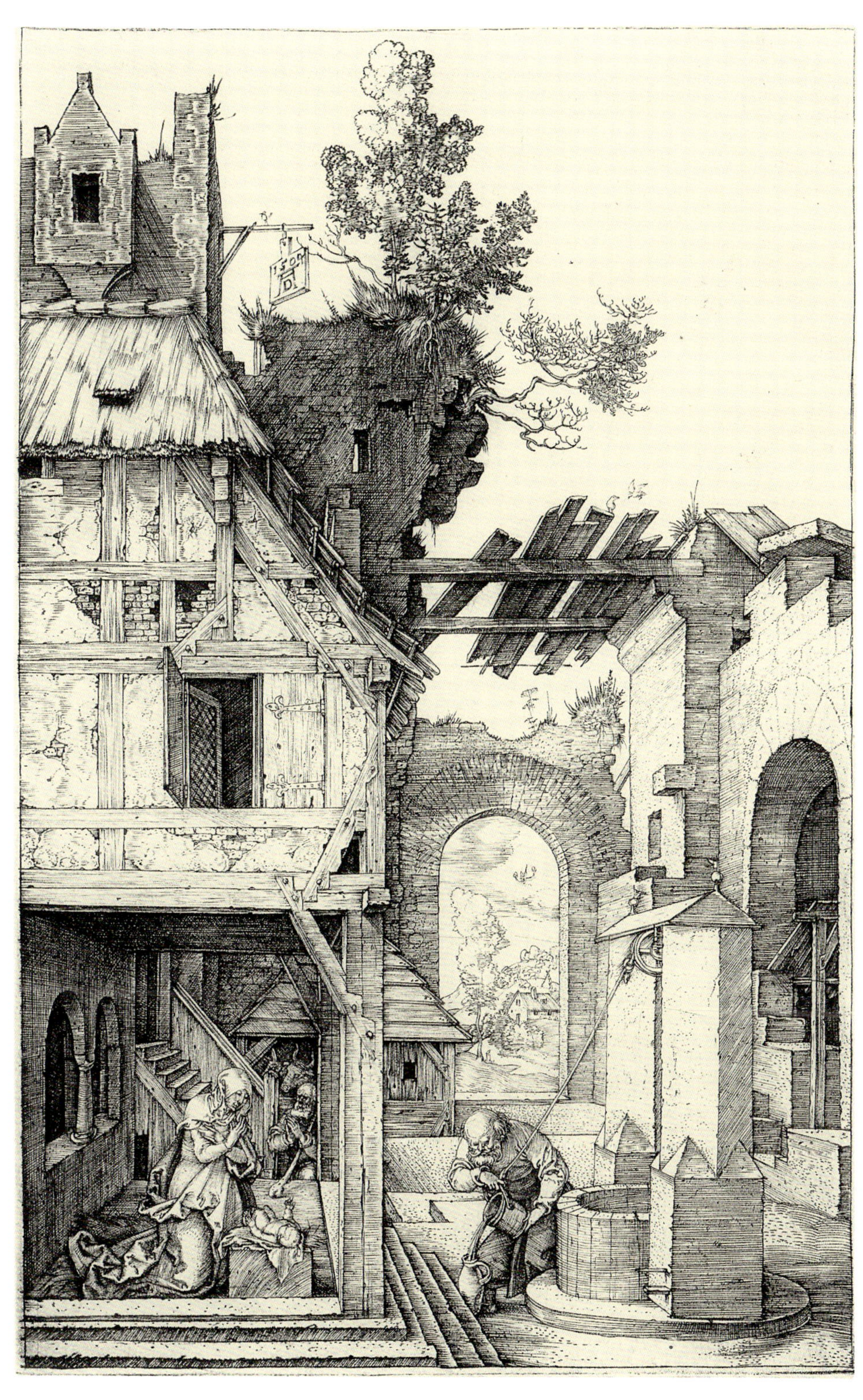

Albrecht Dürer
The Nativity, 1504
Engraving
7 ¼ × 4 ½ inches | 18.4 × 11.4 cm

Henry Koerner
The Stairs, 1950–1951
Oil on Masonite
29 ¾ × 38 inches | 75.6 × 96.5 cm

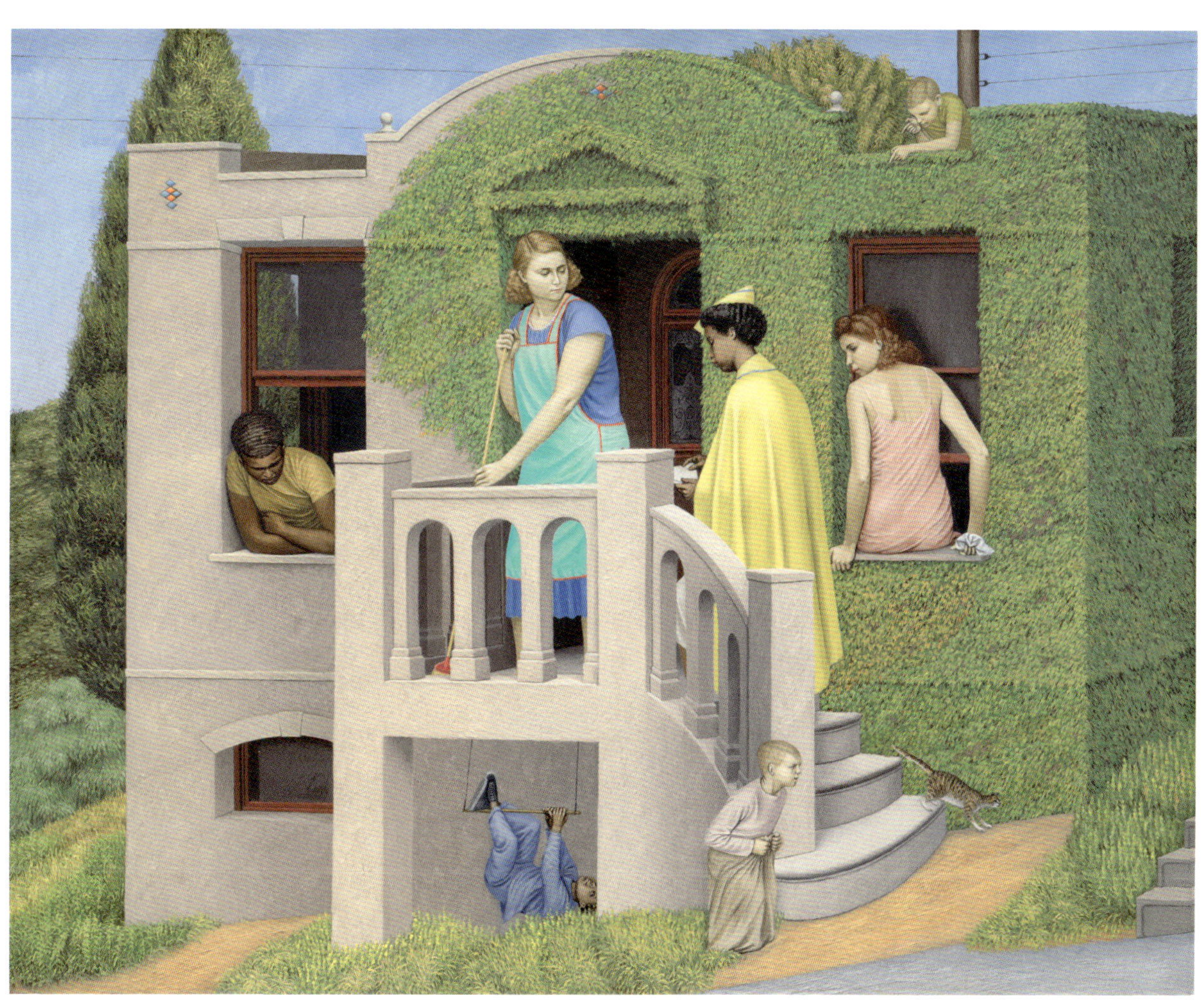

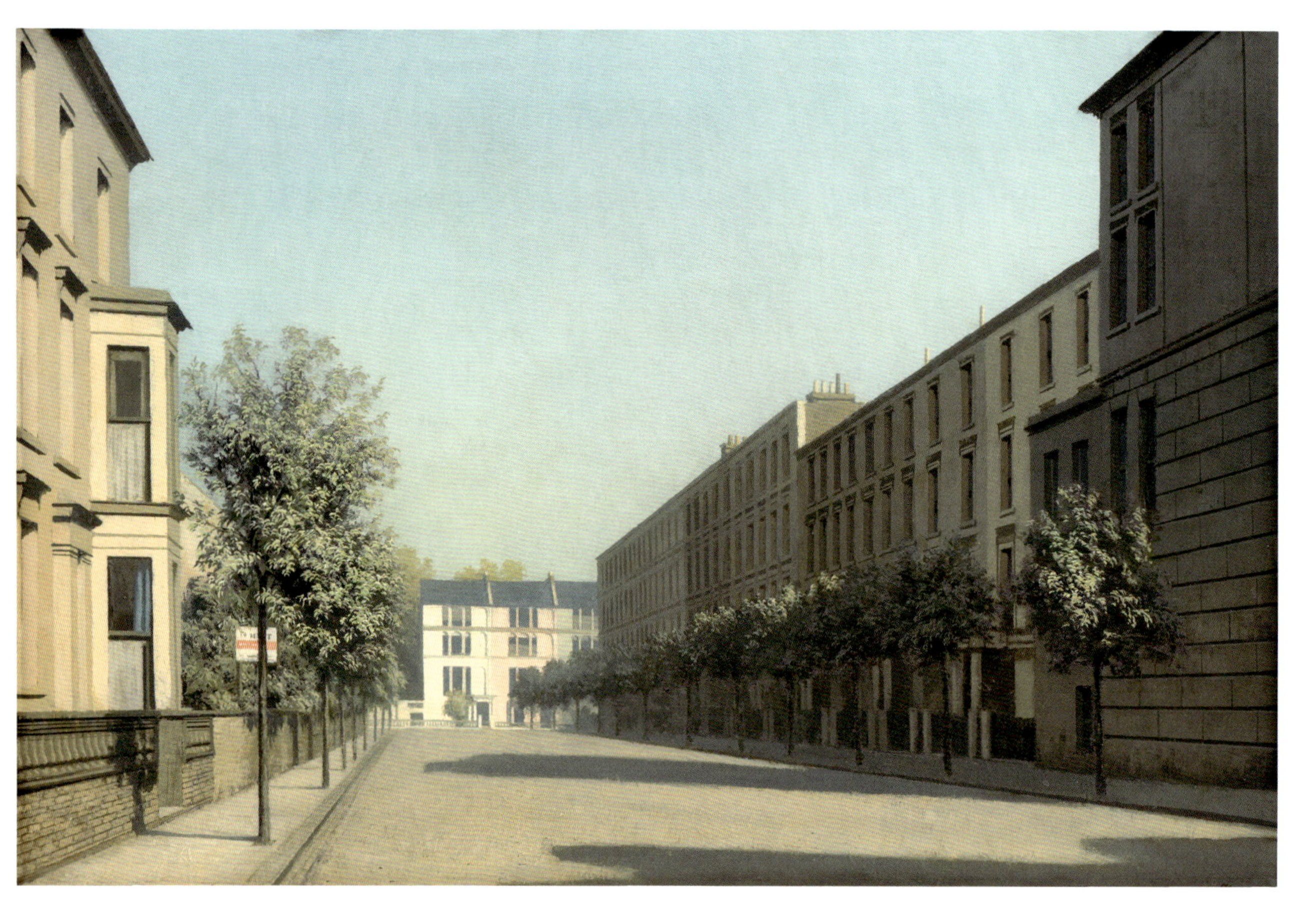

Algernon Newton
Spring Morning, Campden Hill, 1940
Oil on canvas
20 × 30 inches | 50.8 × 76.2 cm

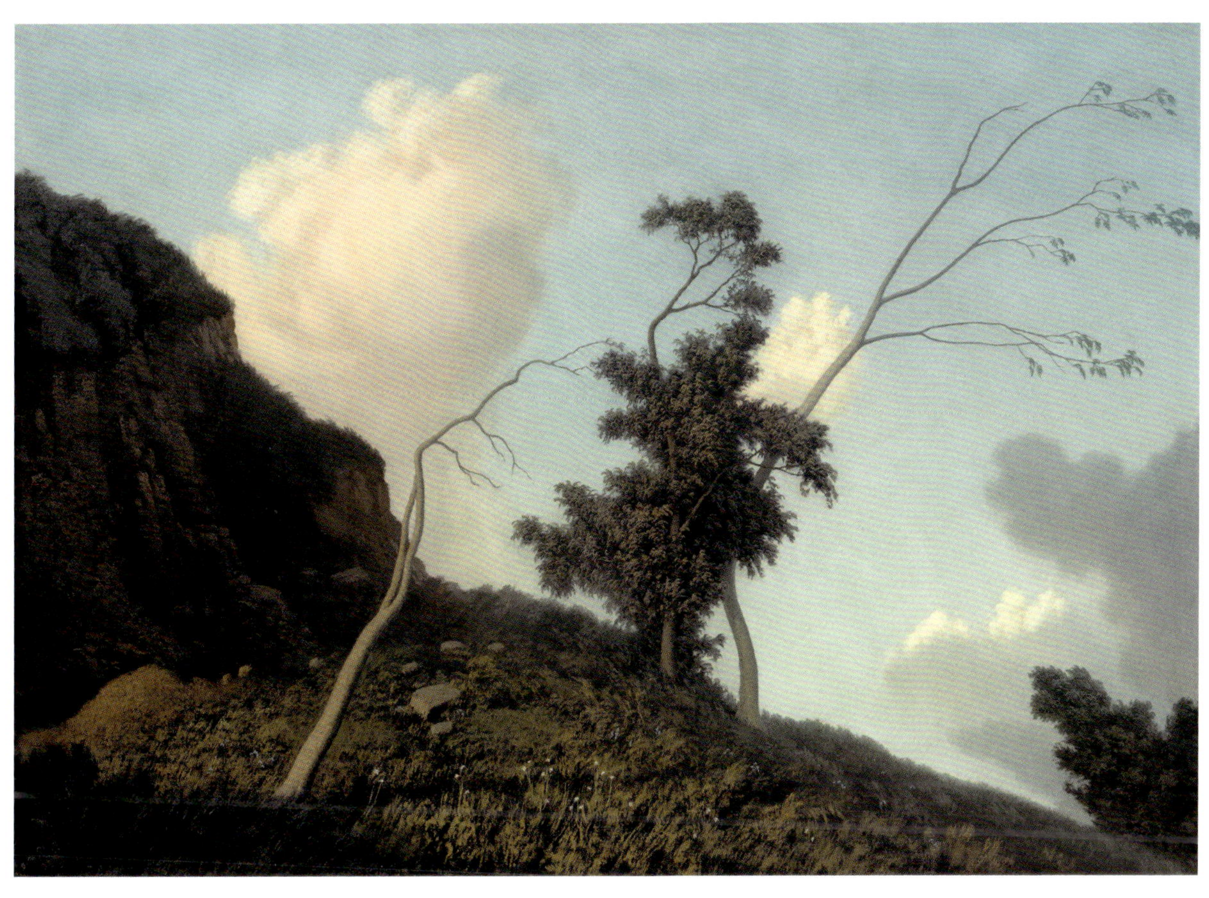

Algernon Newton
The Pink Cloud, 1947
Oil on canvas
33 ⅞ × 48 inches | 86 × 121.9 cm

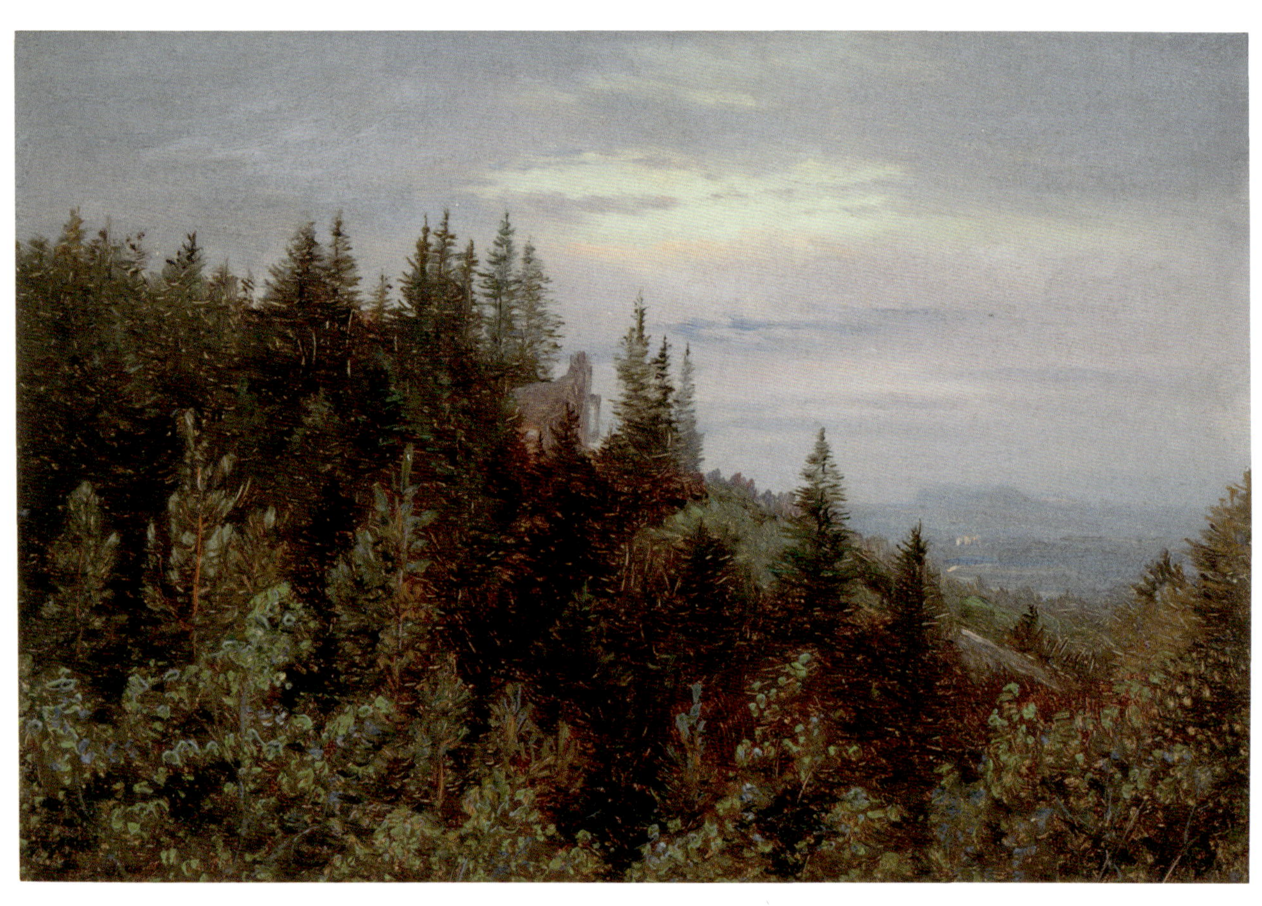

Carl Gustav Carus
Evening Light near Pillnitz, c. 1835
Oil on cardboard
5 ¼ × 7 ¾ inches | 13.3 × 19.7 cm

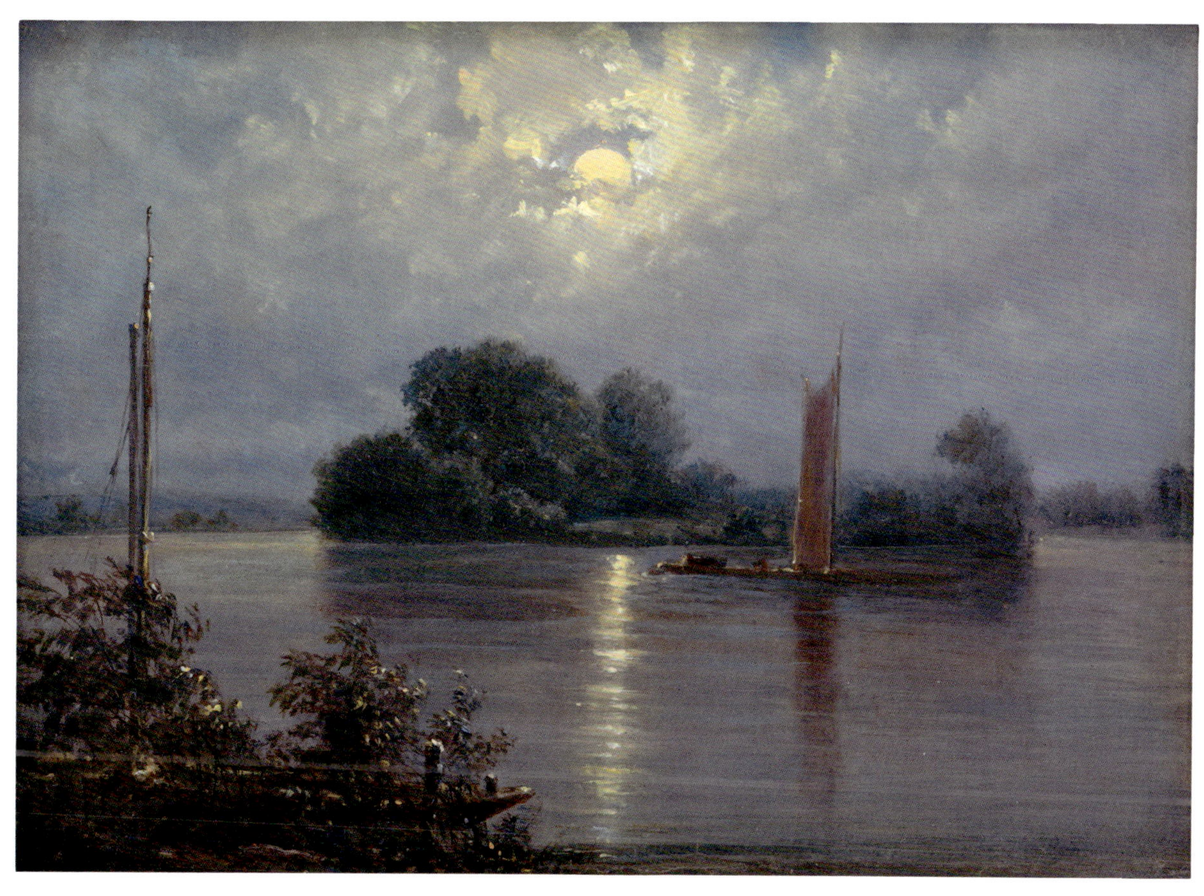

Carl Gustav Carus
Full Moon near Pillnitz, c. 1844
Oil on cardboard
7 × 9 ⅝ inches | 17.8 × 24.4 cm

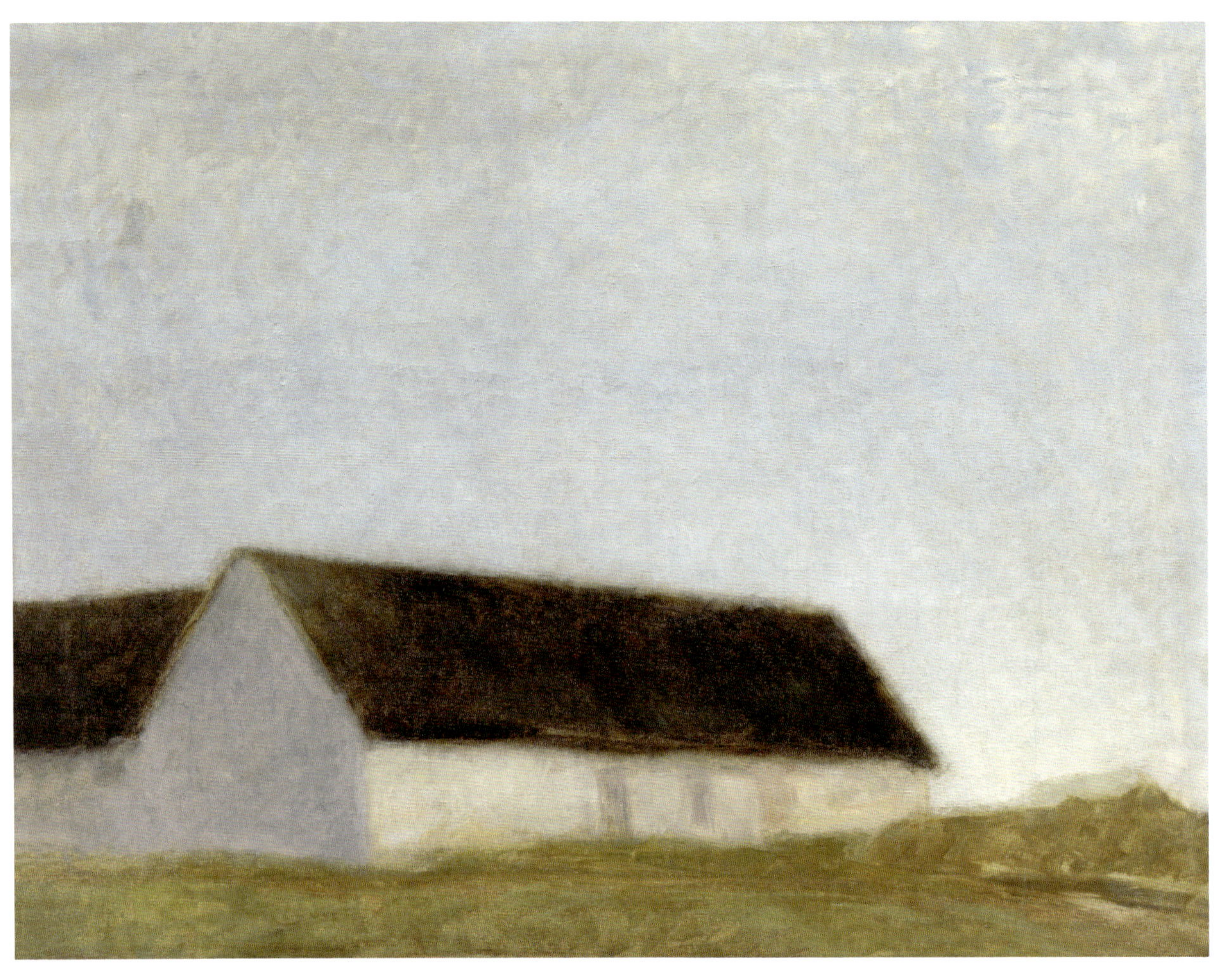

Vilhelm Hammershøi
Parti fra Vejle, Bondelænge [*Farmstead near Vejle*], c. 1883
Oil on linen
19 ¾ × 26 ⅛ inches | 50.2 × 66.4 cm

Lucas Arruda
Untitled (from the Deserto-Modelo series), 2017
Oil on canvas
12 × 13 ⅜ inches | 30.5 × 34 cm

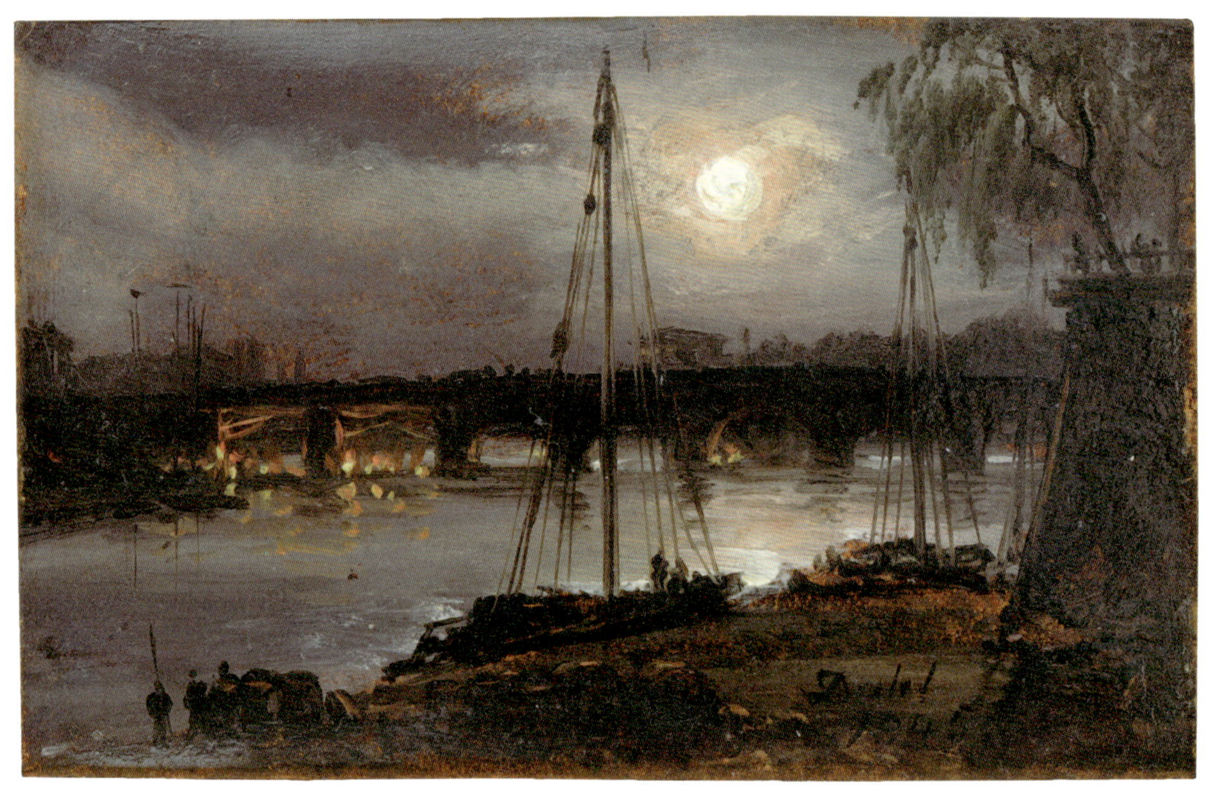

Johan Christian Dahl
The Augustusbrücke in Dresden under Repair, 1845
Oil on cardboard
2 ¾ × 4 ¼ inches | 7 × 10.8 cm

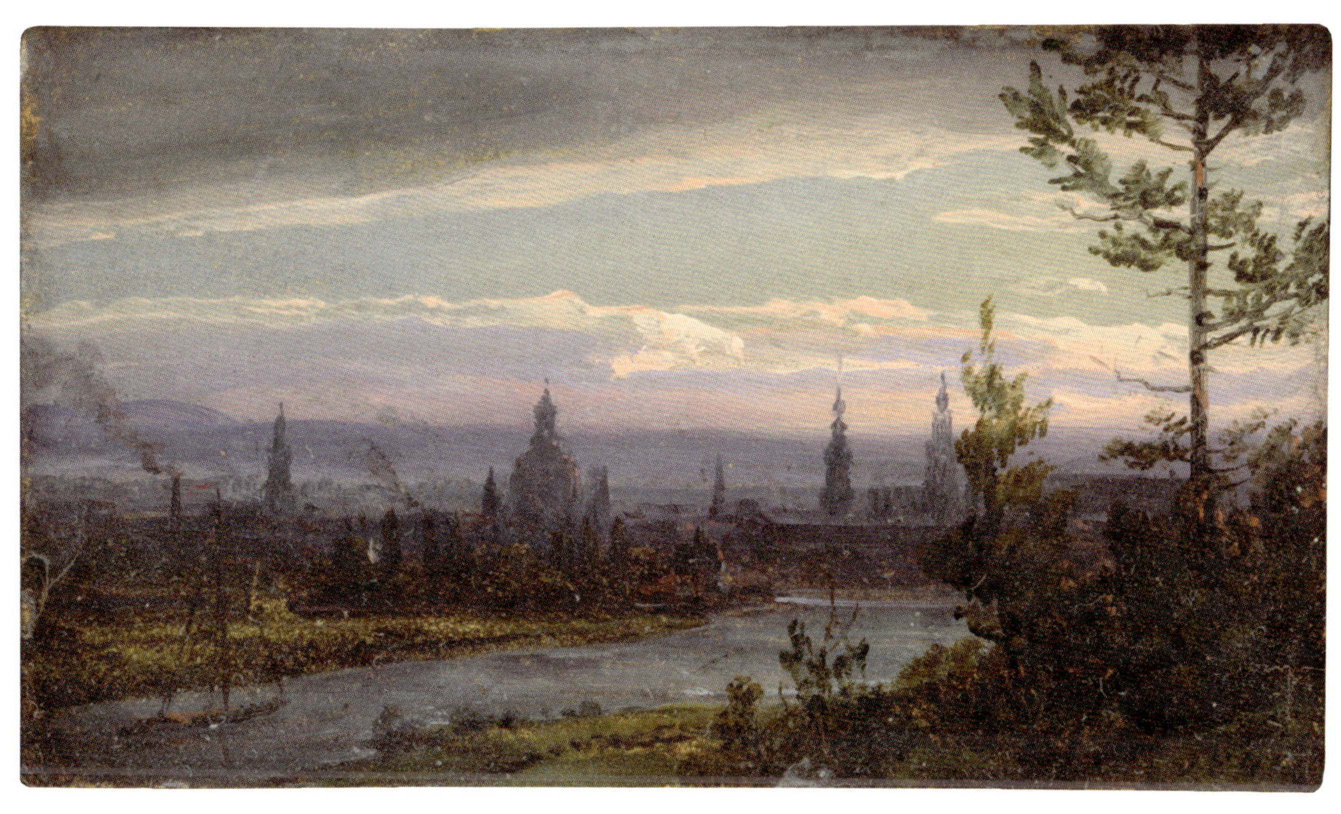

Johan Christian Dahl
Sunset over Dresden, 1841
Oil on cardboard
2 ¾ × 4 ½ inches | 7 × 11.4 cm

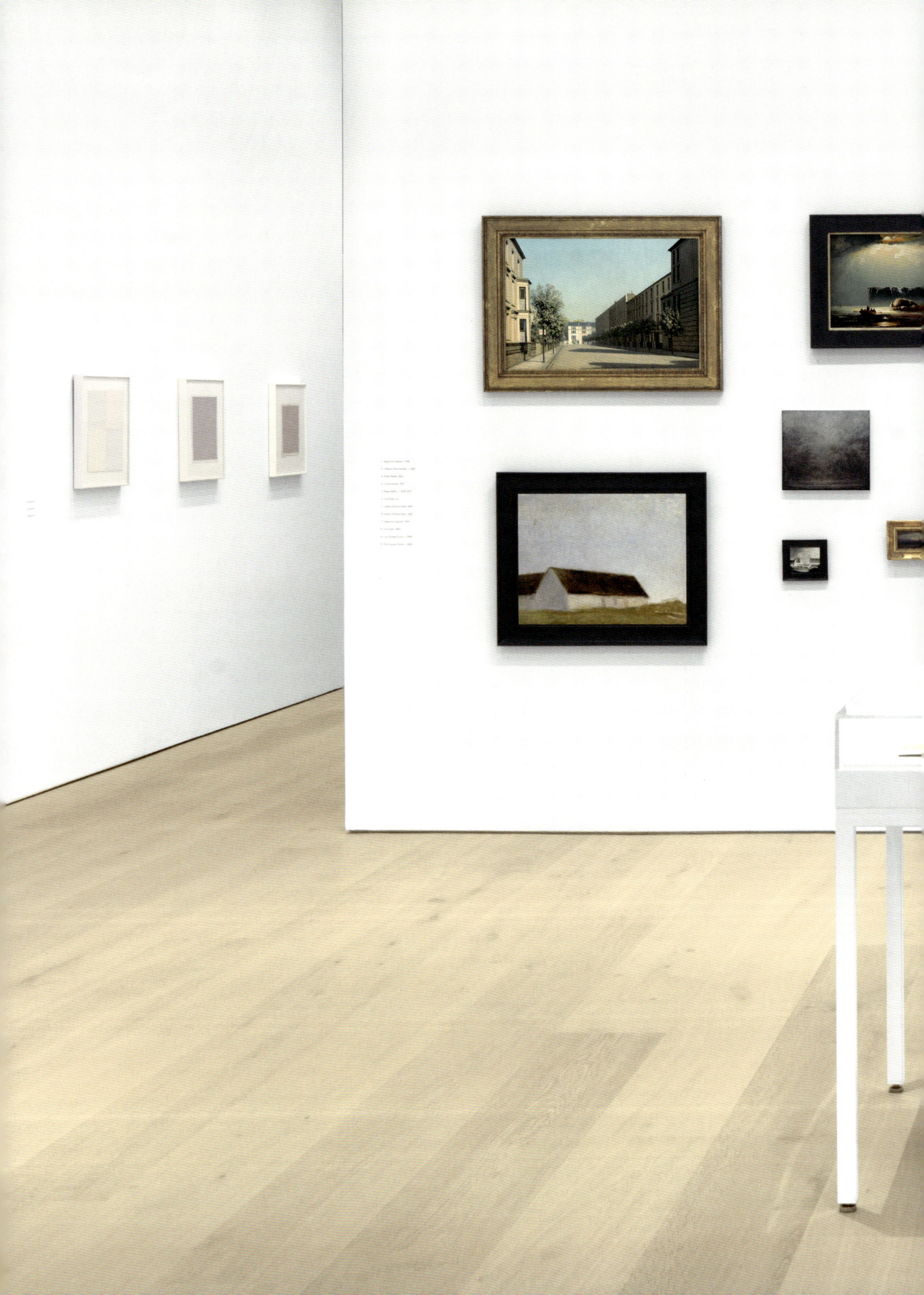

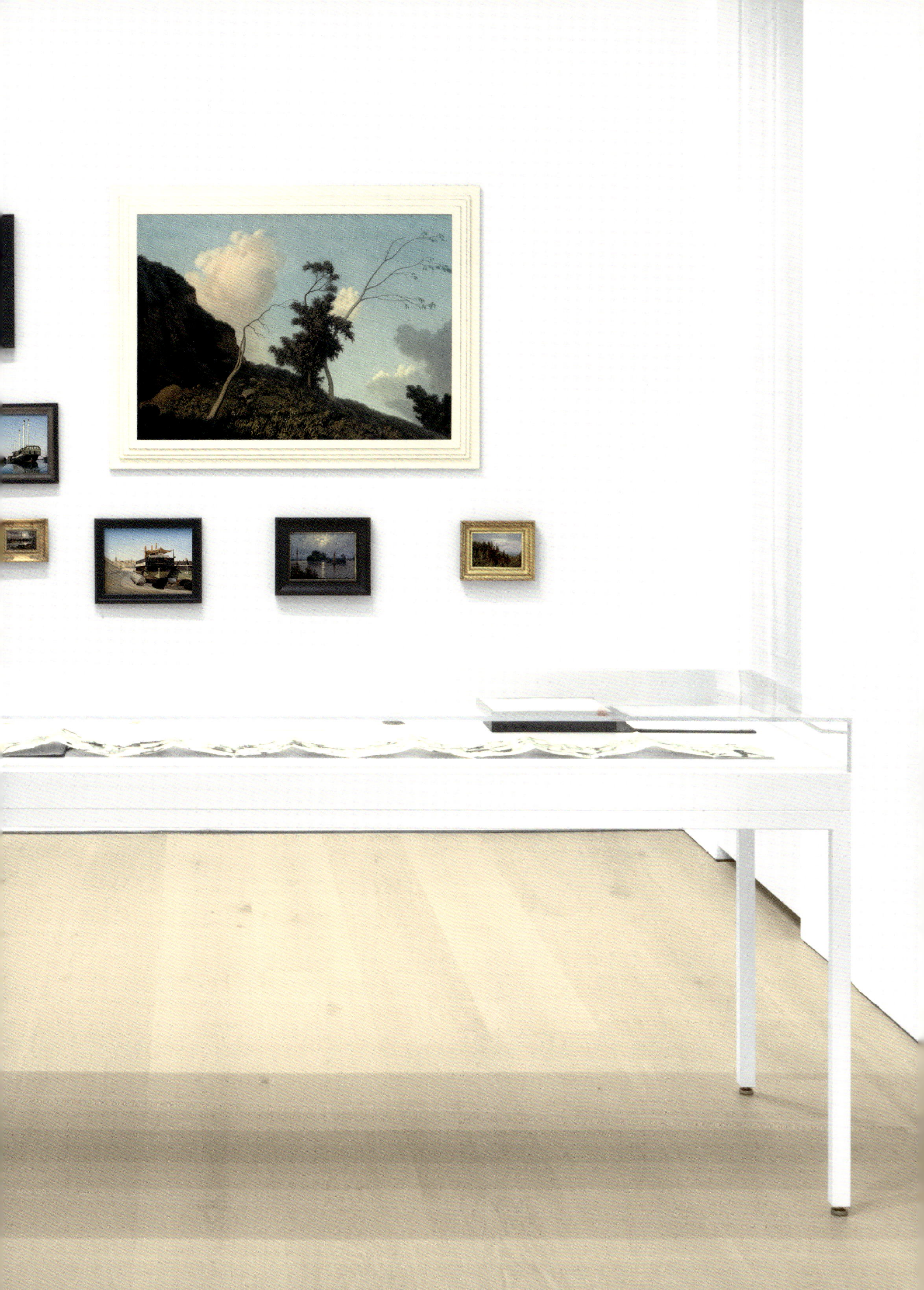

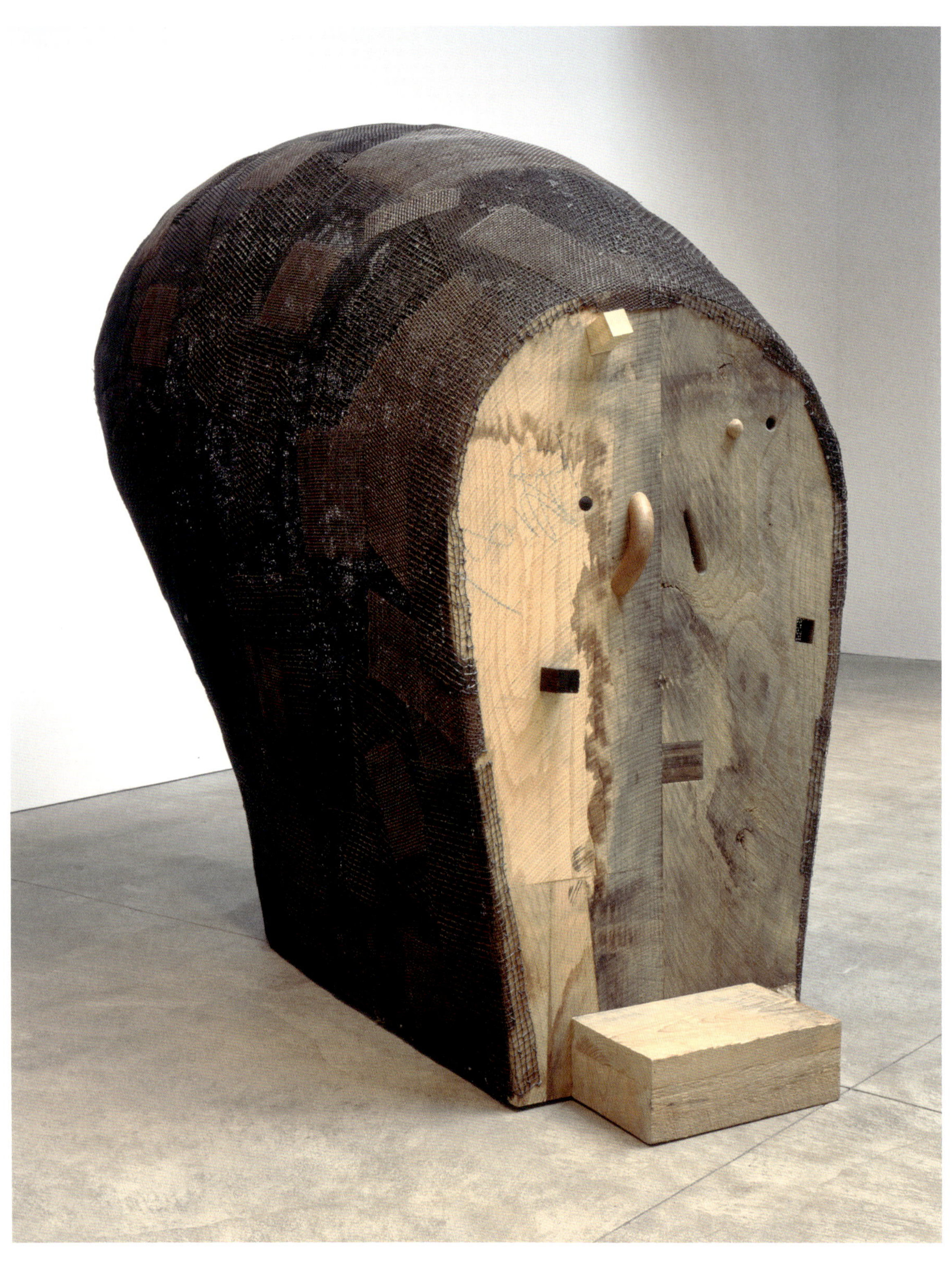

Martin Puryear
Confessional, 1996–2000
Wire mesh, tar, and wood
77 ⅞ × 99 ¾ × 45 ¼ inches | 197.8 × 253.4 × 114.9 cm

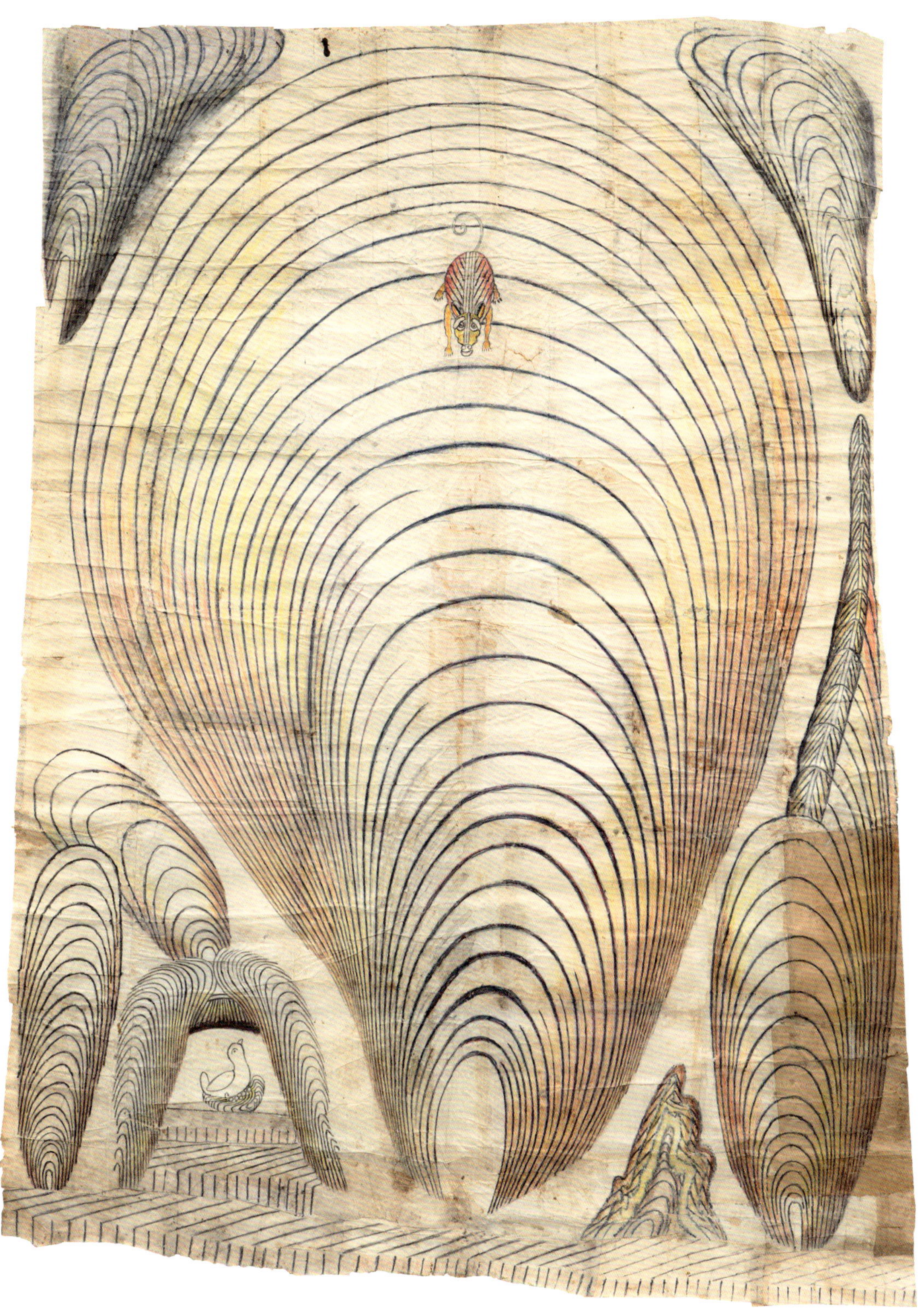

Martin Ramírez
Untitled (Cat, Bird, and Tunnels), c. 1950
Ink, crayon, and graphite on collaged paper
61 × 45 inches | 154.9 × 114.3 cm

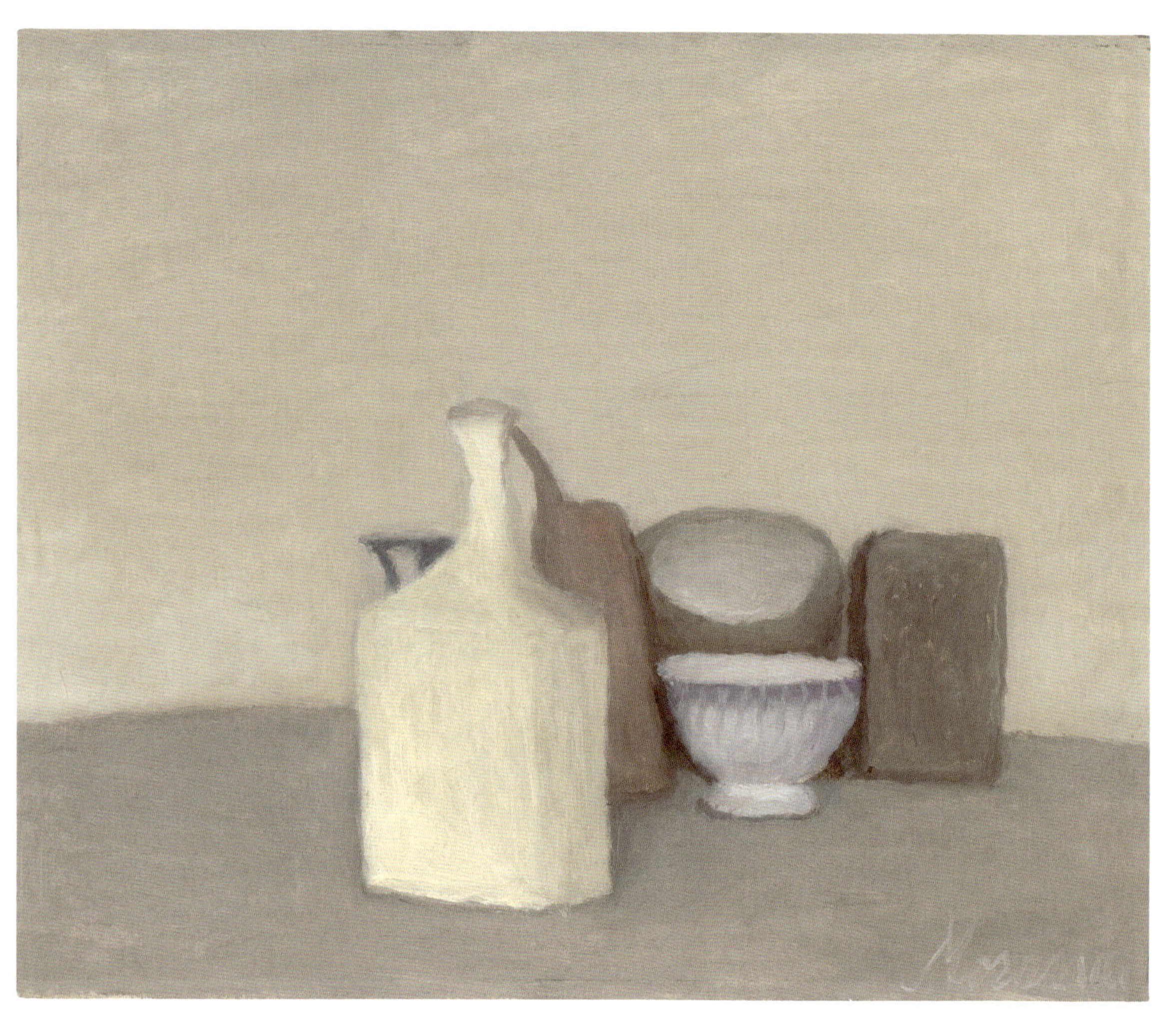

Giorgio Morandi
Natura morta (*Still Life*), 1946
Oil on canvas
14 ⅞ × 18 ⅛ inches | 37.9 × 46 cm
Vitali No. 533

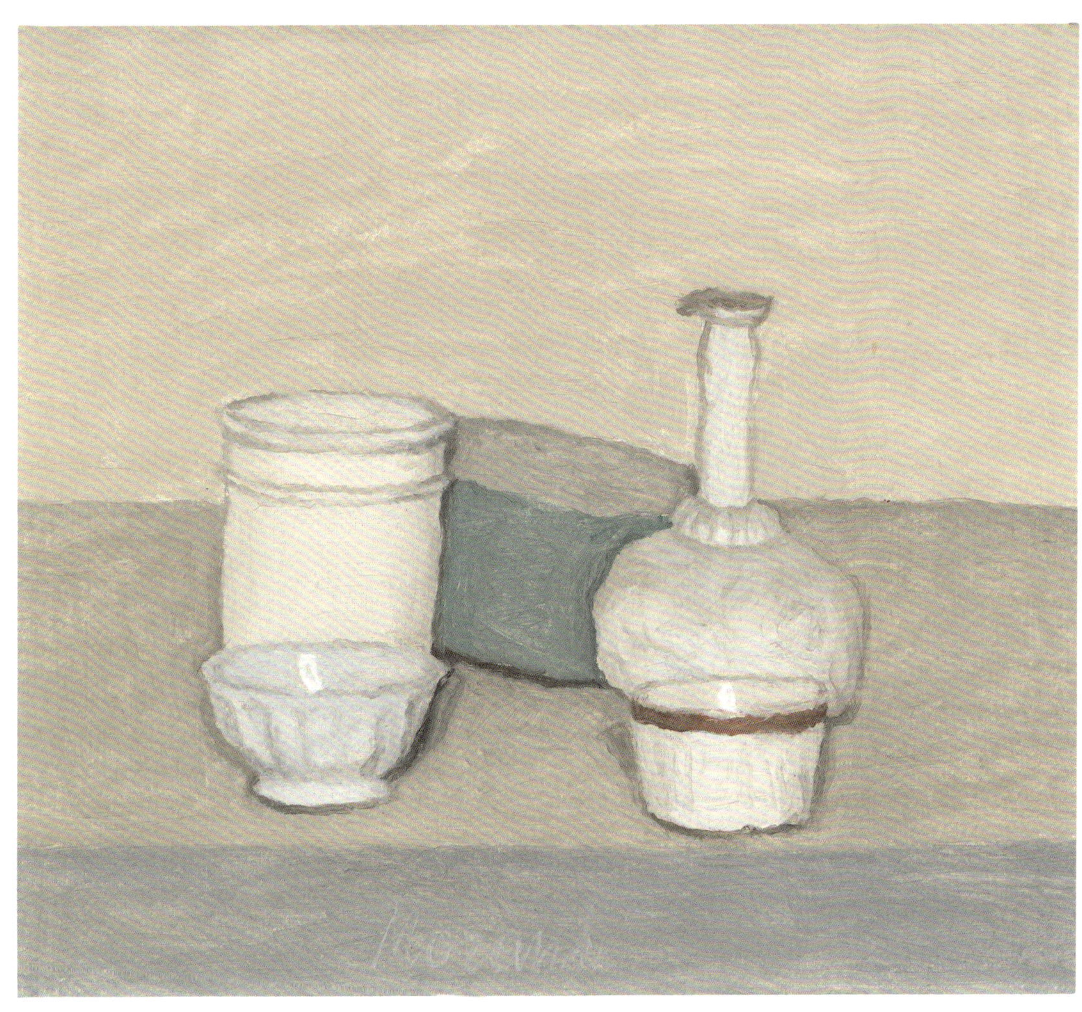

Giorgio Morandi
Natura morta (Still Life), 1952
Oil on canvas
14 ⅛ × 15 ⅝ inches | 36 × 39.8 cm
Vitali No. 837

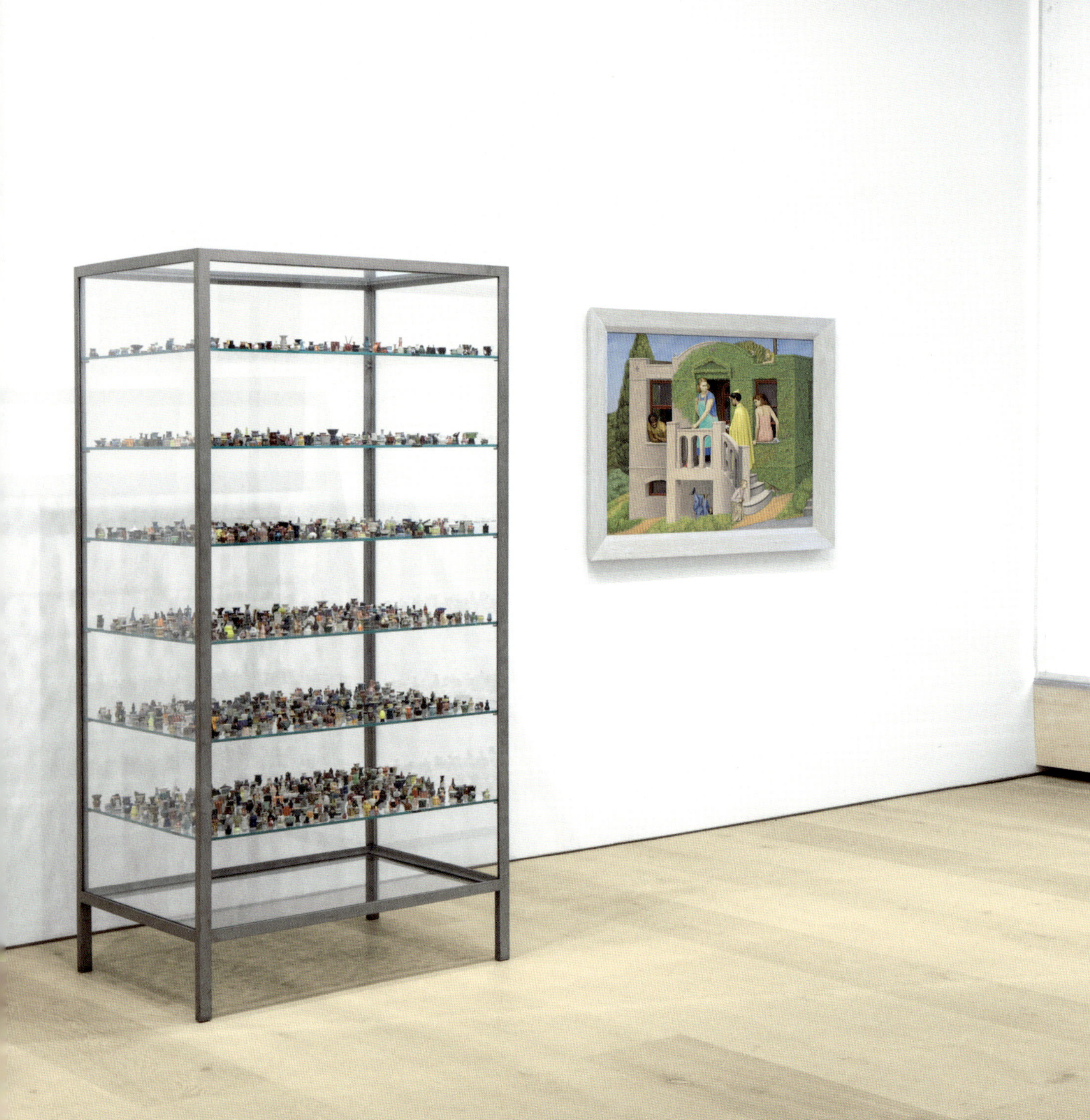

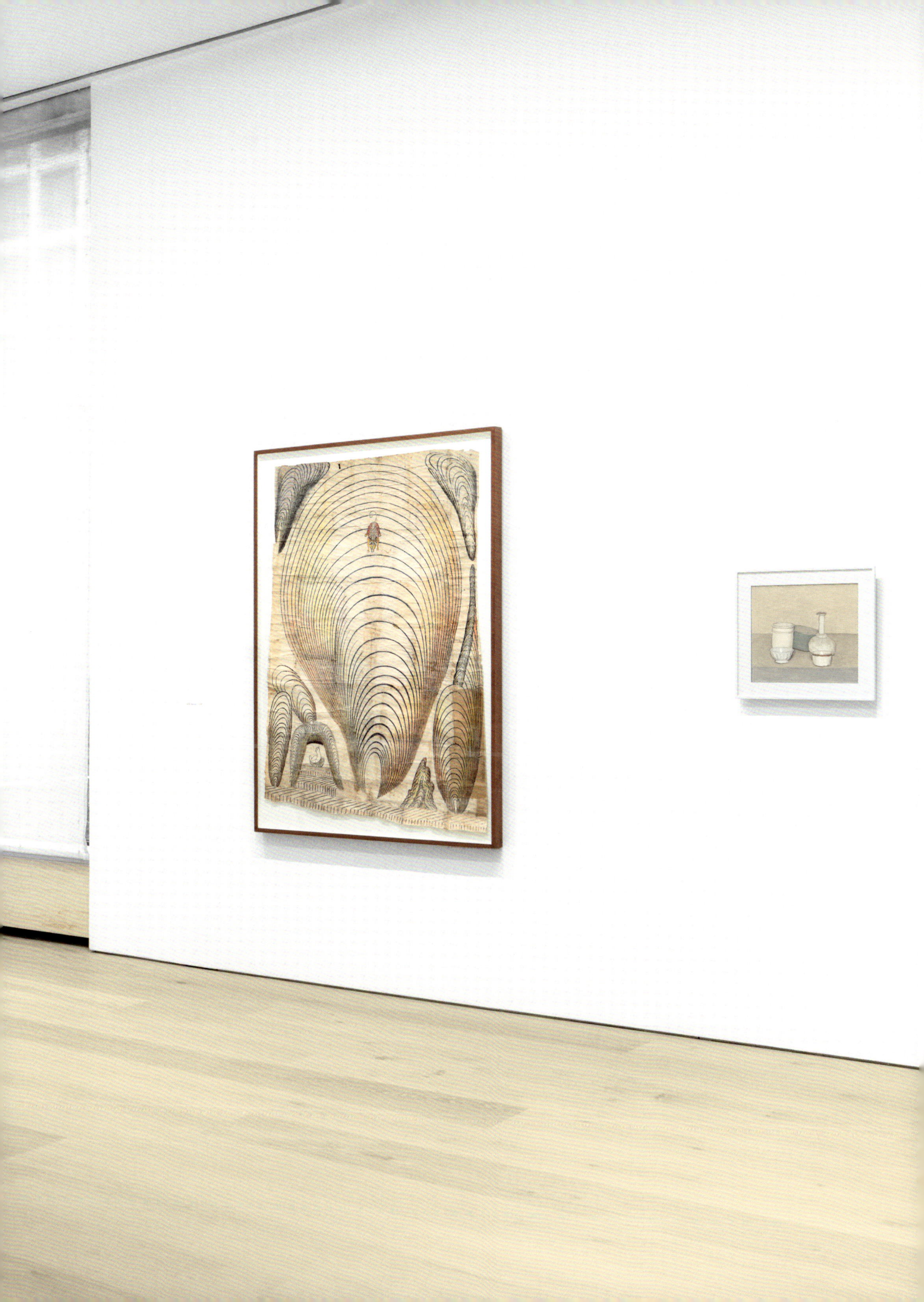

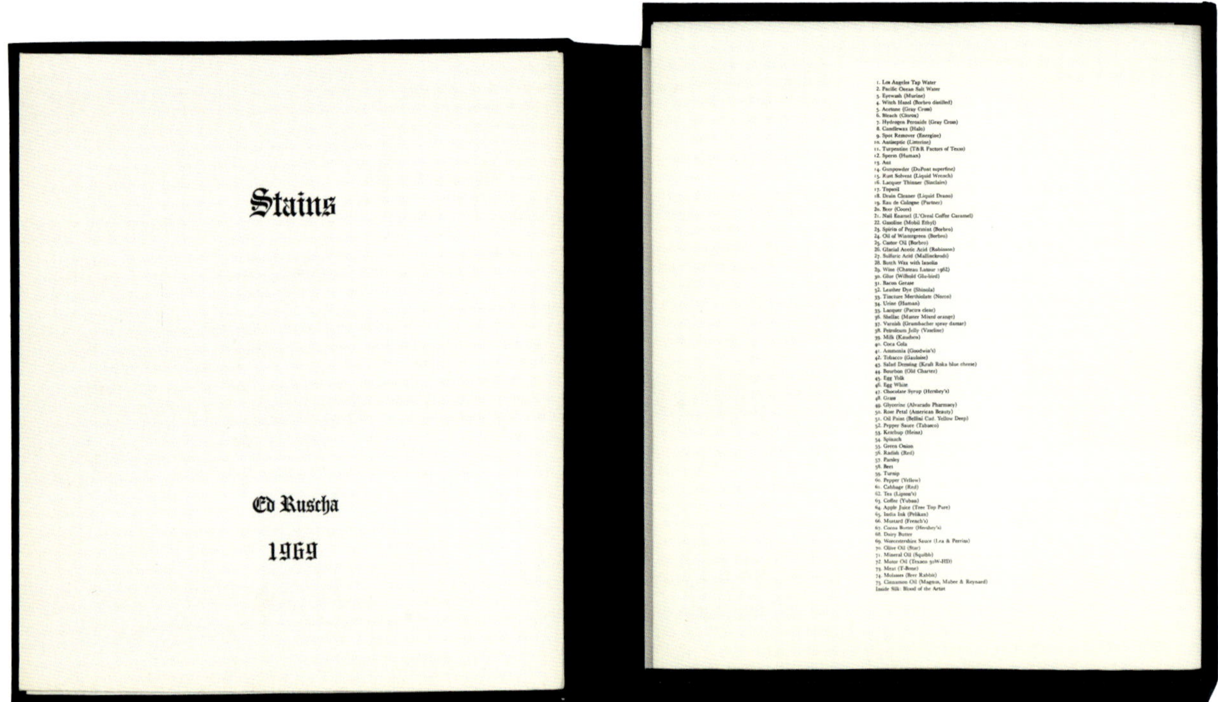

Ed Ruscha
Stains, 1969
Portfolio box and seventy-five
works on paper with animal,
vegetable, mineral, and chemical stains
Overall: 12 × 11 inches | 30.5 × 27.9 cm

Clockwise from top left:

2   Pacific Ocean Salt Water
6   Bleach (Clorox)
8   Candlewax (Halo)
7   Hydrogen Peroxide (Gray Cross)

Jean-Michel Basquiat
Untitled (Subject), 1985
Acrylic and oil stick on canvas
60 × 48 inches | 152.4 × 121.9 cm

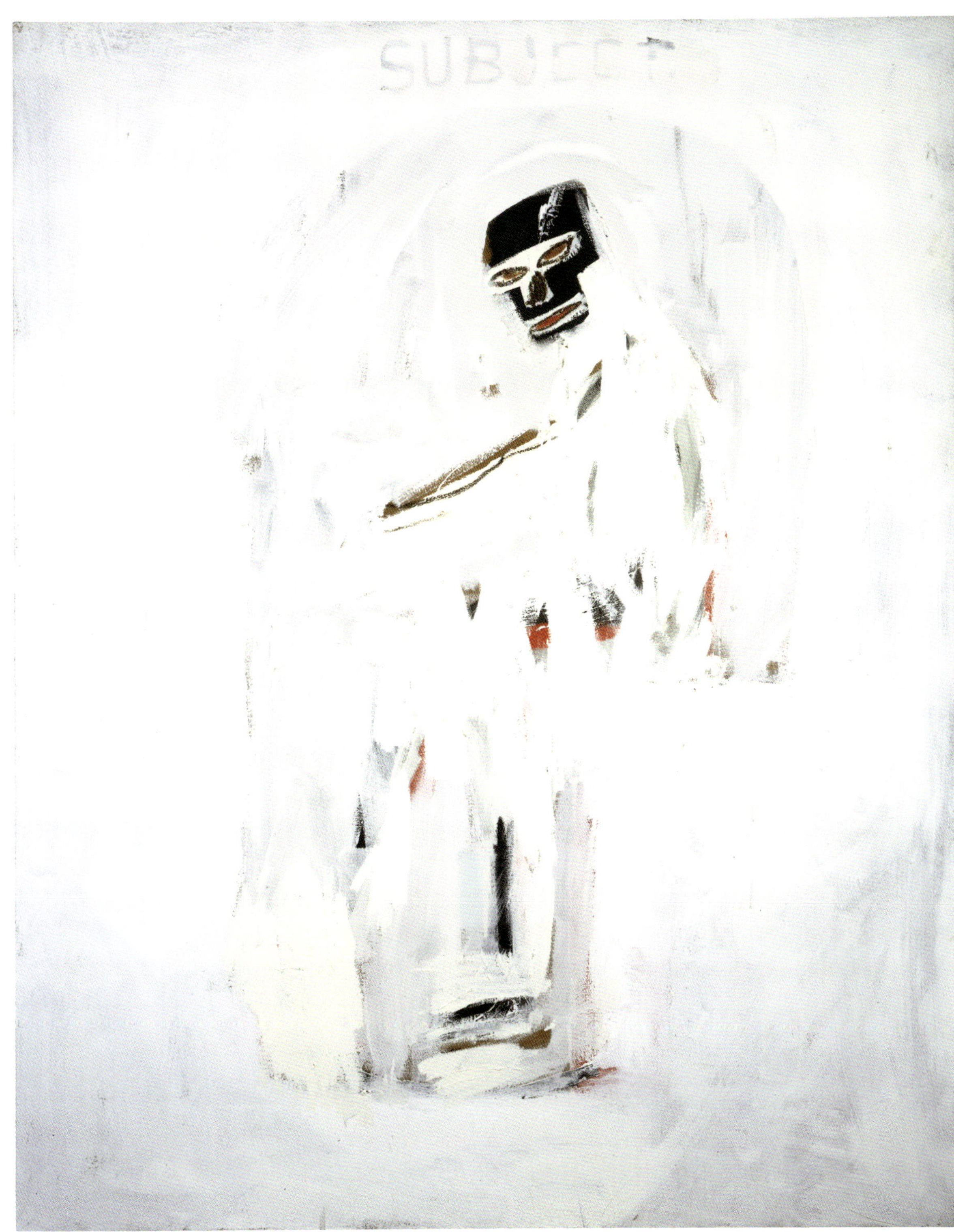
SUBJECT

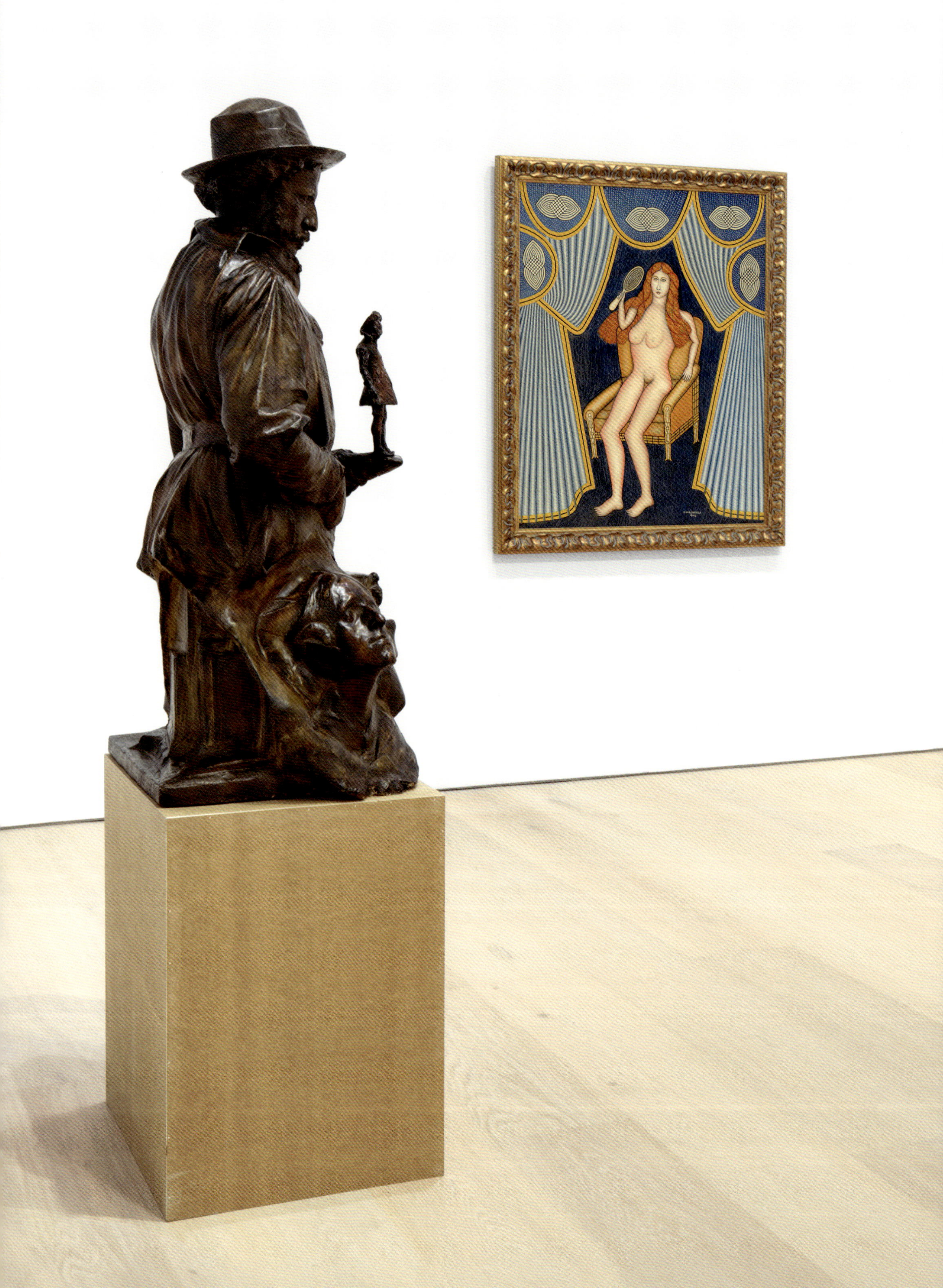

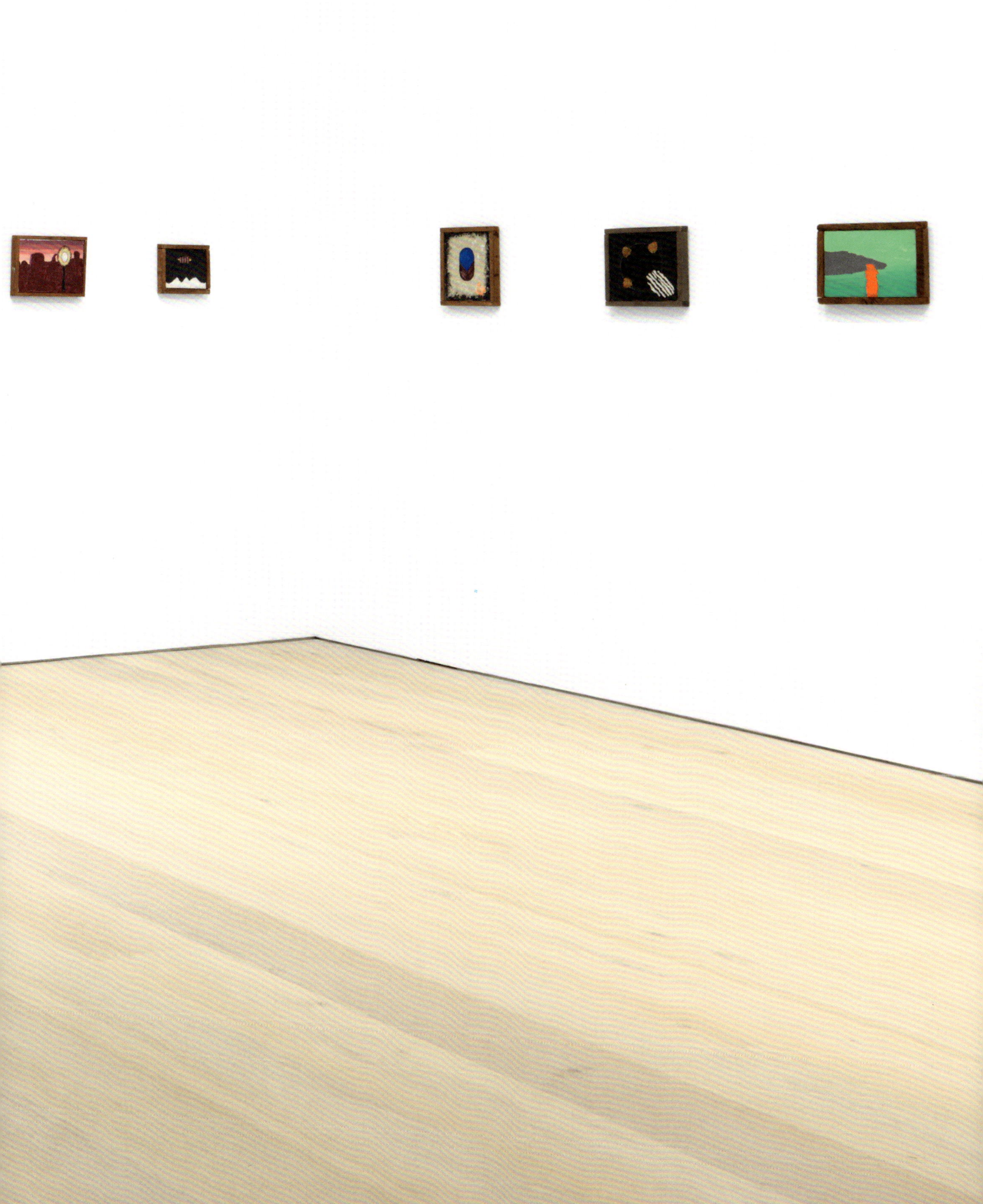

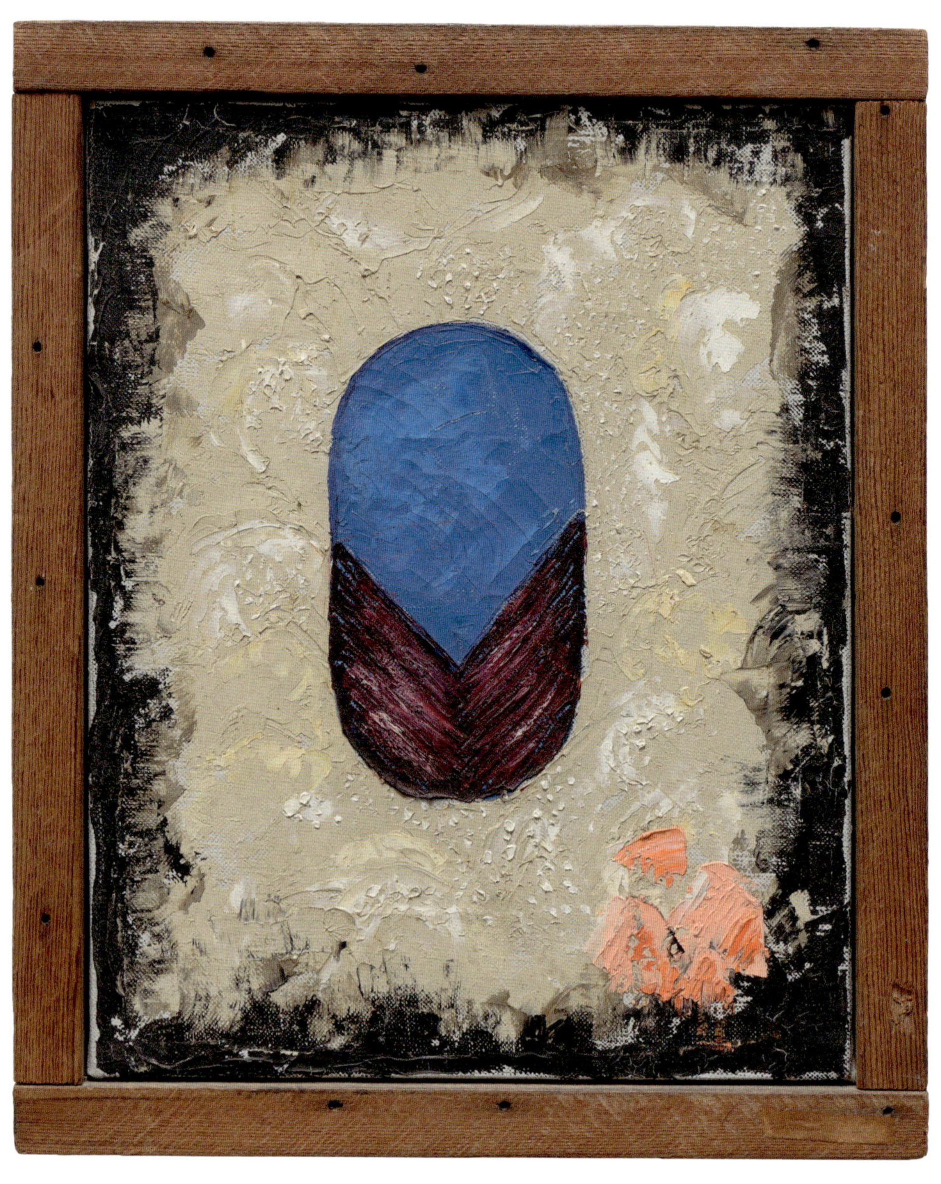

Forrest Bess
Untitled (No. 11), 1950
Oil on canvas, in artist's frame
10 × 8 inches | 25.4 × 20.3 cm

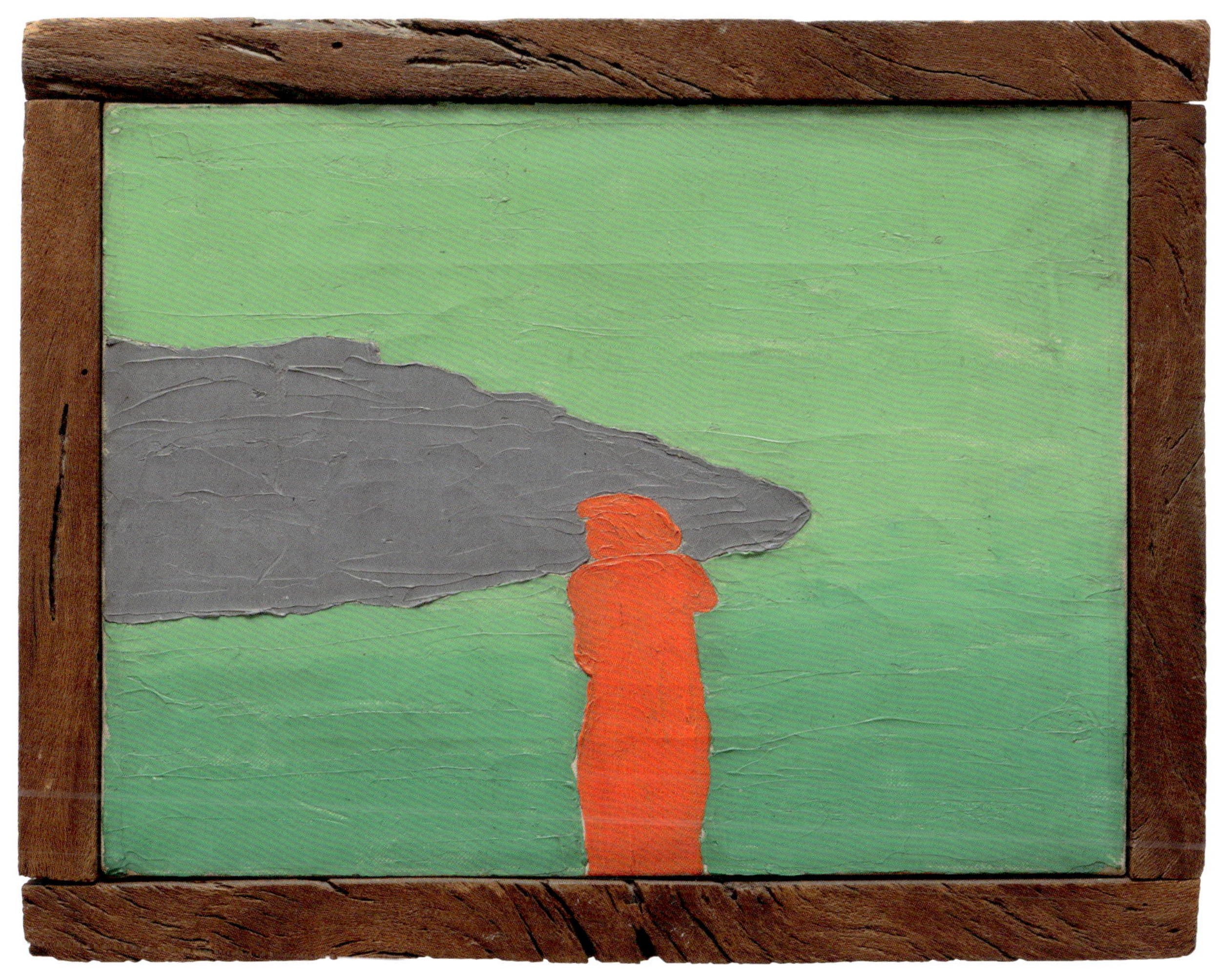

Forrest Bess
Untitled (No. 5), 1949
Oil on canvas, in artist's frame
8 ⅛ × 11 ⅛ inches | 20.6 × 28.3 cm

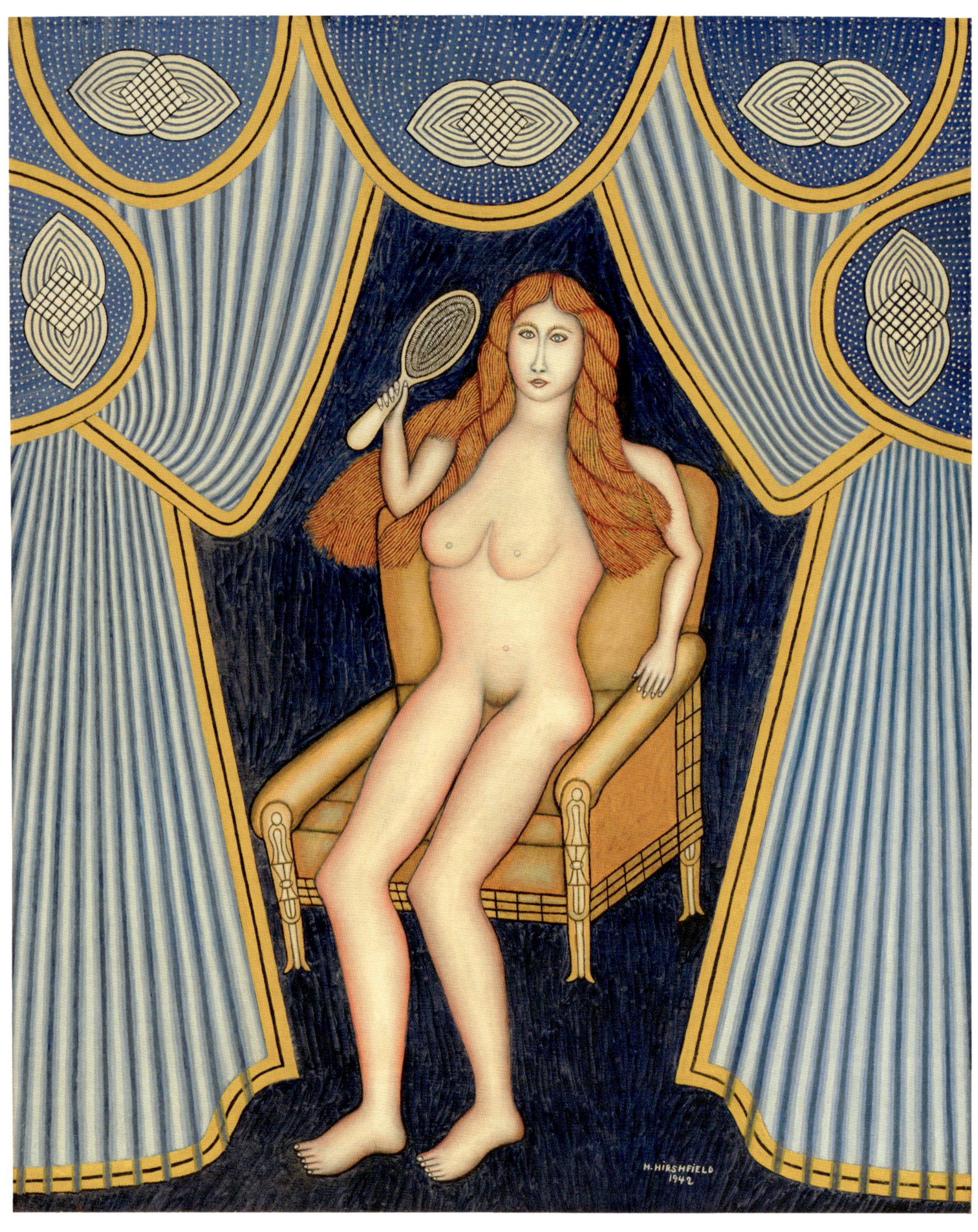

Morris Hirshfield
American Beauty (Nude with Mirror), 1942
Oil on canvas
48 × 40 inches | 121.9 × 101.6 cm

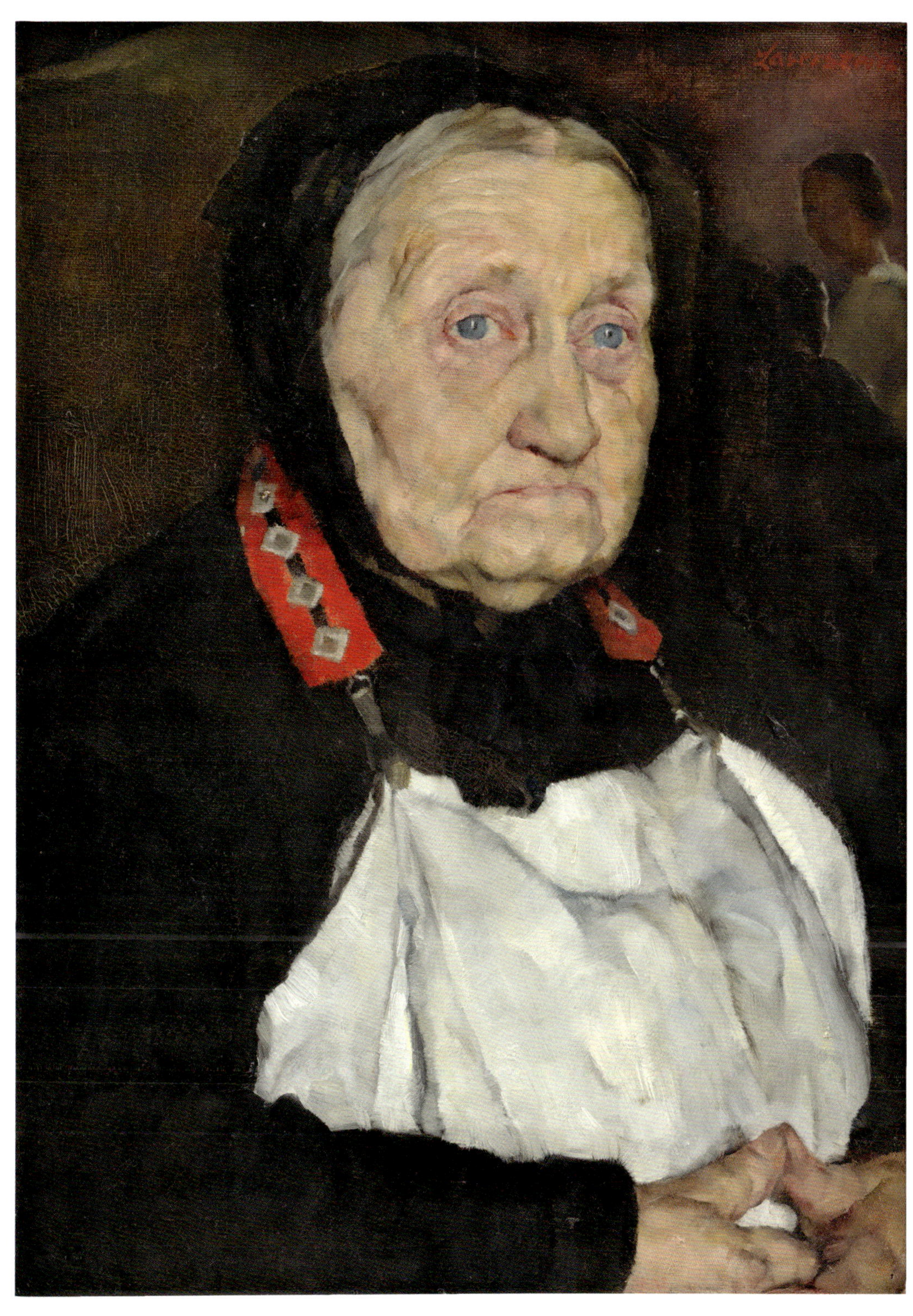

Lotte Laserstein
Meine Großmutter (My Grandmother), 1924
Oil on canvas
18 ⅝ × 13 ⅝ inches | 47.3 × 34.6 cm

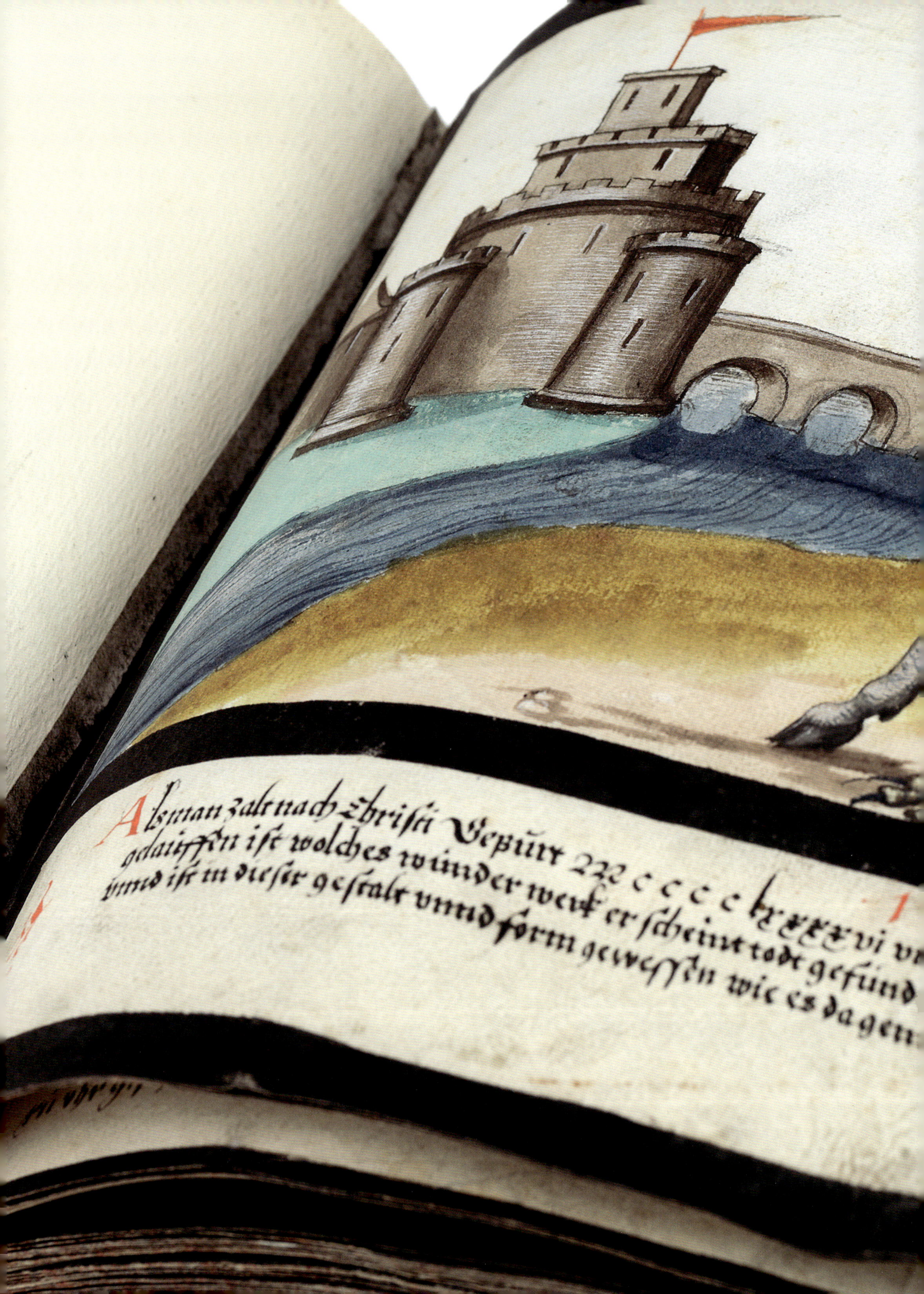

Als man zalt nach Christi Geburt MCCCC lxxxvi vn-
gelauffen ist wolches wunderweis erscheint tode gefund
unnd ist in dieser gestalt unnd form gewesen wie es da geu

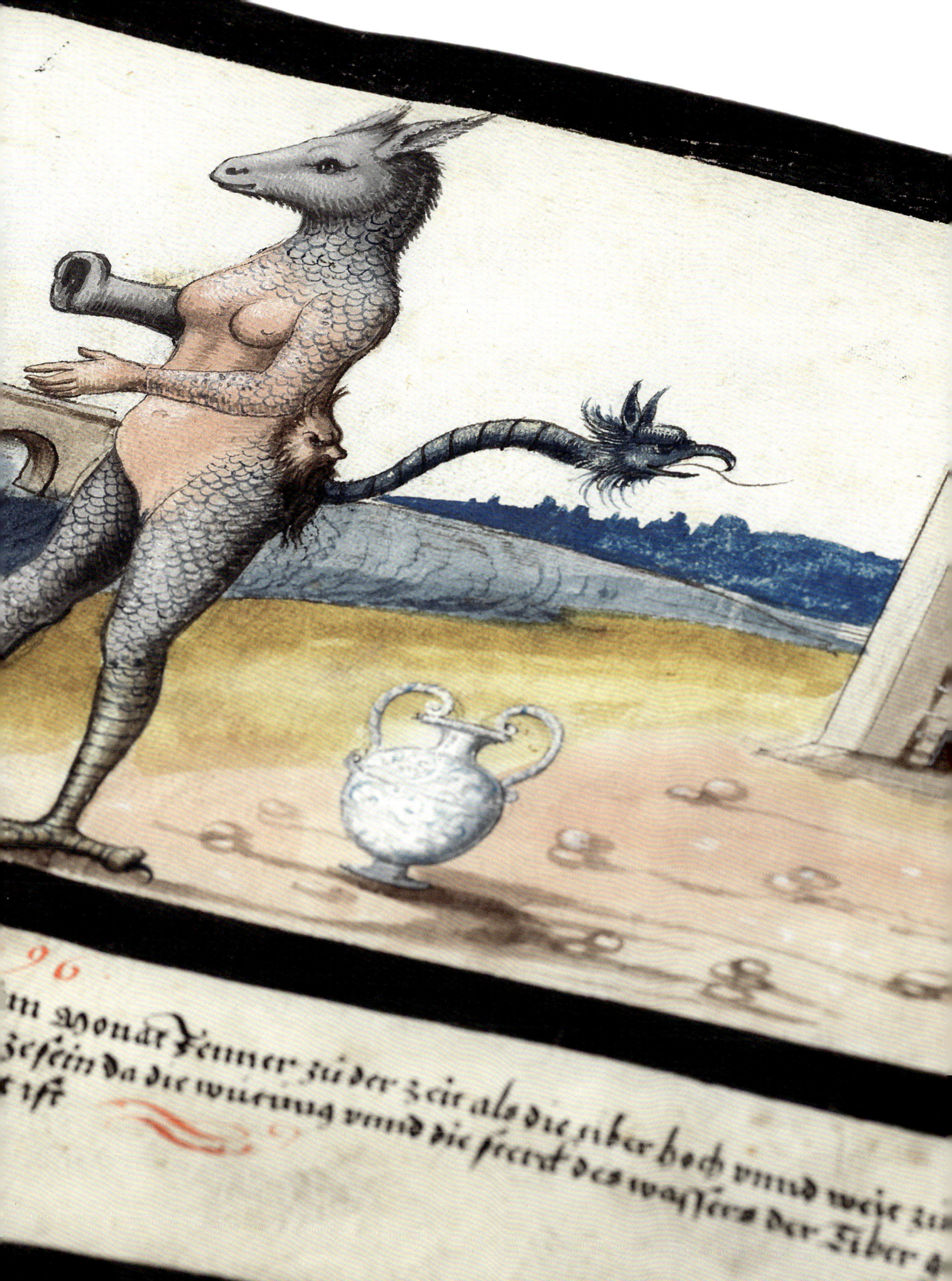

...m Monat Jenner zu der zeit als die Tiber hoch vnnd weit zu
...zesein da die wuerung vnnd die spertd des wassers der Tiber
...e ist

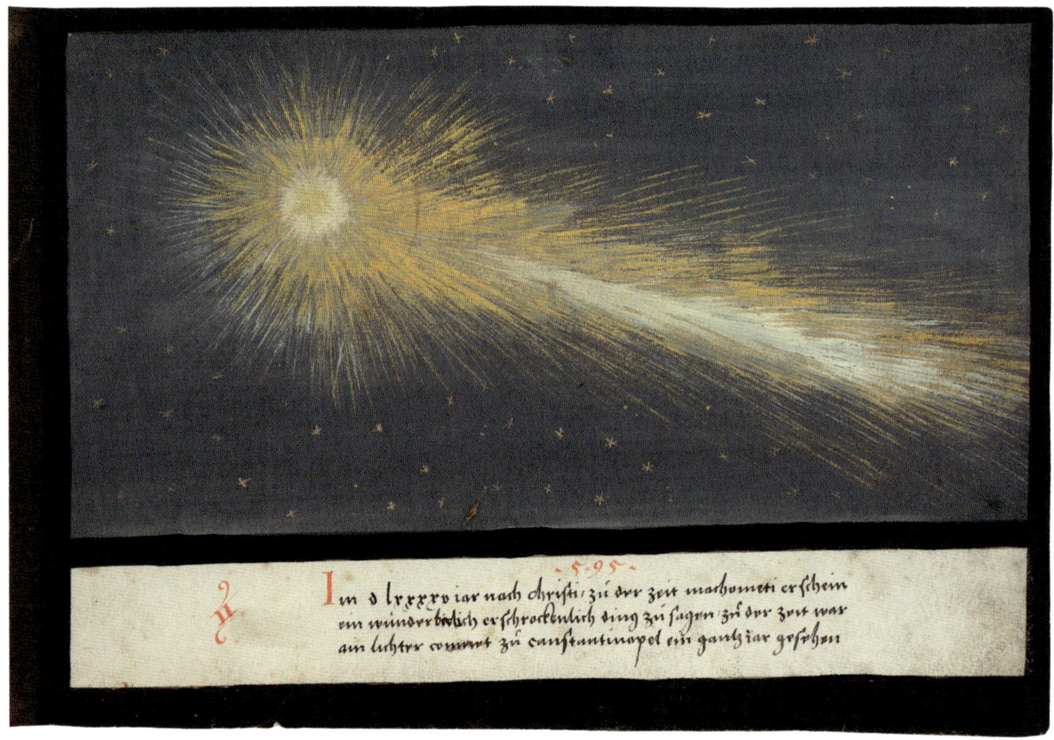

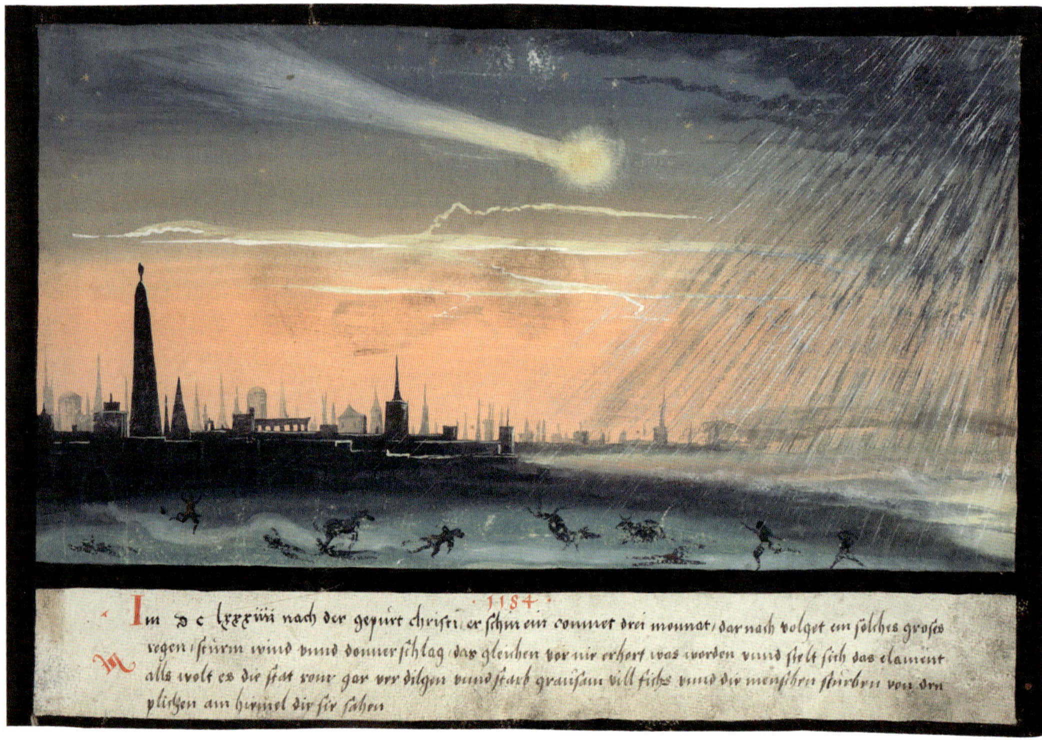

Anonymous
Wunderzeichenbuch (*Book of Miracles*), c. 1552
Gouache, watercolor, and inscriptions on paper; 167 works
Each: 8 ½ × 13 inches | 21.6 × 33 cm

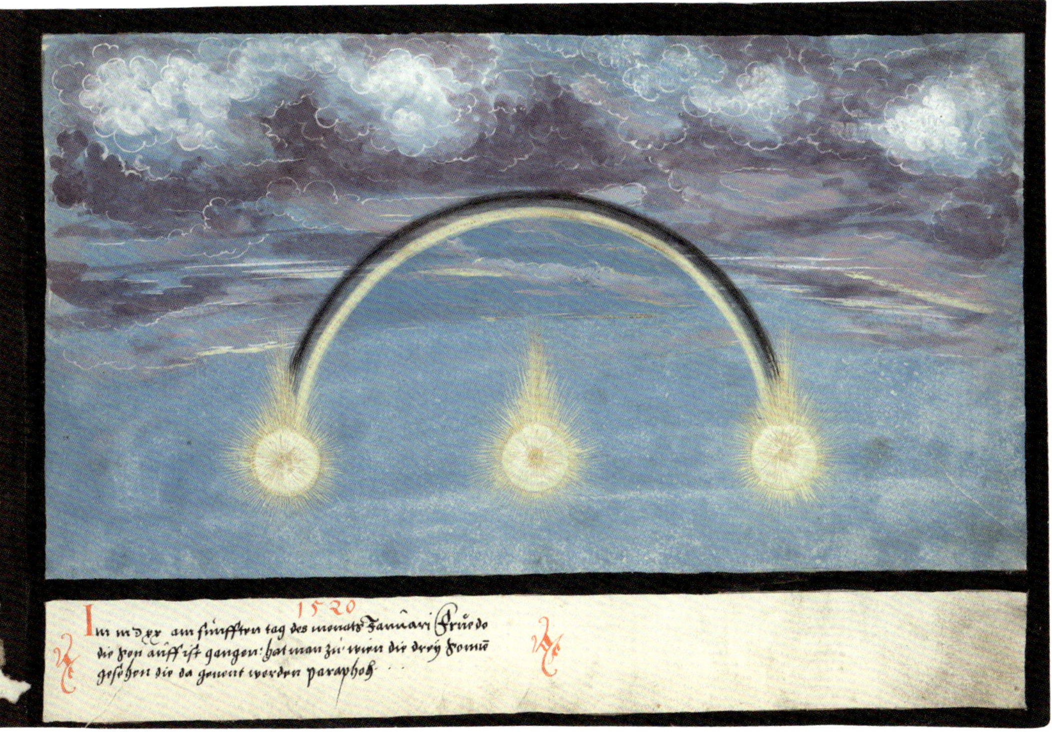

1520
Im m d xx am fünfften tag des monats Januari frü do
die son auff ist gangen: hat man zu wien die drey sonnū
gesehen die da genent werden paraphoß

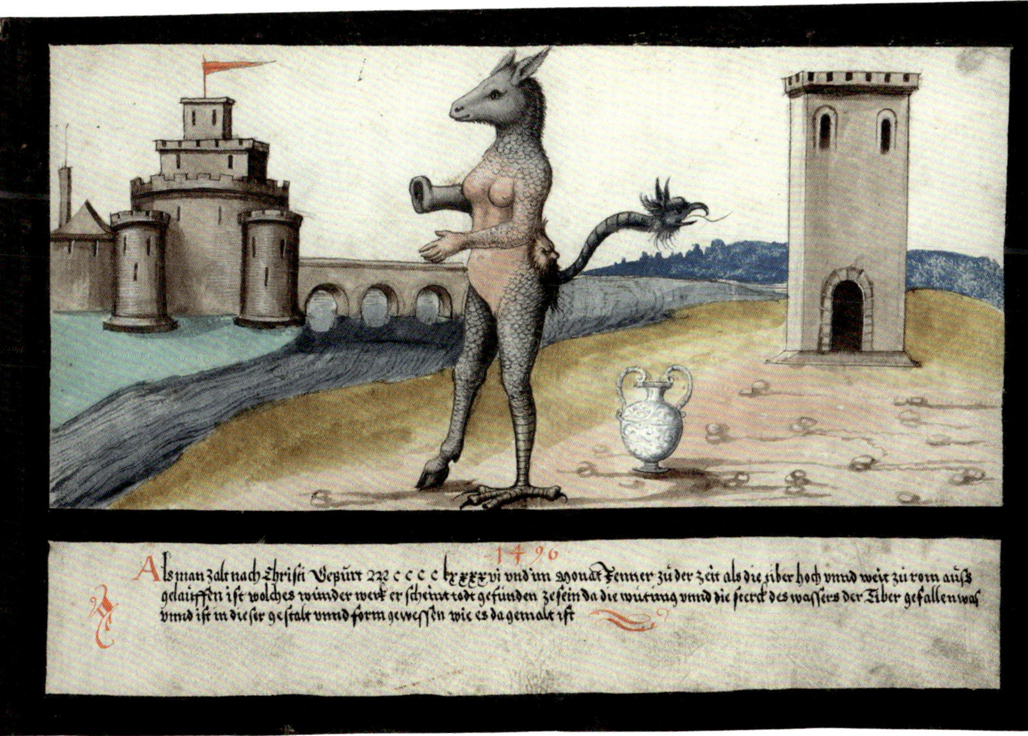

1496
Als man zalt nach Christi Gepürt m c c c c lxxxxvi vnd im Monat Jenner zu der zeit als die Tiber hoch vnnd weit zu rom auß
gelauffen ist welches wunder werck er scheint todt gefunden zesein da die wüetung vnnd die sterck des wassers der Tiber gefallen was
vnnd ist in dieser gestalt vnnd form gewessen wie es da gemalt ist

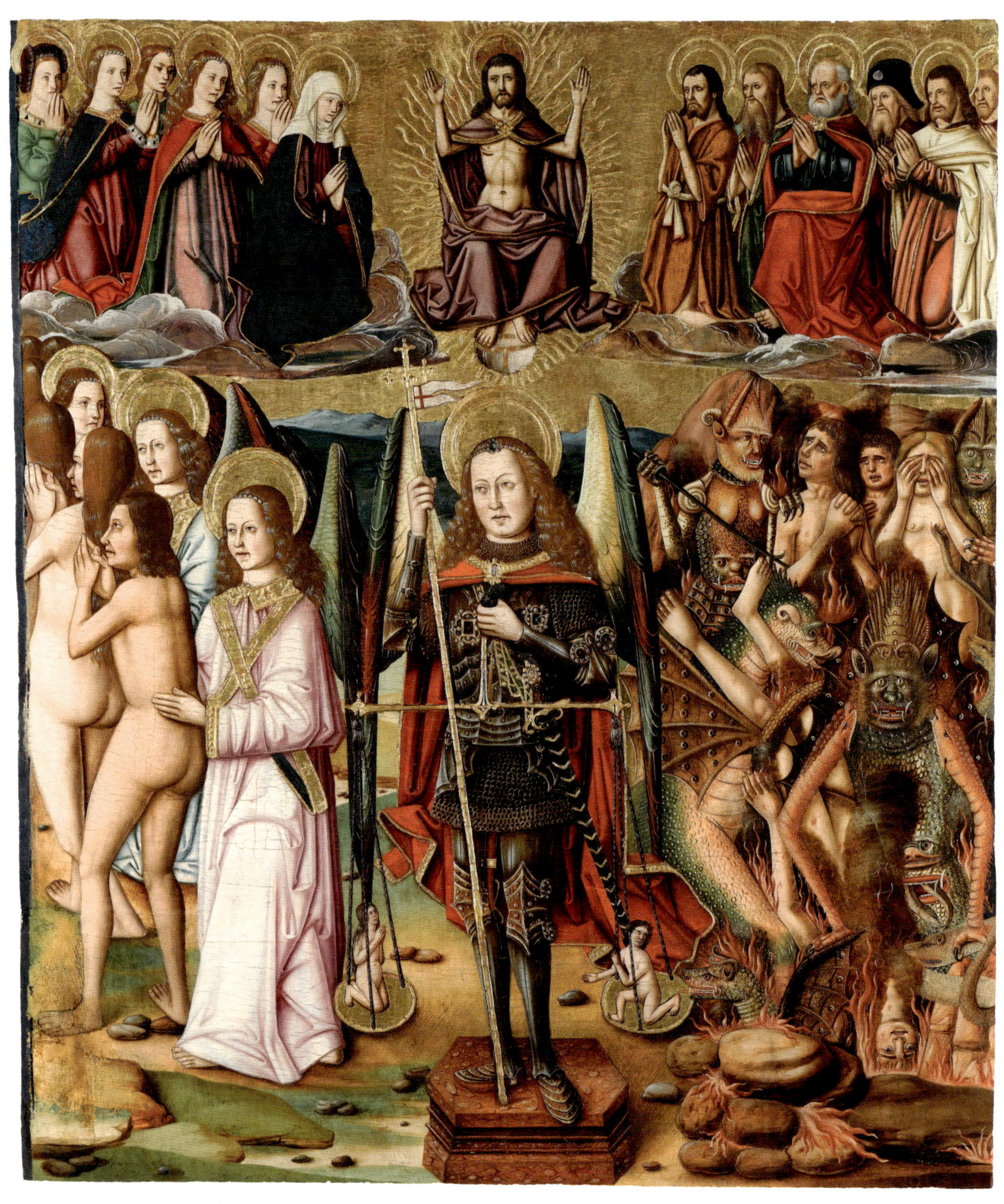

Miguel Ximénez
The Last Judgment with
Saint Michael Weighing Human Souls, 1450
Oil on panel
44 ½ × 37 ⅜ inches | 113 × 94.9 cm

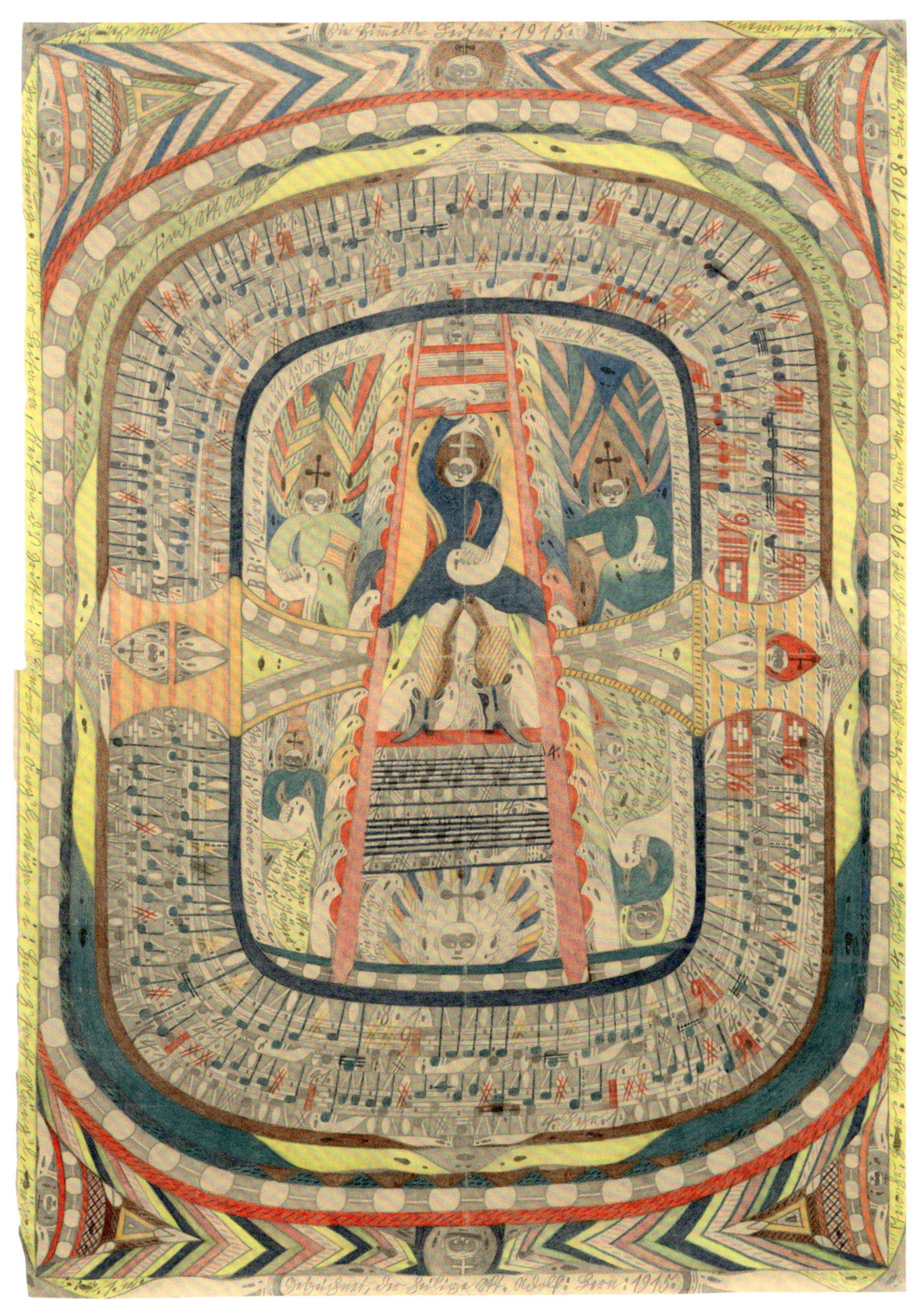

Adolf Wölfli
Die Himmels Leiter (*The Ladder to Heaven*), 1915
Graphite and colored pencil on paper
39 ¼ × 28 ¼ inches | 99.7 × 71.8 cm

Tony Fitzpatrick
James "Cool Papa" Bell, 1990
Colored pencil on paper
26 ¼ × 22 ¼ inches | 66.7 × 56.5 cm

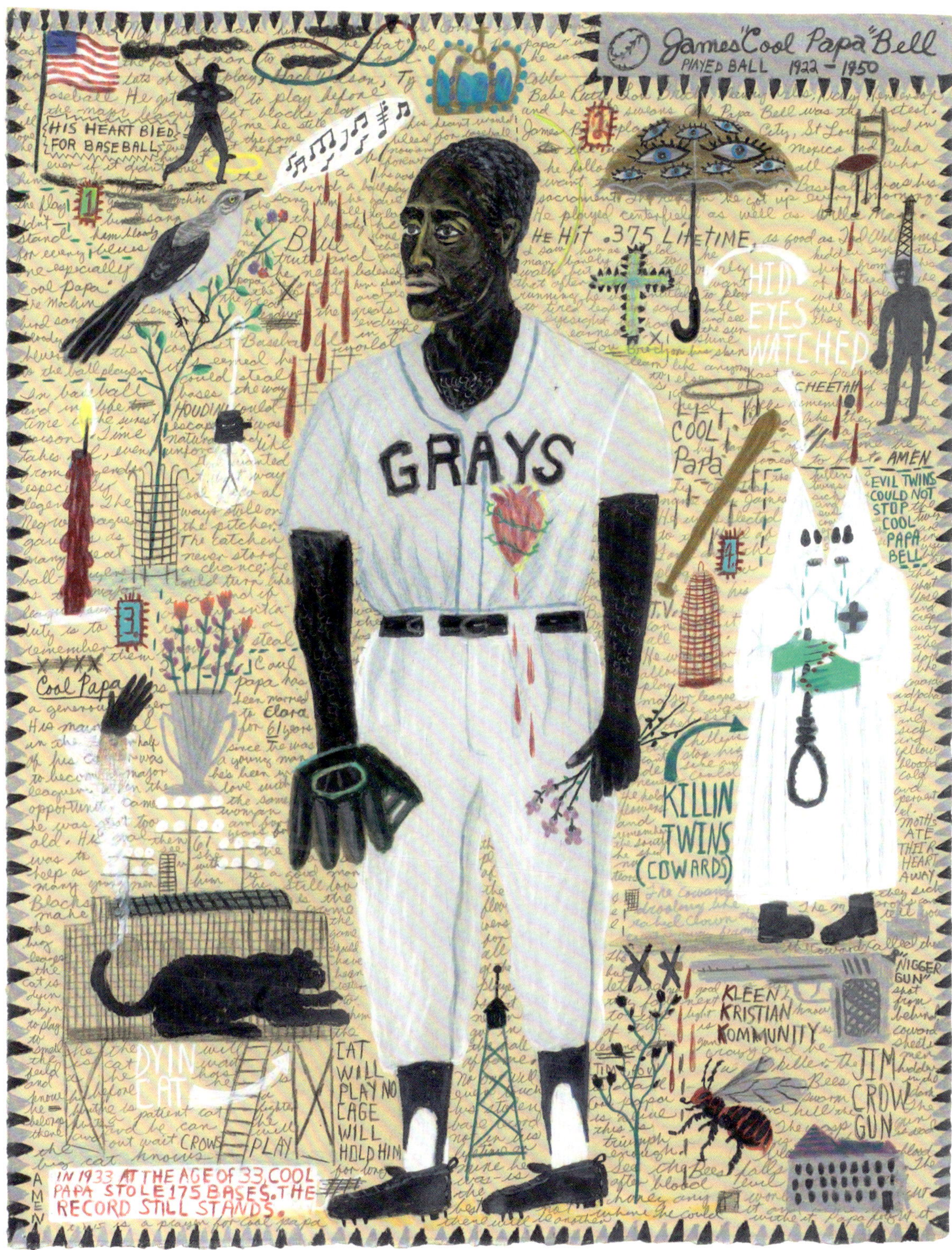

James "Cool Papa" Bell
PLAYED BALL 1922-1950
HIS HEART BLED FOR BASEBALL
GRAYS
HE HIT .375 LIFETIME
HID EYES WATCHED
CHEETAH
COOL Papa
AMEN
EVIL TWINS COULD NOT STOP THE COOL PAPA BELL
KILLIN TWINS (COWARDS)
Cool Papa
Blue
HOUDINI
DYIN EAT
CAT WILL PLAY NO CAGE WILL HOLD HIM
EAT WILL PLAY NO CAGE WILL PLAY CROW PLAY
AMEN
KLEEN KRISTIAN KOMMUNITY
"NIGGER GUN"
JIM CROW GUN
IN 1933 AT THE AGE OF 33 COOL PAPA STOLE 175 BASES. THE RECORD STILL STANDS.

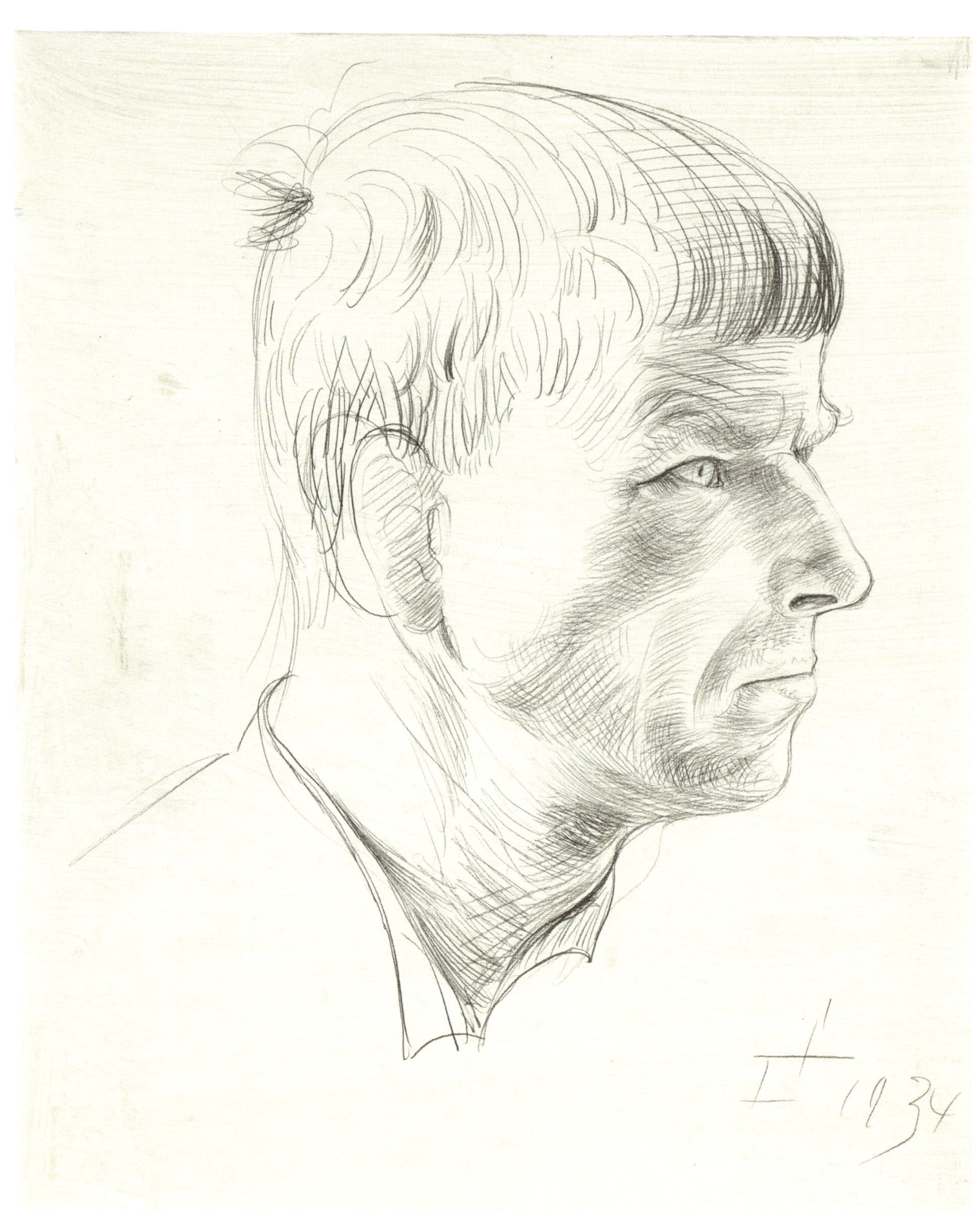

Otto Dix
Selbst (Self-Portrait), 1934
Silverpoint on prepared cardboard
14 ⅜ × 12 ⅝ inches | 36.5 × 32.1 cm

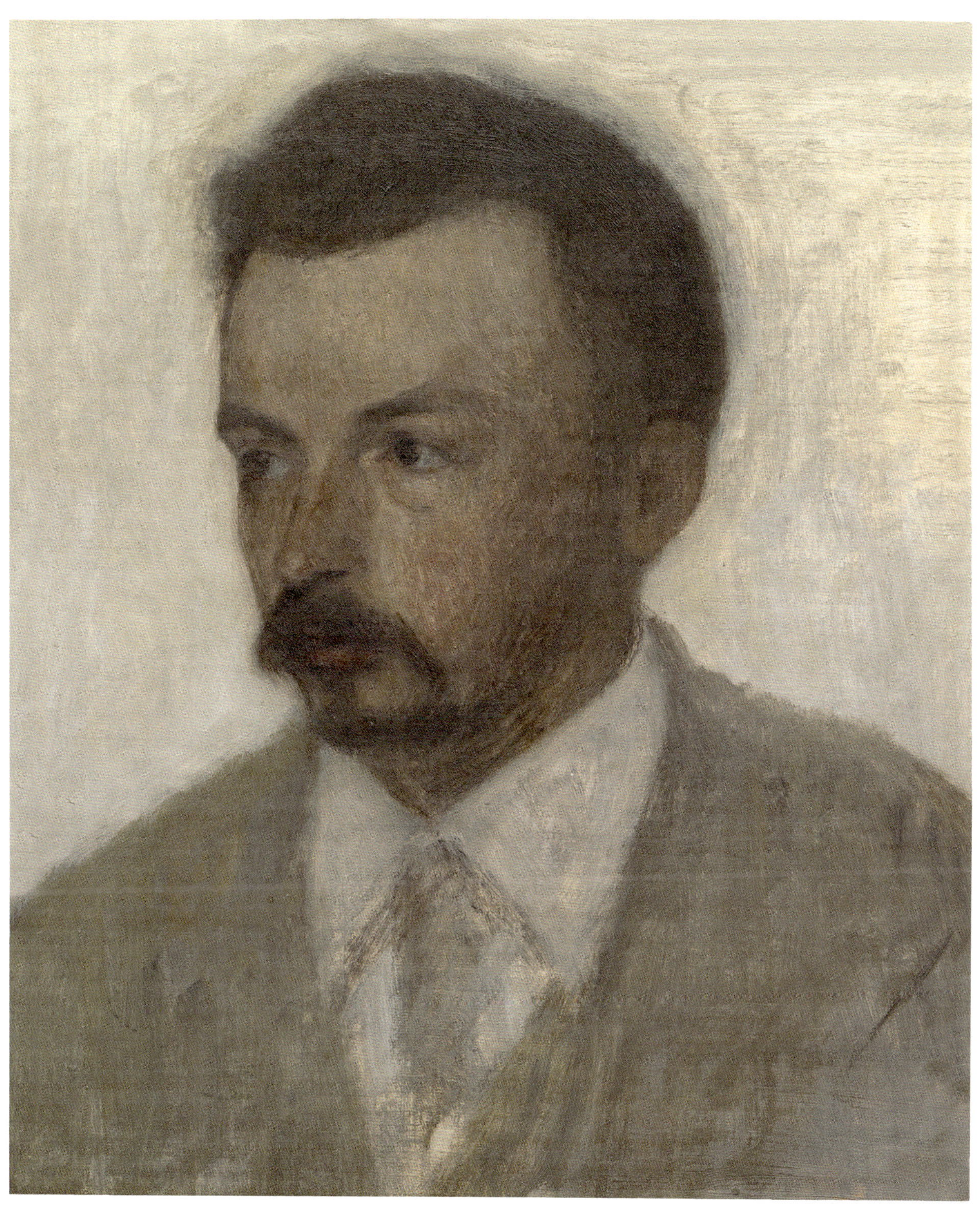

Vilhelm Hammershøi
Self-Portrait, 1895
Oil on canvas
13 ⅛ × 11 ⅛ inches | 33.3 × 28.3 cm

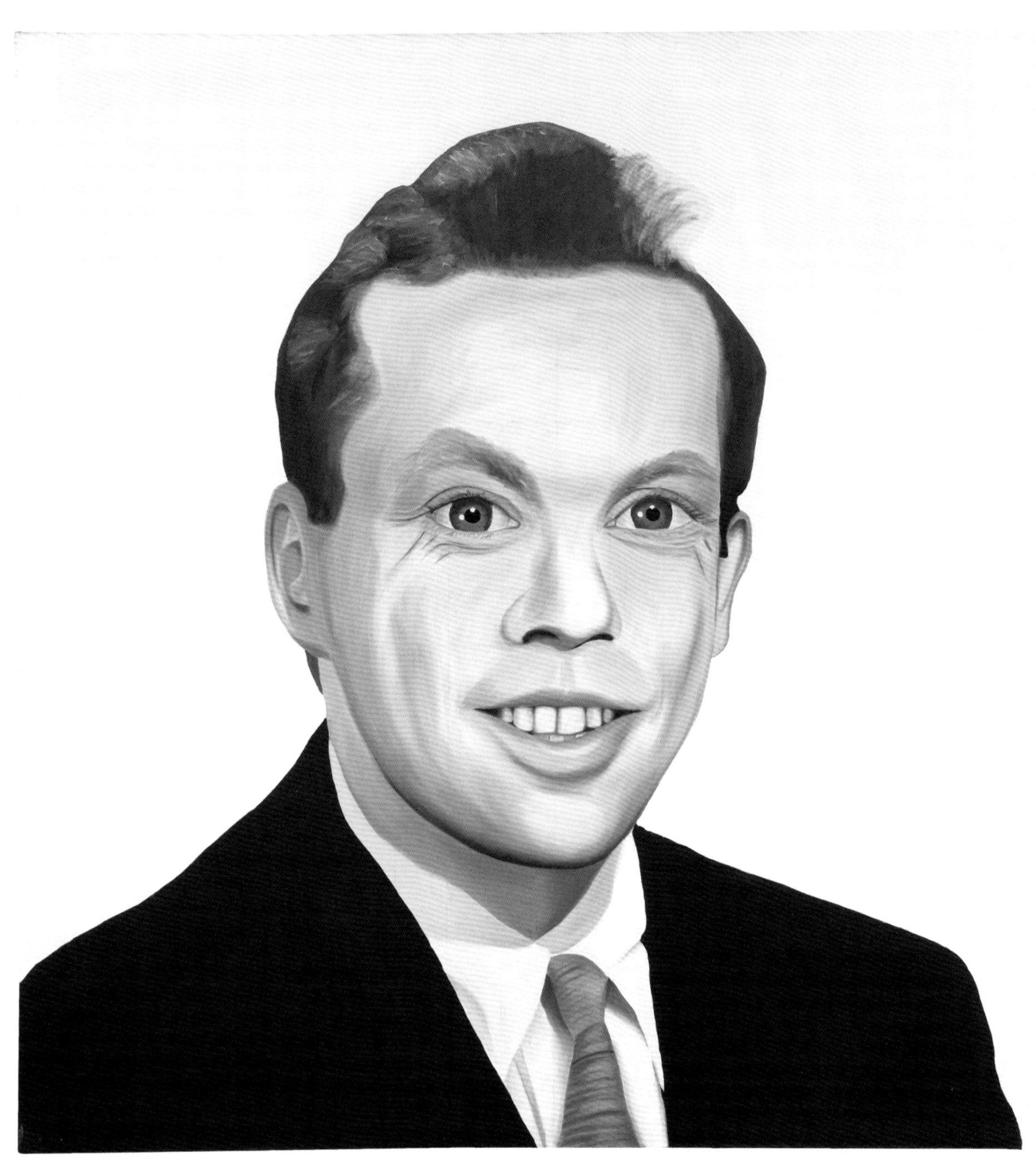

Paul Laffoley
Self-Portrait, 1969
Oil on canvas
49 × 49 inches | 124.5 × 124.5 cm

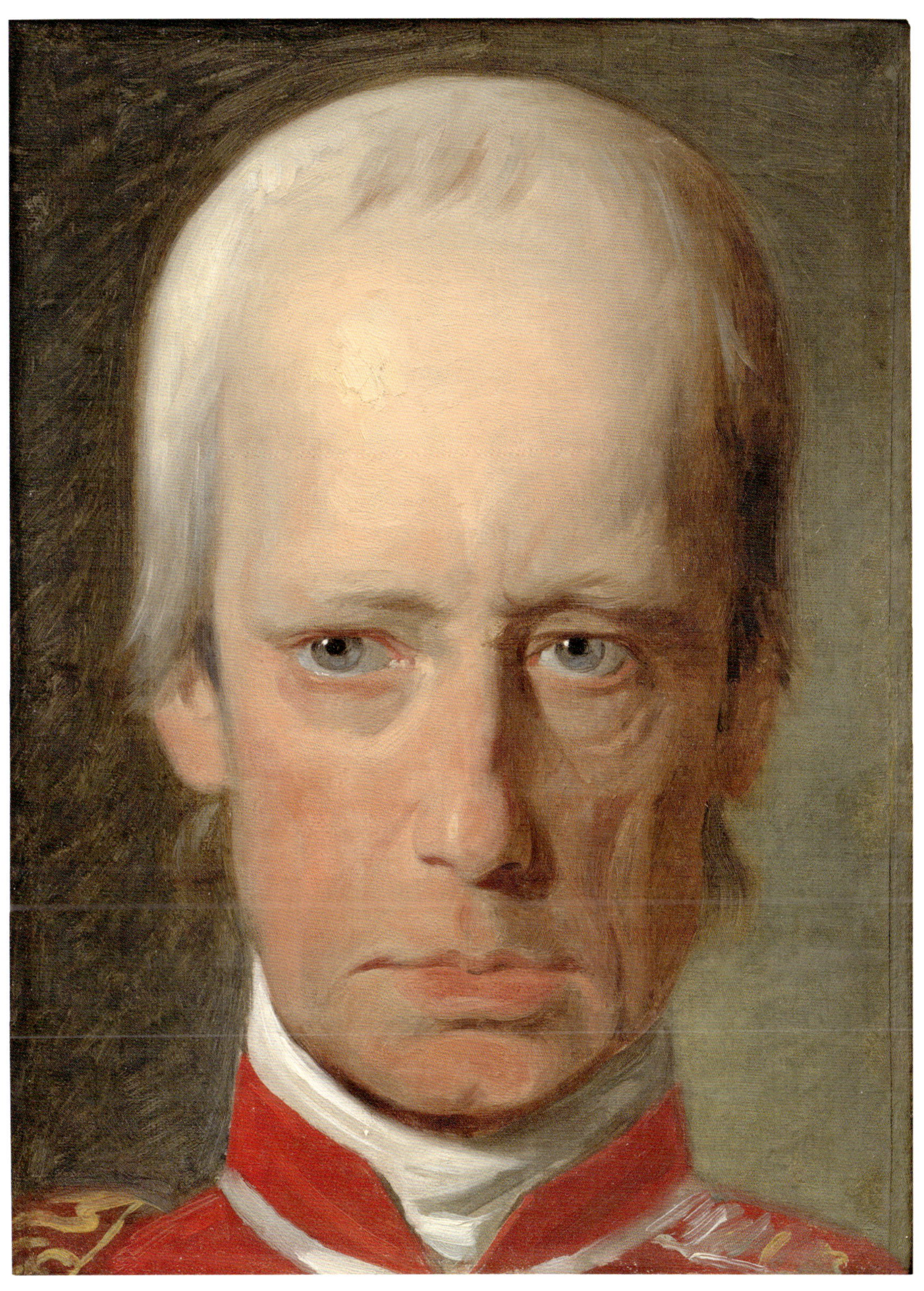

Friedrich von Amerling
Kaiser Franz I of Austria, Study for the
Official Portrait, Executed during His Majesty's
Luncheon, March 27th, 1832, 1832
Oil on canvas
11 ¾ × 8 ⅝ inches | 29.9 × 21.9 cm

Carlo Bugatti
Self-Portrait, n.d.
Oil on canvas
19 ⅞ × 16 inches | 50.5 × 40.6 cm

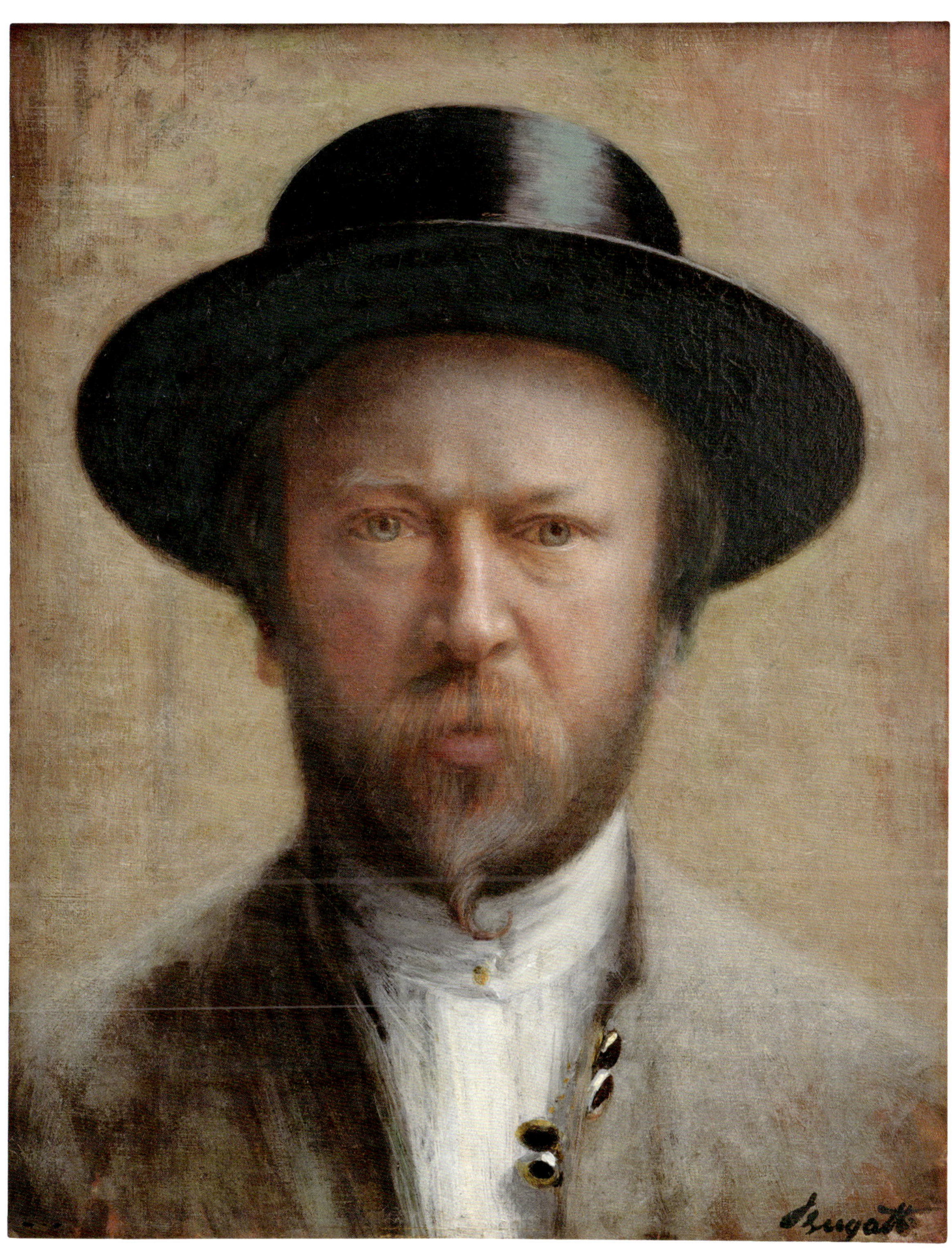

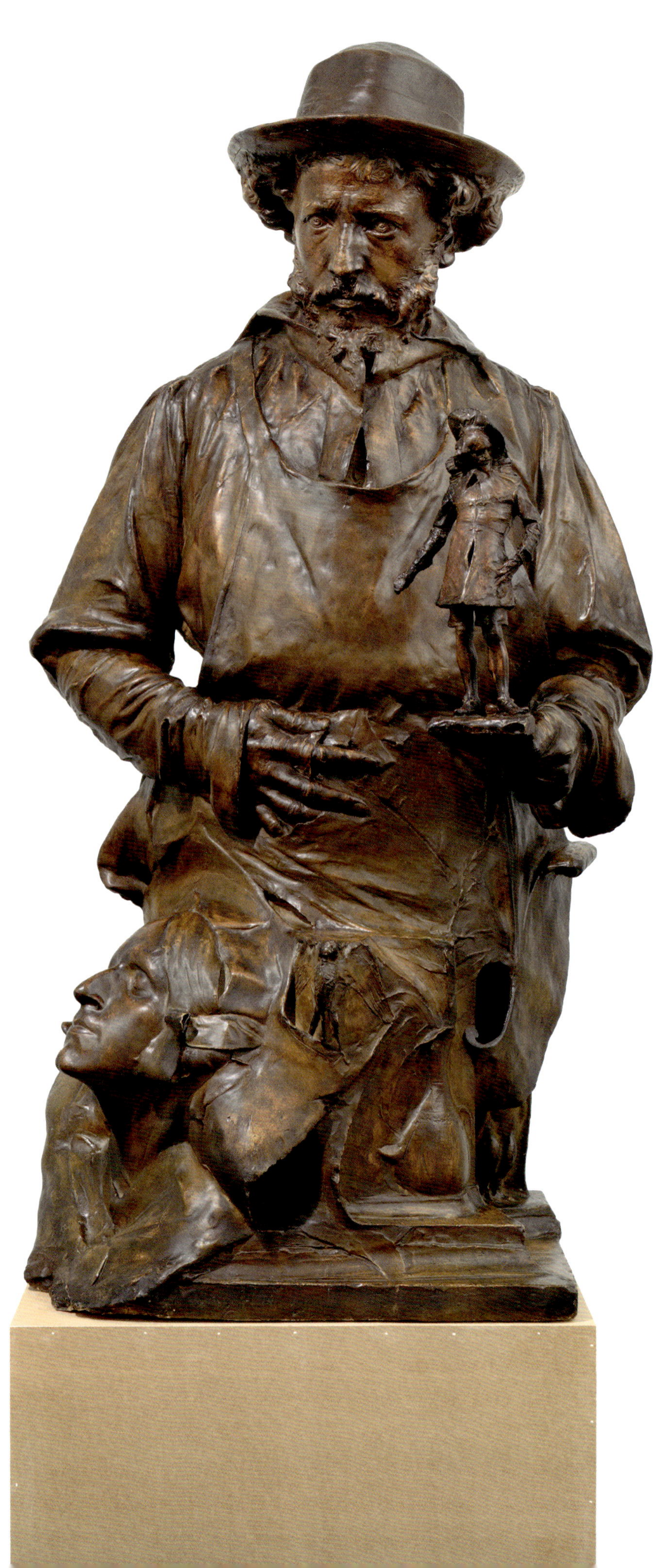

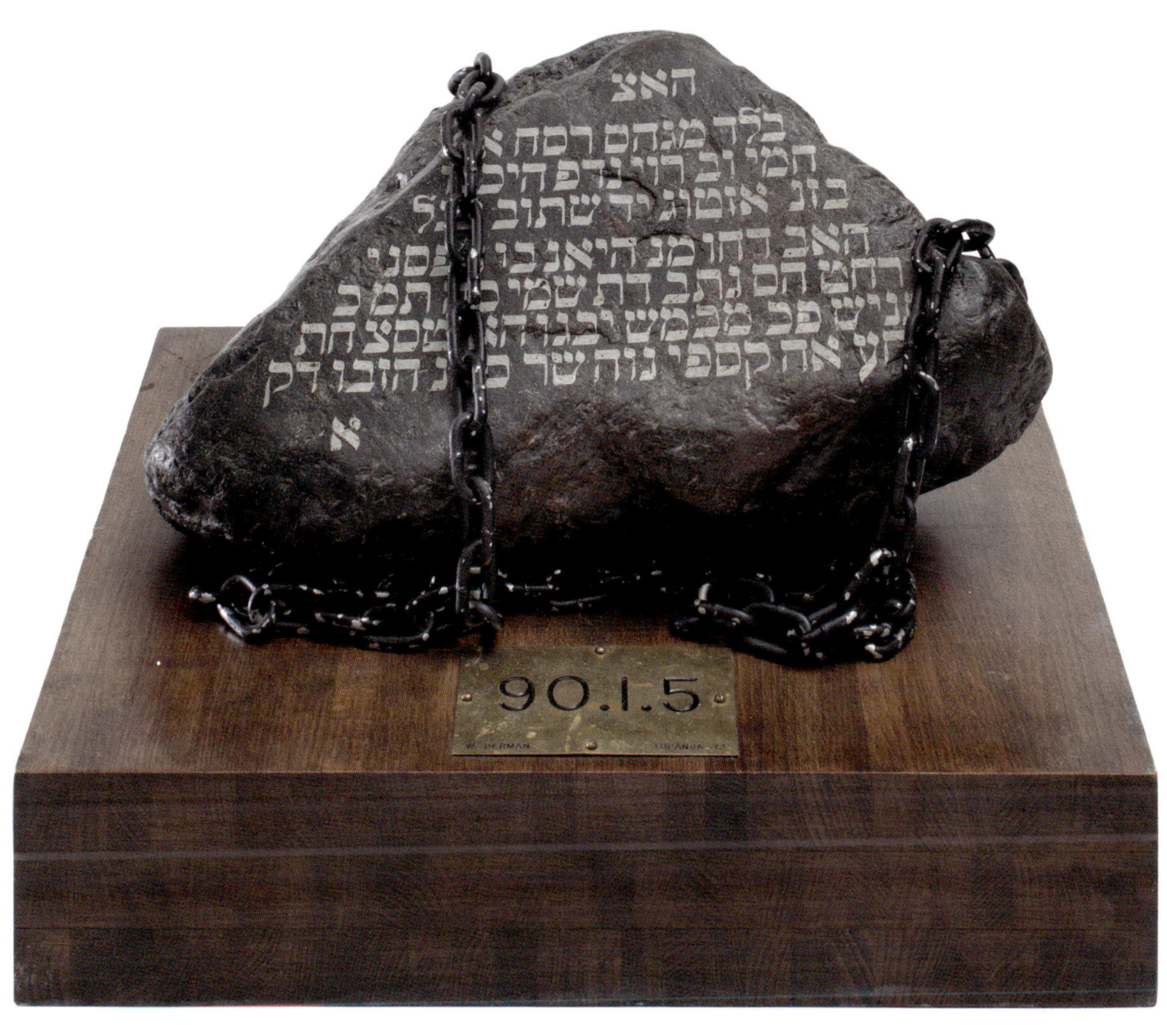

Jean Carriès
Mon Portrait, c. 1888
Patinated plaster
50 ½ × 27 ⅛ × 23 ¼ inches
128.3 × 68.9 × 59.1 cm

Wallace Berman
Untitled, 1973
Rock, chain, and brass plate on walnut base
22 × 18 × 15 inches
55.9 × 45.7 × 38.1 cm

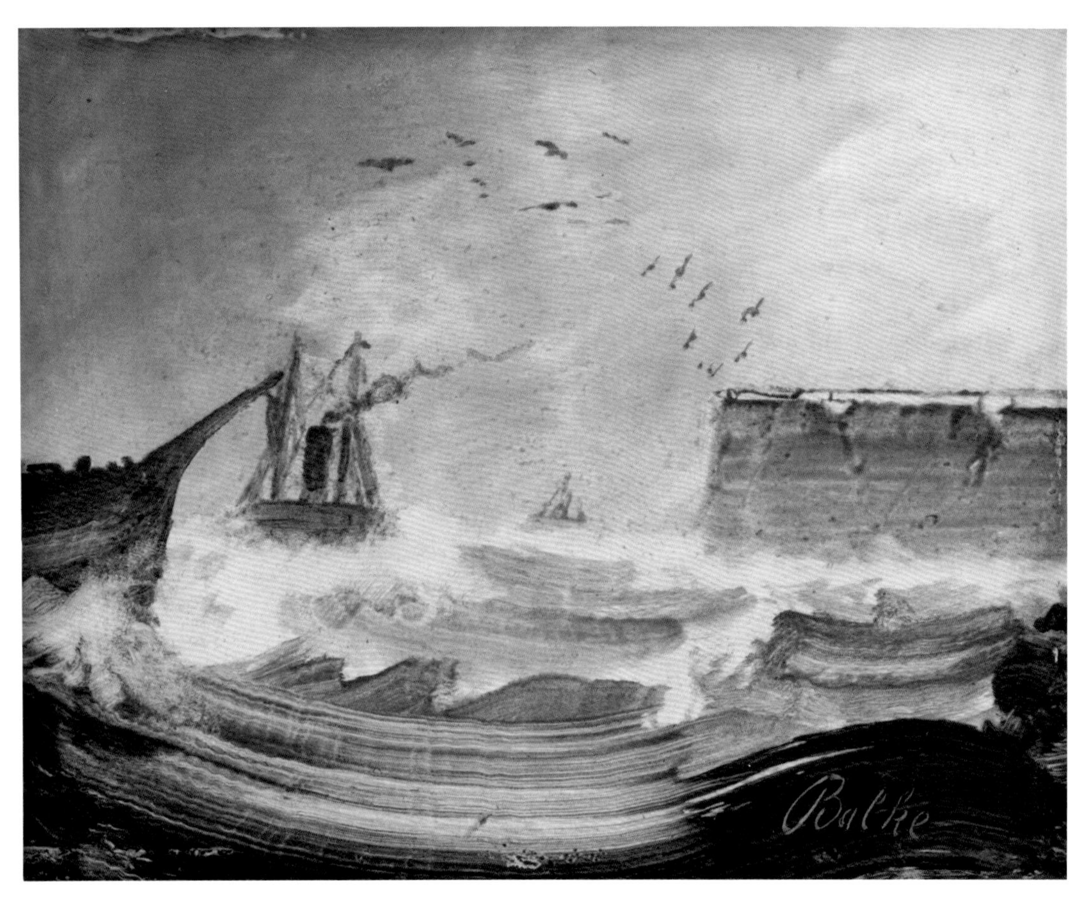

Peder Balke
Ships in a Storm, c. 1870–1879
Oil on panel
3 ¾ × 4 ½ inches | 9.5 × 11.4 cm

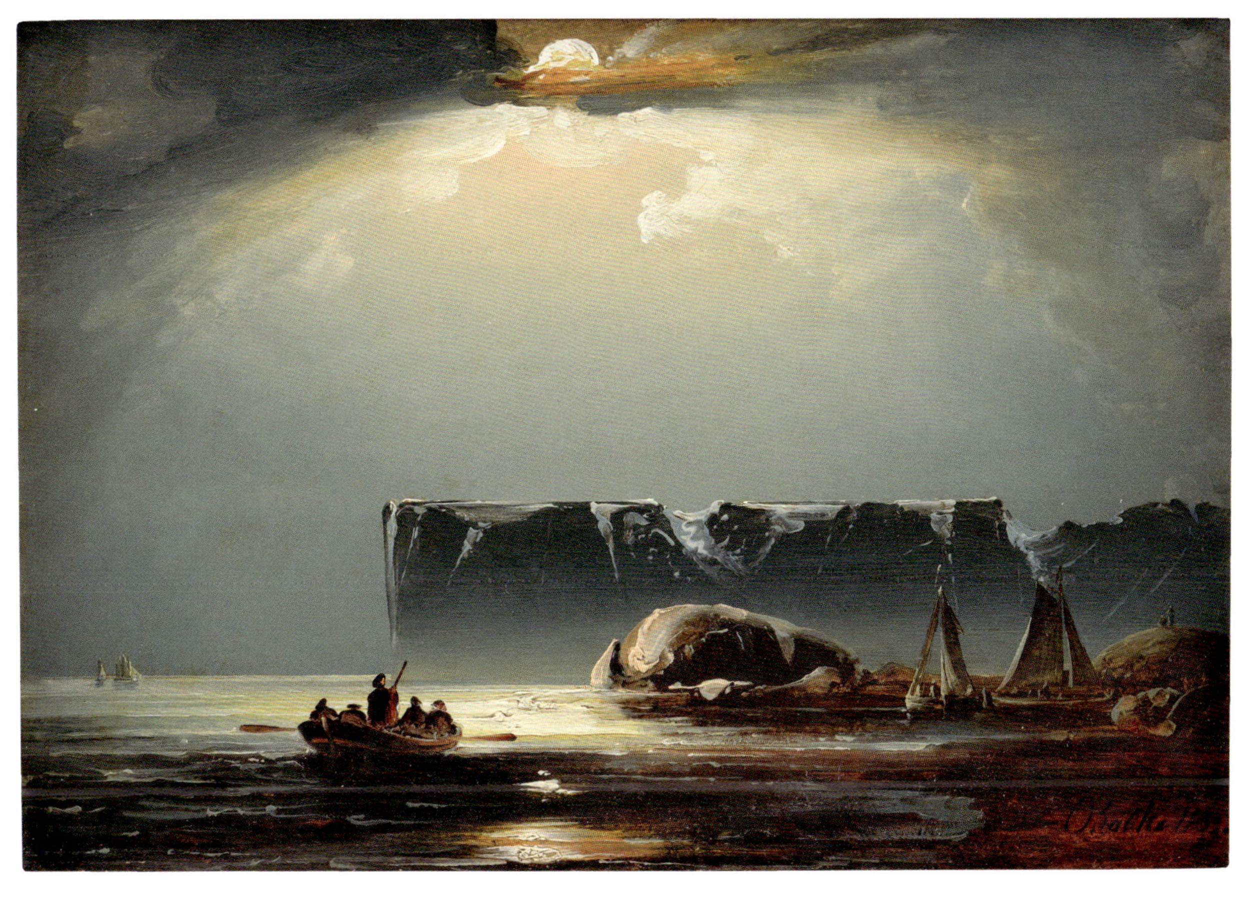

Peder Balke
Fra Nordkapp (From the North Cape), 1853
Oil on paper on board
14 ¼ × 19 ⅞ inches | 36.2 × 50.5 cm

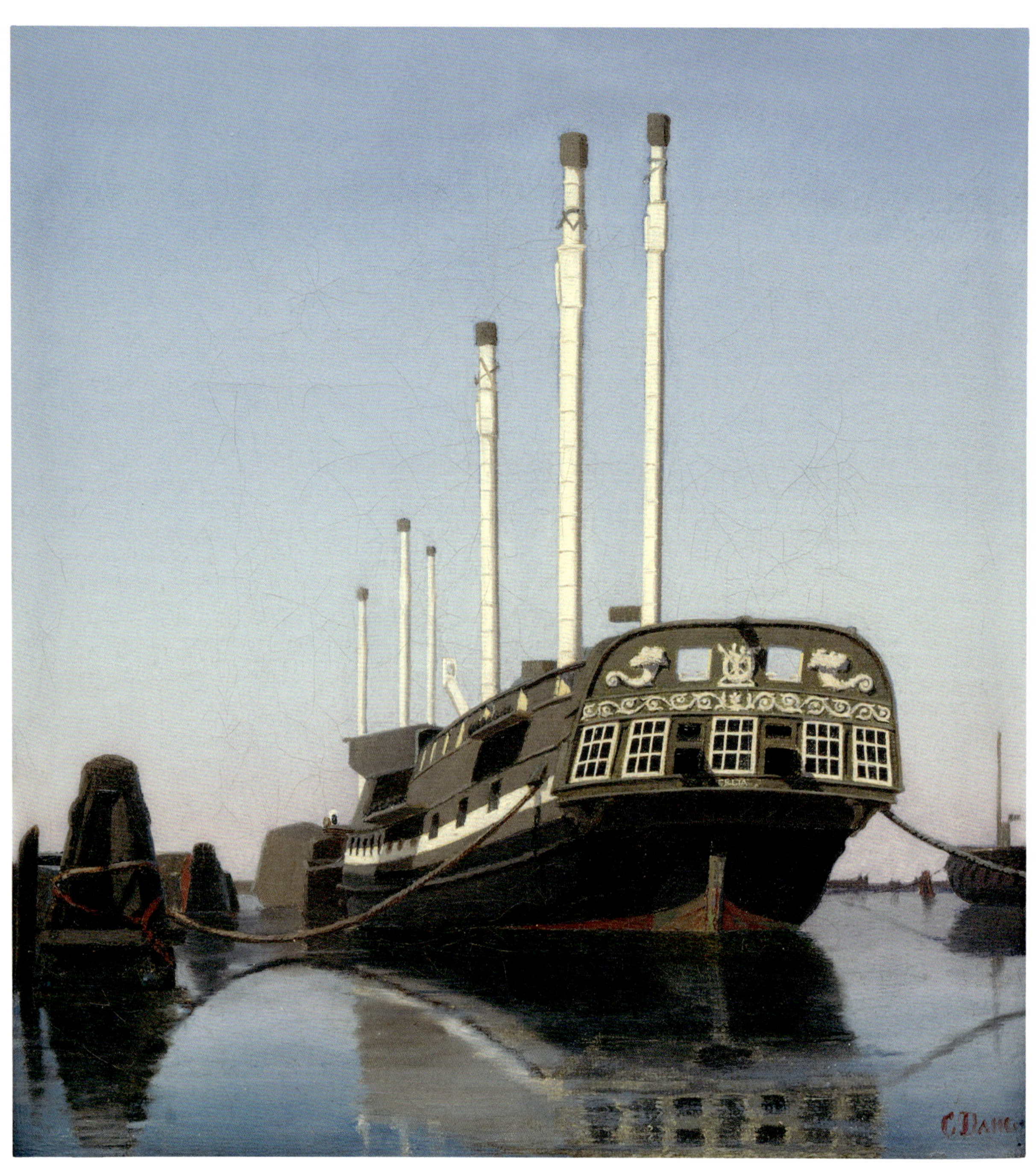

Carl Dahl
The Frigate Freya, c. 1824–1853
Oil on canvas
8 ¾ × 8 ⅛ inches | 22.2 × 20.6 cm

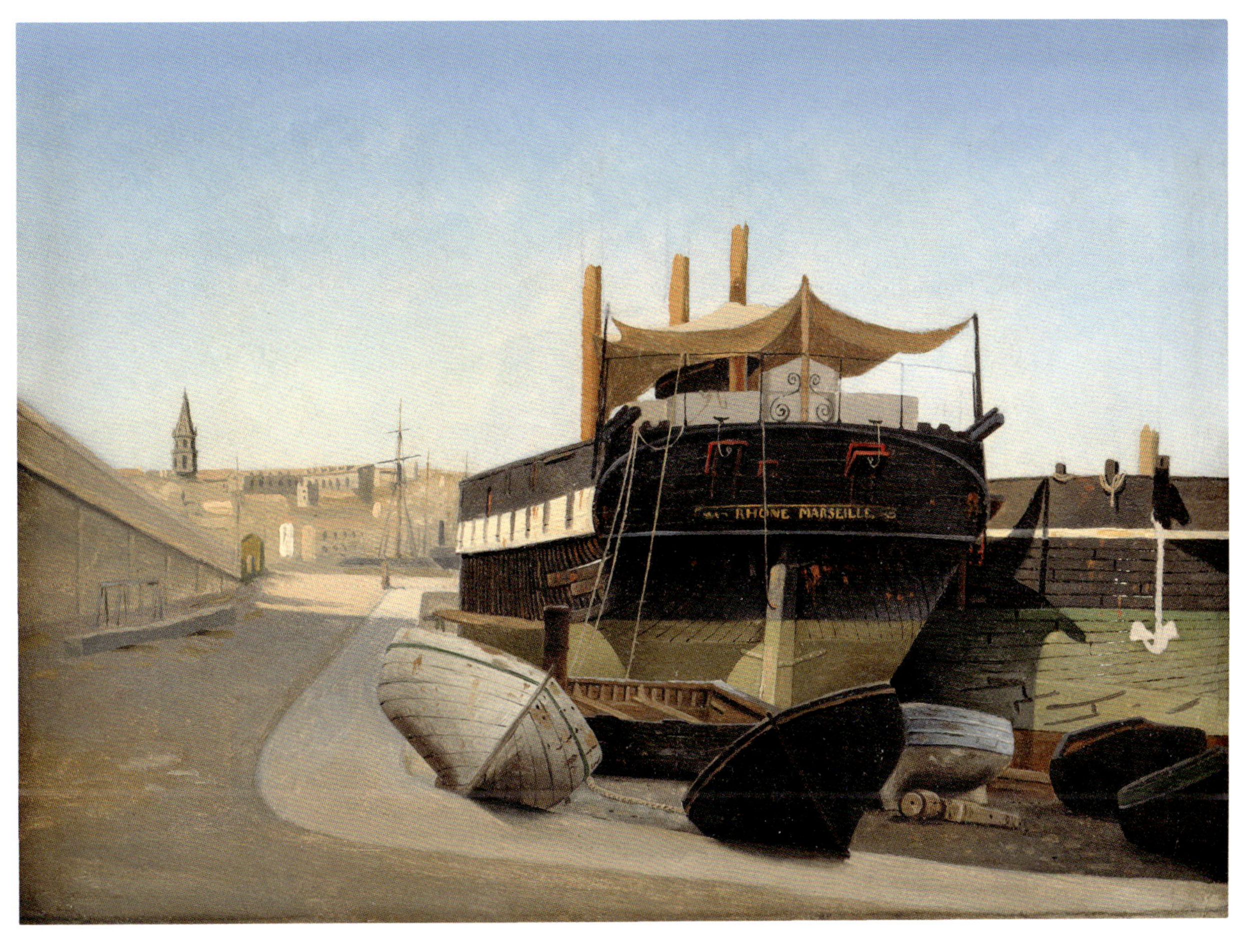

Carl Dahl
The Sailing Ship Rhone in Dock in Marseille, 1852
Oil on paper, laid down on canvas
10 x 14 inches | 25.6 x 35.6 cm

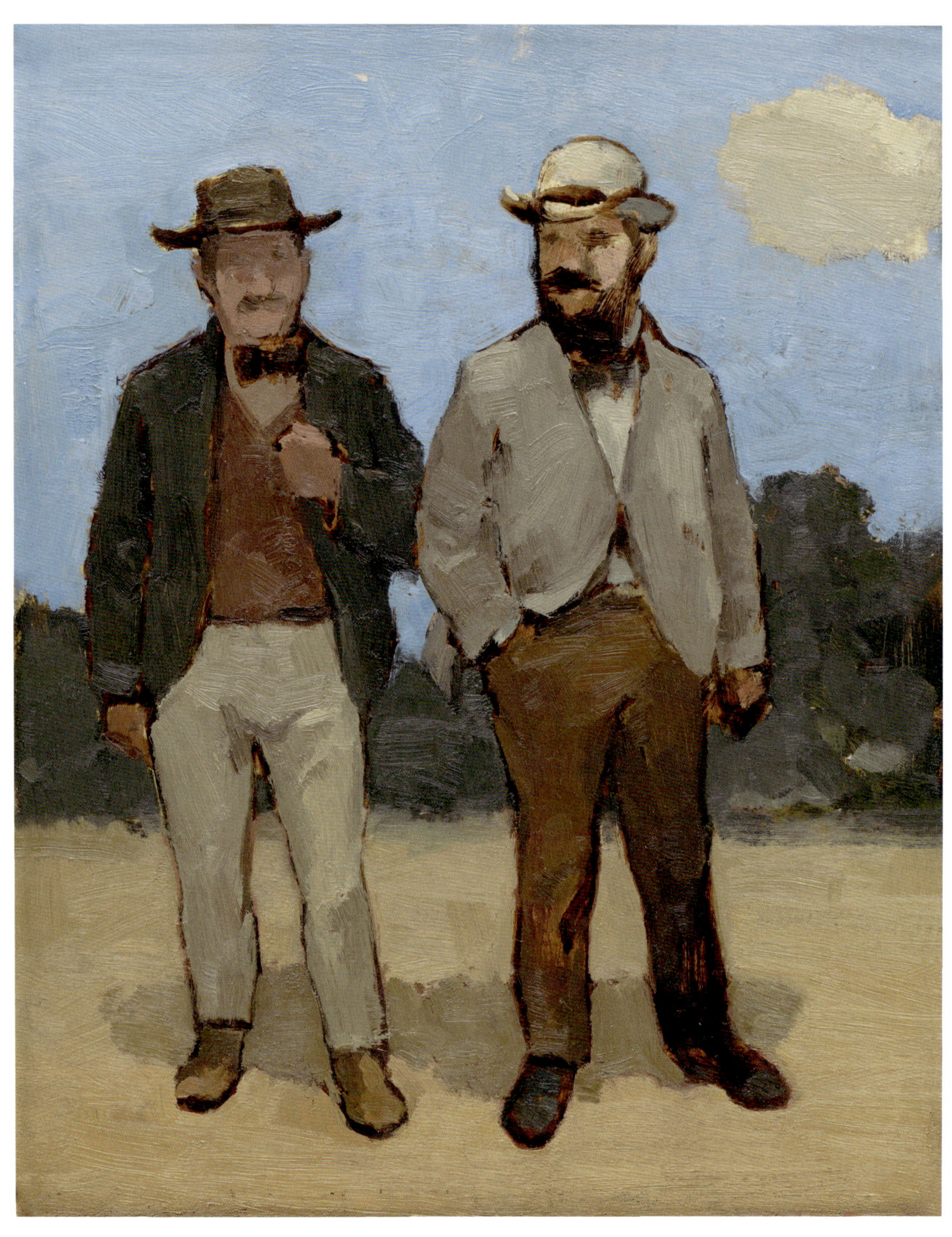

Albert York
Two Men on a Moonlit Road, 1978
Oil on Masonite
12 × 9 ¾ inches | 30.5 × 24.8 cm

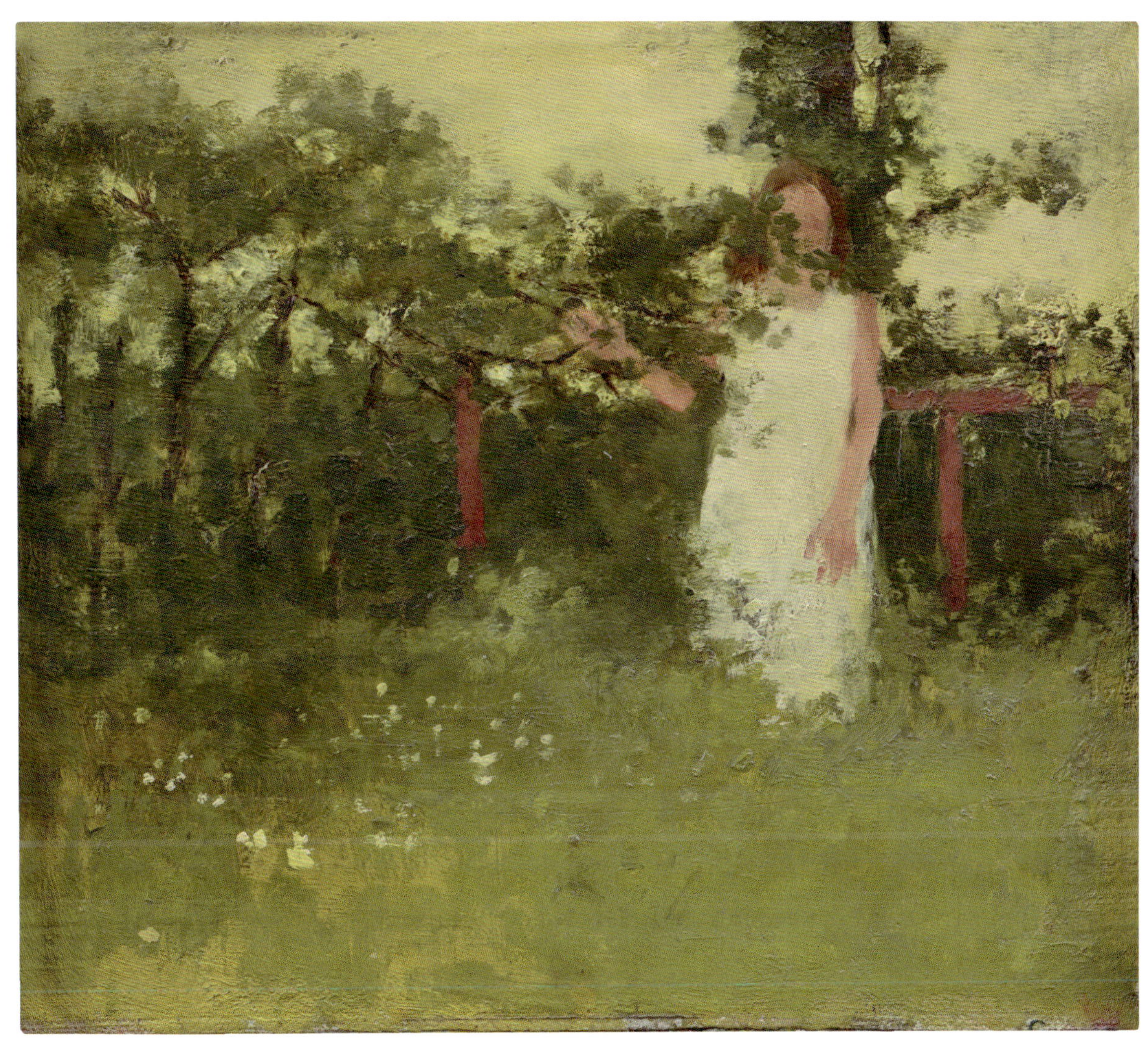

Albert York
Spring, c. 1963
Oil on canvas on Masonite
8 ⅞ × 10 ¼ inches | 22.5 × 26 cm

Alfred Jensen
The Ionic Order, 1979
Oil on canvas
79 × 145 ½ inches | 200.7 × 369.6 cm

TIME
DER
S

2 × 18 = 36	1.
4 × 18 = 72	2.
6 × 18 = 108	3.
8 × 18 = 144	4.
10 × 18 = 180	5.
12 × 18 = 216	6.
14 × 18 = 252	7.
16 × 18 = 288	8.
18 × 18 = 324	9.
20 × 18 = 360	10.

ST
IS
TED
E.

21 × 21 = 441	10.
23 × 21 = 483	9.
25 × 21 = 525	8.
27 × 21 = 567	7.
29 × 21 = 609	6.
31 × 21 = 651	5.
33 × 21 = 693	4.
35 × 21 = 735	3.
37 × 21 = 777	2.
39 × 21 = 819	1.

= 36 + 819 = 855	1.
= 72 + 777 = 849	2.
= 108 + 735 = 843	3.
= 144 + 693 = 837	4.
= 180 + 651 = 831	5.
= 216 + 609 = 825	6.
= 252 + 567 = 819	7.
= 288 + 525 = 813	8.
= 324 + 483 = 807	9.
= 360 + 441 = 801	10.

MERCURY-TIME
6 YEARS OF 116 DAYS
= 696.

1.	3×9=27
2.	5×9=45
3.	7×9=63
4.	9×9=81
5.	11×9=99
6.	13×9=117
7.	15×9=135
8.	17×9=153
9.	19×9=171
9.	22×8=176
8.	24×8=192
7.	26×8=208
6.	28×8=224
5.	30×8=240
4.	32×8=256
3.	34×8=272
2.	36×8=288
1.	38×8=304

4×8=32	1.
6×8=48	2.
8×8=64	3.
10×8=80	4.
12×8=96	5.
14×8=112	6.
16×8=128	7.
18×8=144	8.
20×8=160	9.
21×9=189	9.
23×9=207	8.
25×9=225	7.
27×9=243	6.
29×9=261	5.
31×9=279	4.
33×9=297	3.
35×9=315	2.
37×9=333	1.

1.	27 + 304 = 331 =	696 = 365 =	32 + 333	1.
2.	45 + 288 = 333 =	696 = 363 =	48 + 315	2.
3.	63 + 272 = 335 =	696 = 361 =	64 + 297	3.
4.	81 + 256 = 337 =	696 = 359 =	80 + 279	4.
5.	99 + 240 = 339 =	696 = 357 =	96 + 261	5.
6.	117 + 224 = 341 =	696 = 355 =	112 + 243	6.
7.	135 + 208 = 343 =	696 = 353 =	128 + 225	7.
8.	153 + 192 = 345 =	696 = 351 =	144 + 207	8.
9.	171 + 176 = 347 =	696 = 349 =	160 + 189	9.

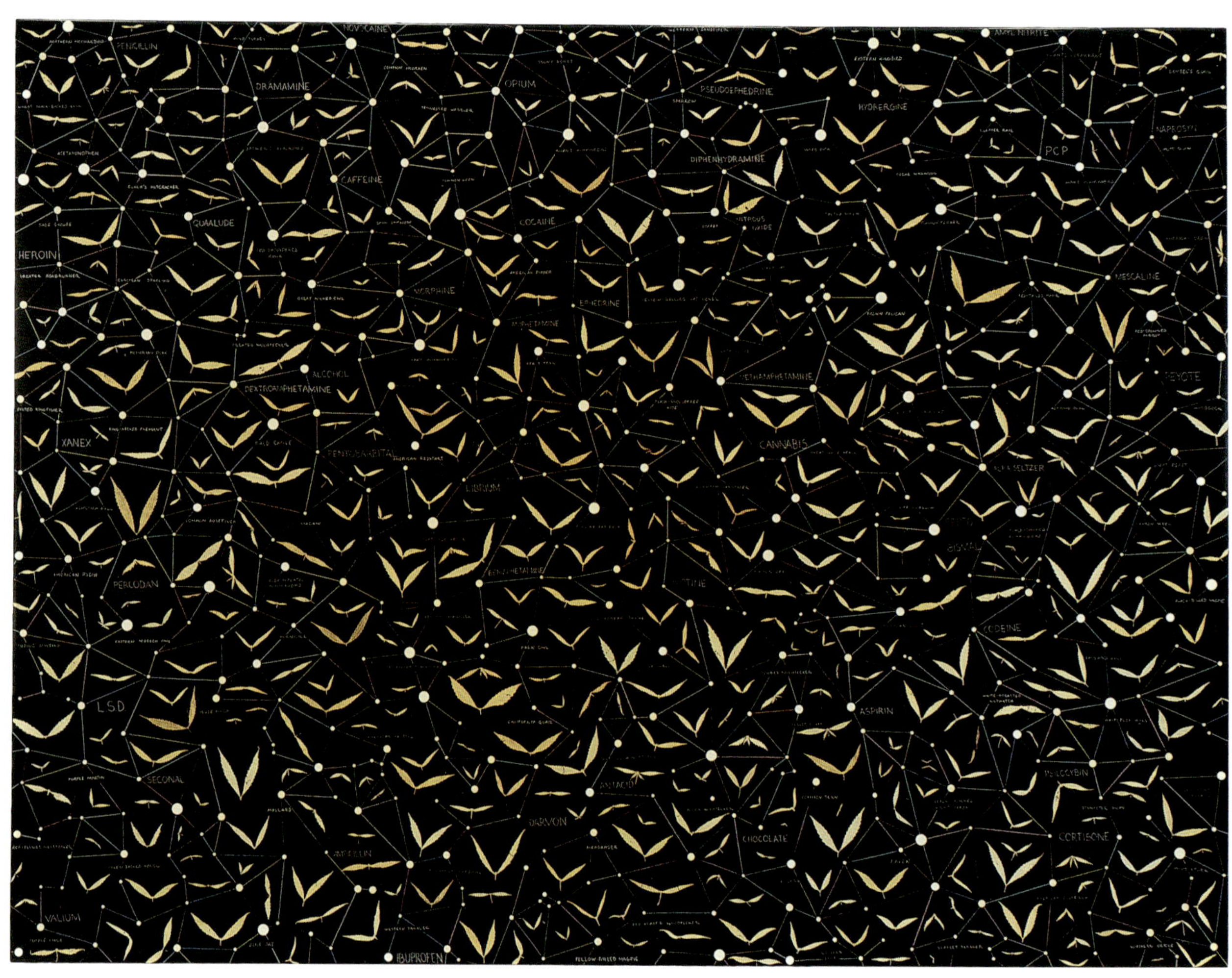

Fred Tomaselli
All the Drugs I Remember Taking,
All the Birds I Remember Seeing, 1996
Aspirin, acetaminophen, hemp leaves, saccharin,
colored pencil, acrylic, and resin on wood panel
54 × 72 inches | 137.2 × 182.9 cm

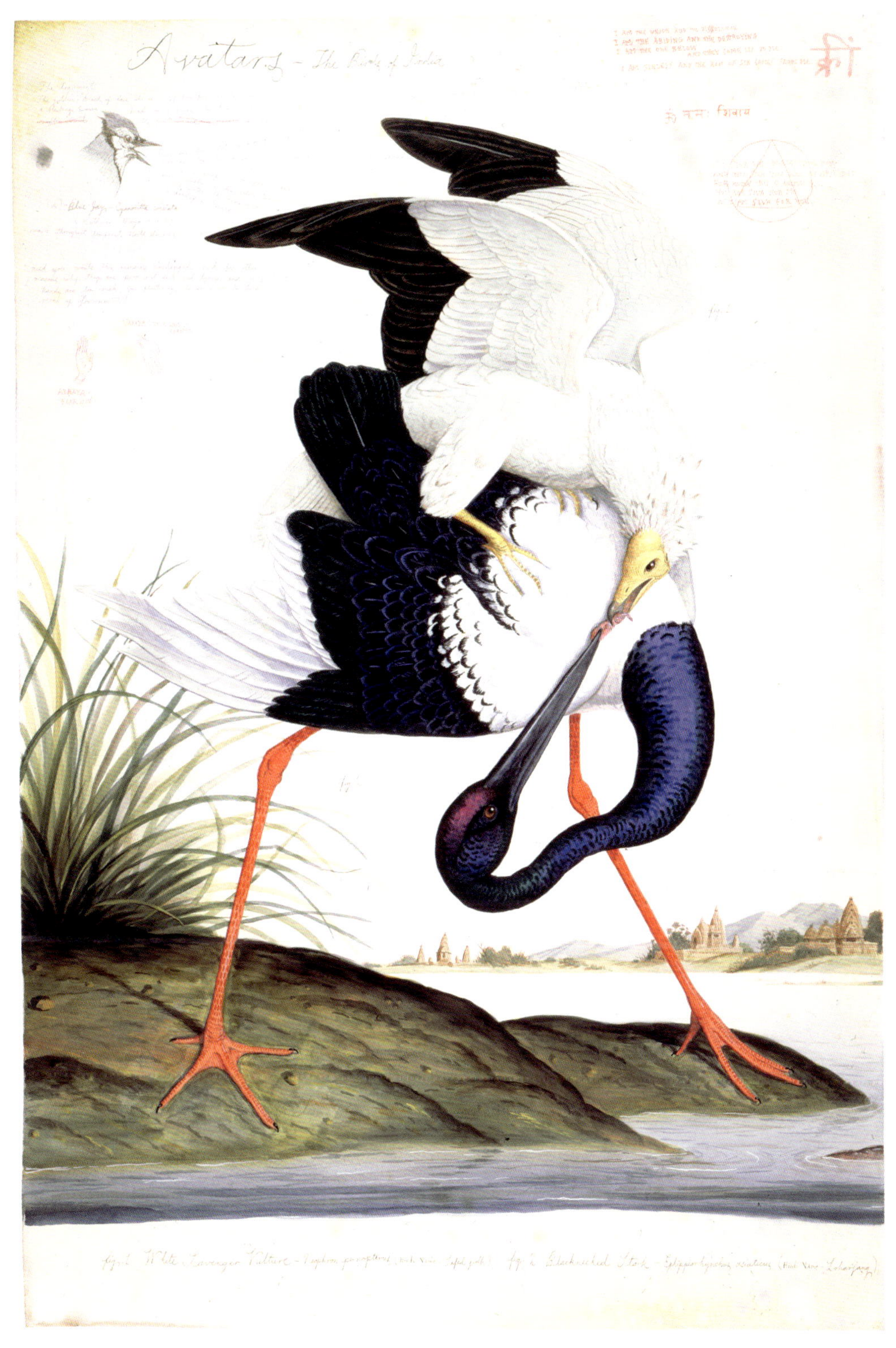

Walton Ford
Avatars—The Birds of India, 1996
Watercolor, gouache, and graphite on paper
59 ¾ × 40 inches | 151.8 × 101.6 cm

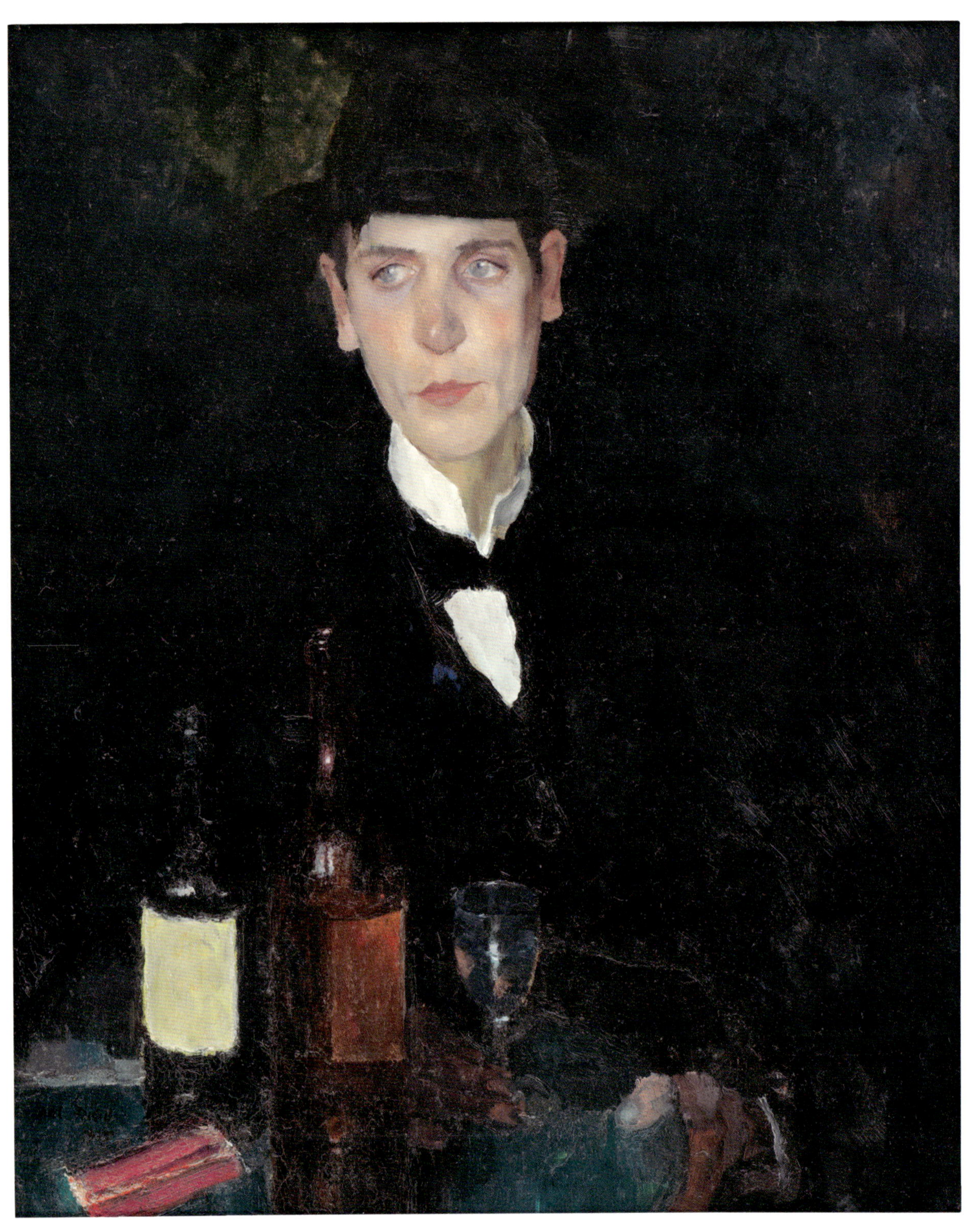

Axel Fridell
Portrait of Einar Forseth, 1915
Oil on canvas
21 ⅞ × 18 ¼ inches | 55.6 × 46.4 cm

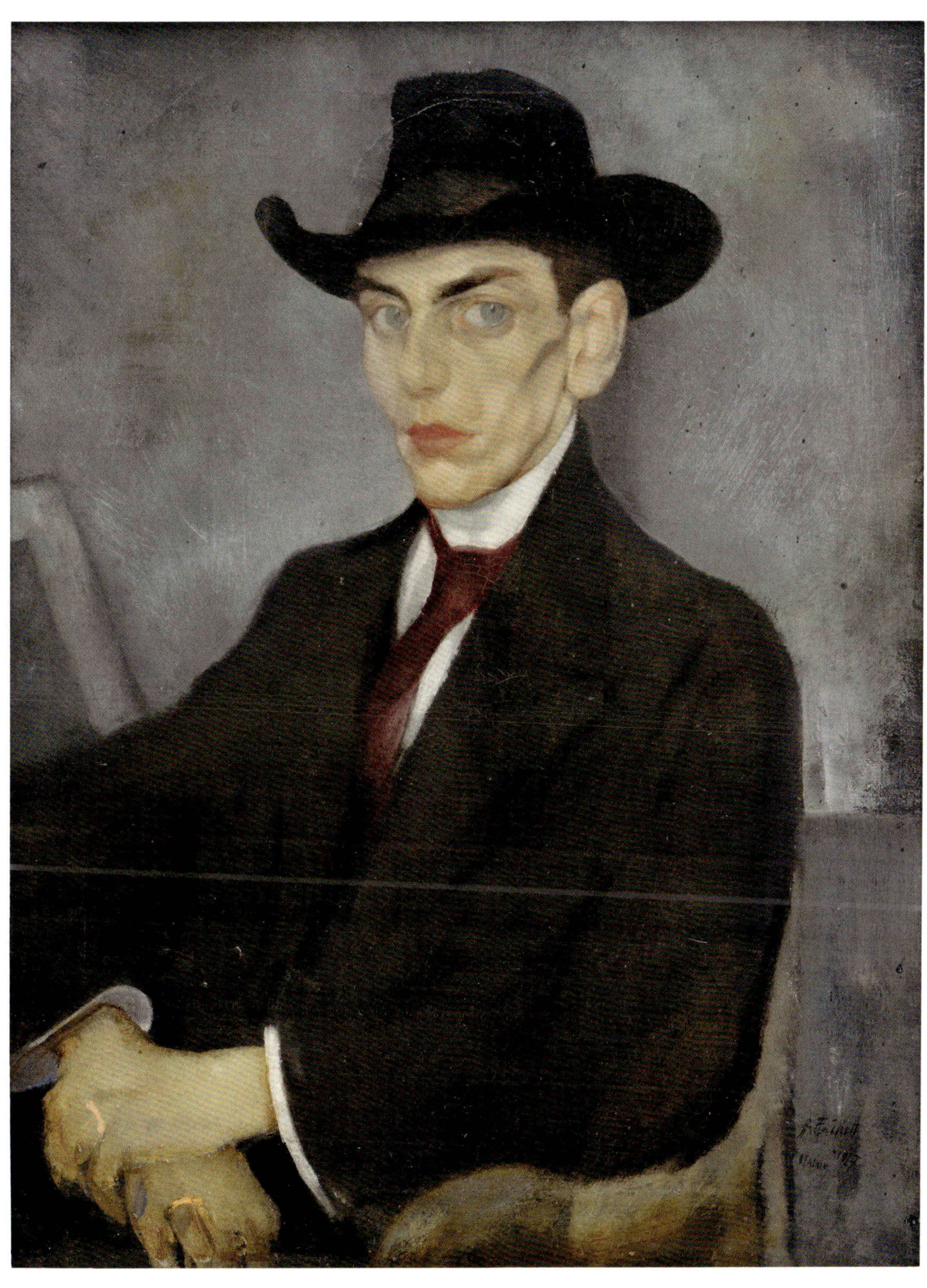

Axel Fridell
Portrait of the Sculptor Natanael Cassén, 1917
Oil on canvas
24 ⅛ × 18 ¼ inches | 61.3 × 46.4 cm

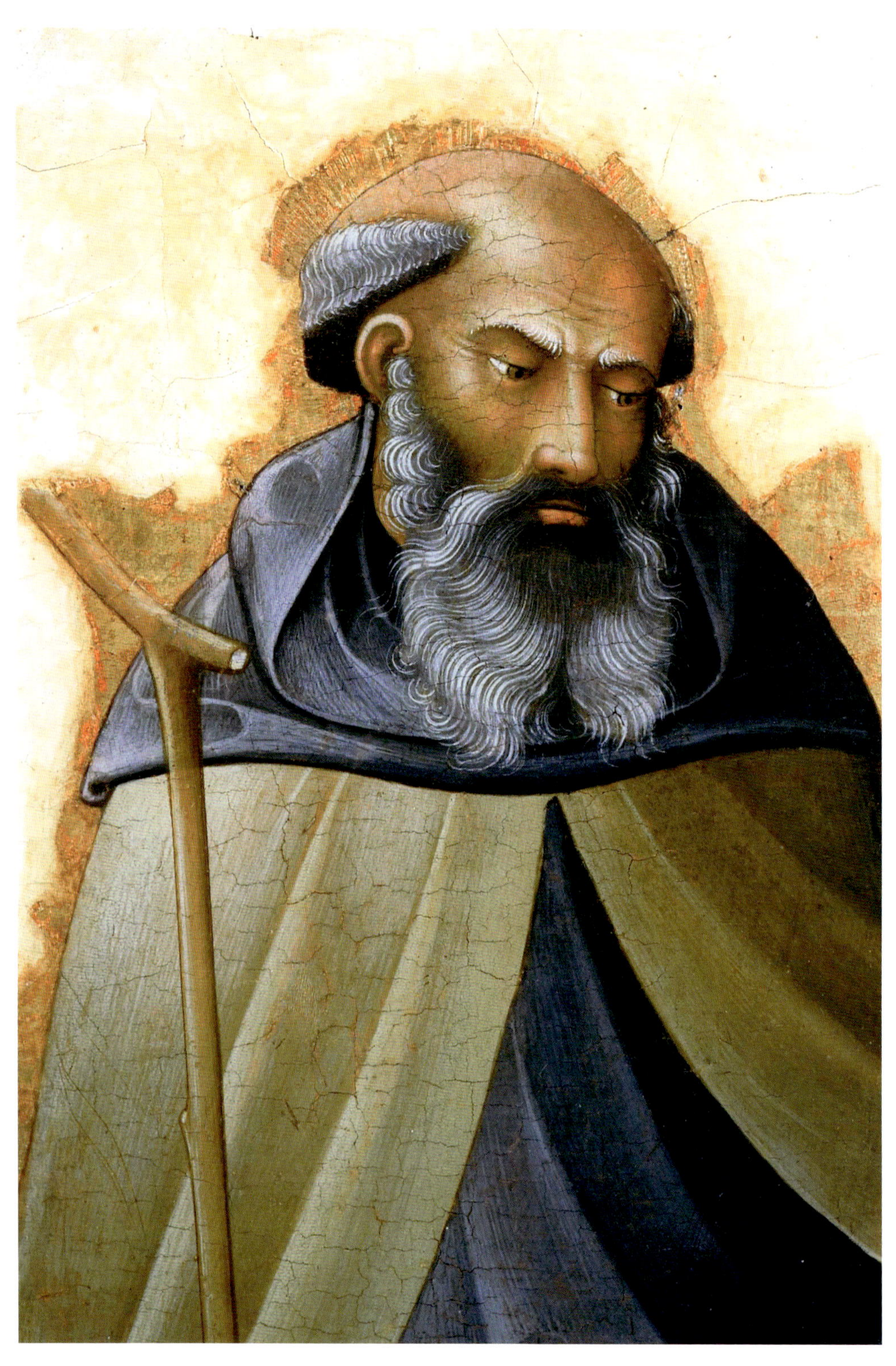

Lorenzo Monaco
Saint Anthony Abbot, 1415–1420
Tempera on panel
13 ¾ × 9 ½ inches | 34.9 × 24.1 cm

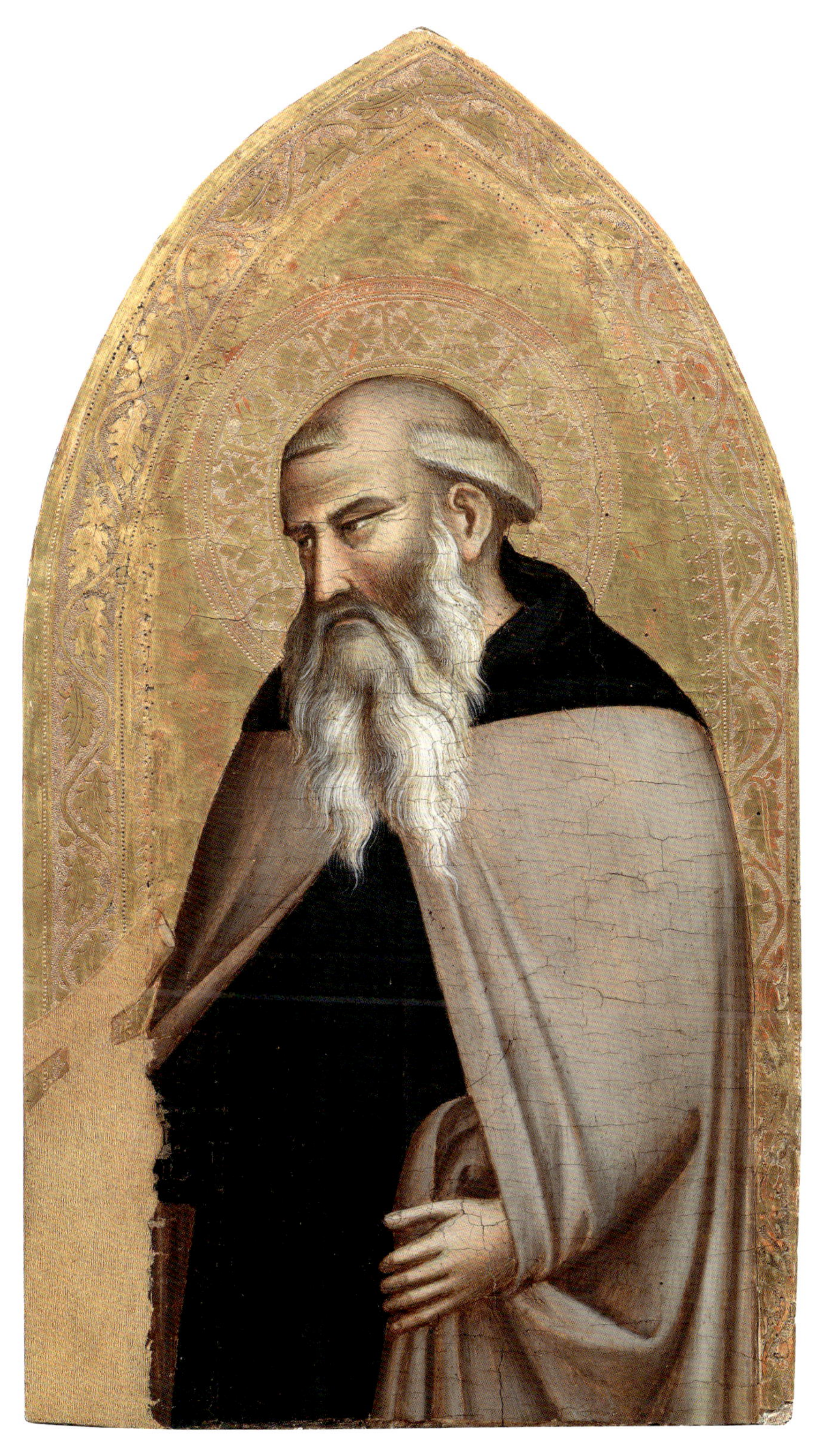

Taddeo Gaddi
Saint Anthony Abbot, c. 1366
Oil on panel
24 ⅜ × 15 ⅛ inches | 61.9 × 38.4 cm

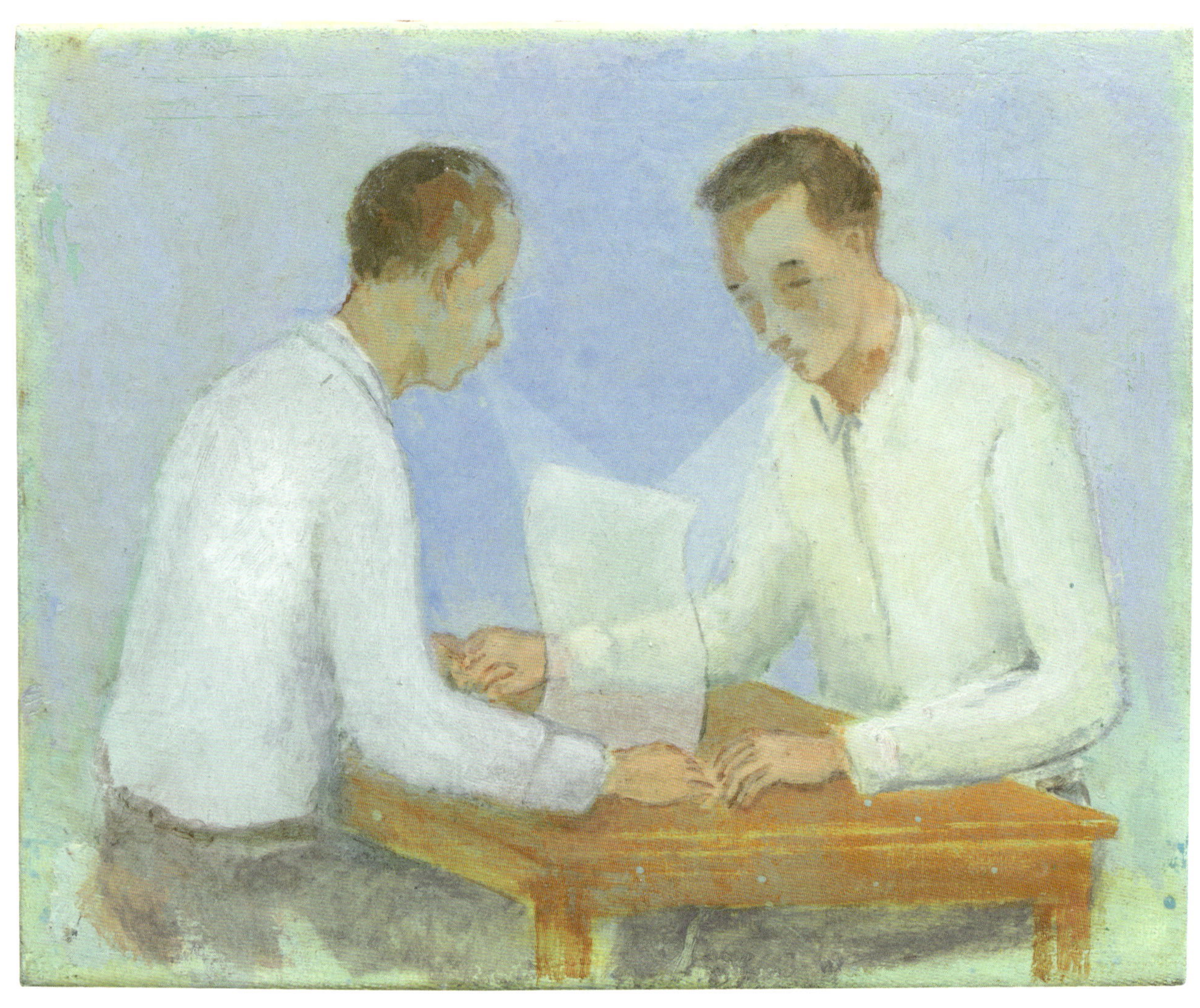

Francis Alÿs
Study for La Leçon de Musique, 1999
Oil and encaustic on canvas
6 ¾ × 8 ¼ inches | 17.1 × 21 cm

134

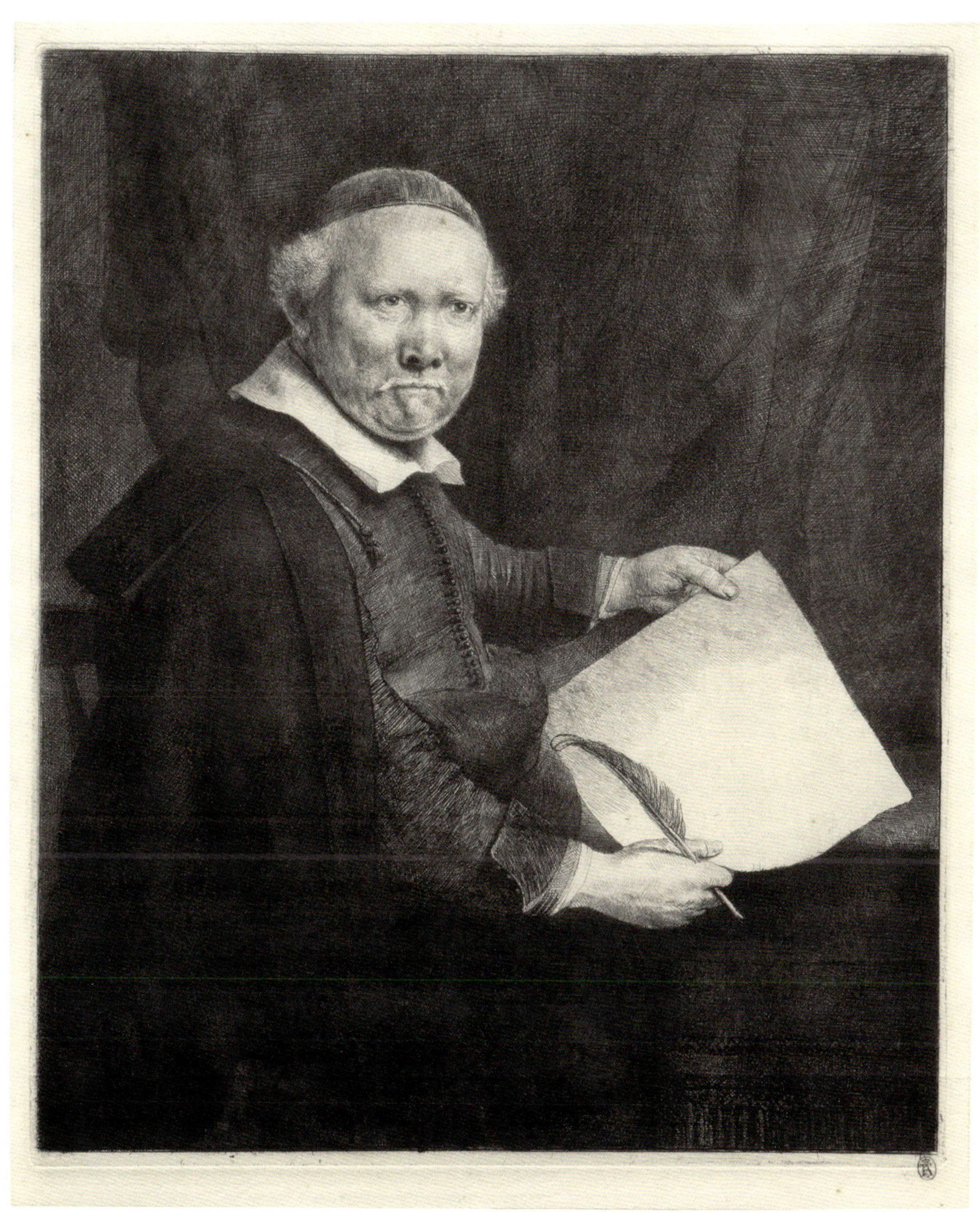

Rembrandt van Rijn
Lieven Willemsz. van Coppenol,
Writing Master (The Larger Plate), 1658
Etching, drypoint, and engraving
14 ¼ × 12 inches | 36.2 × 30.5 cm

135

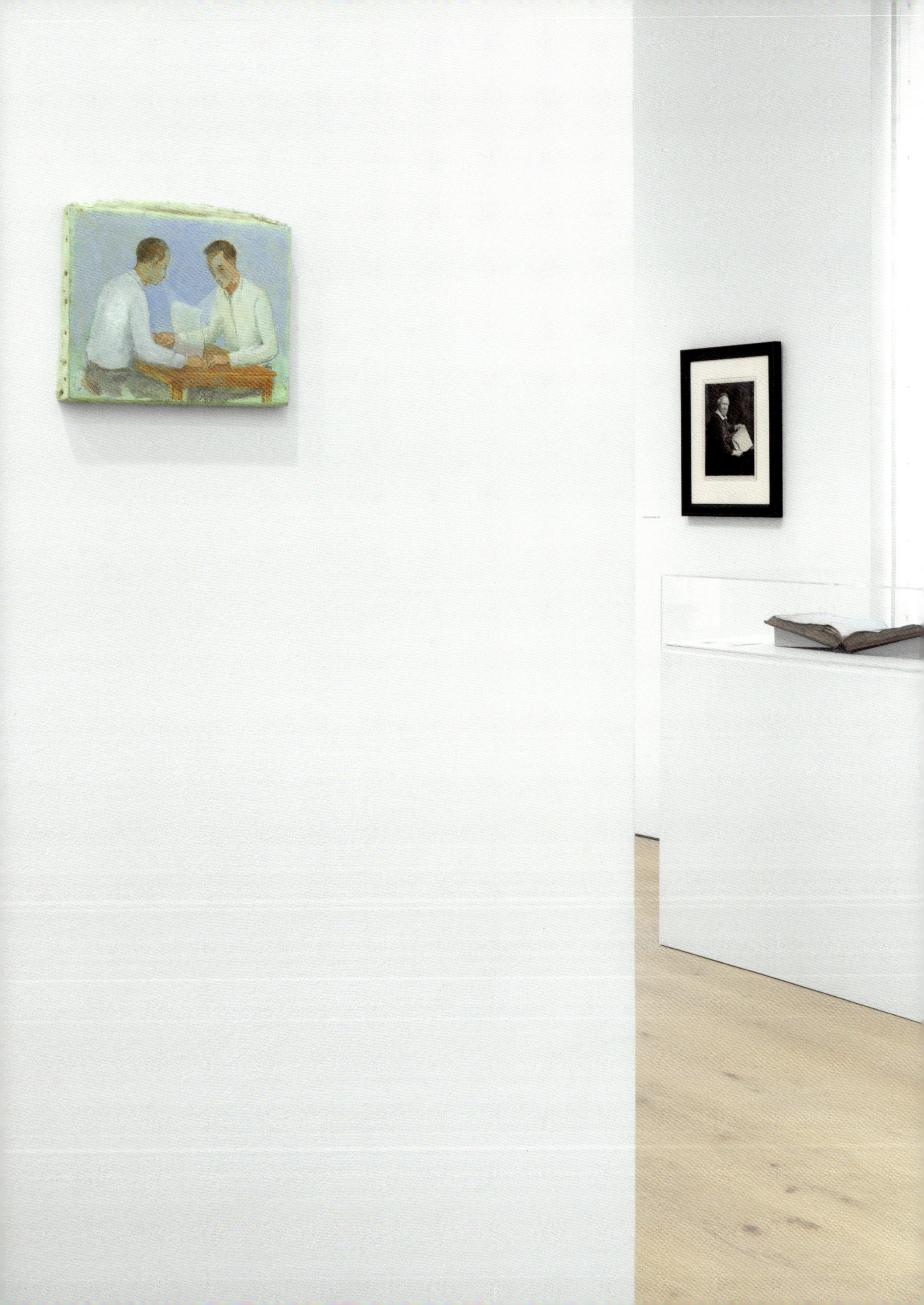

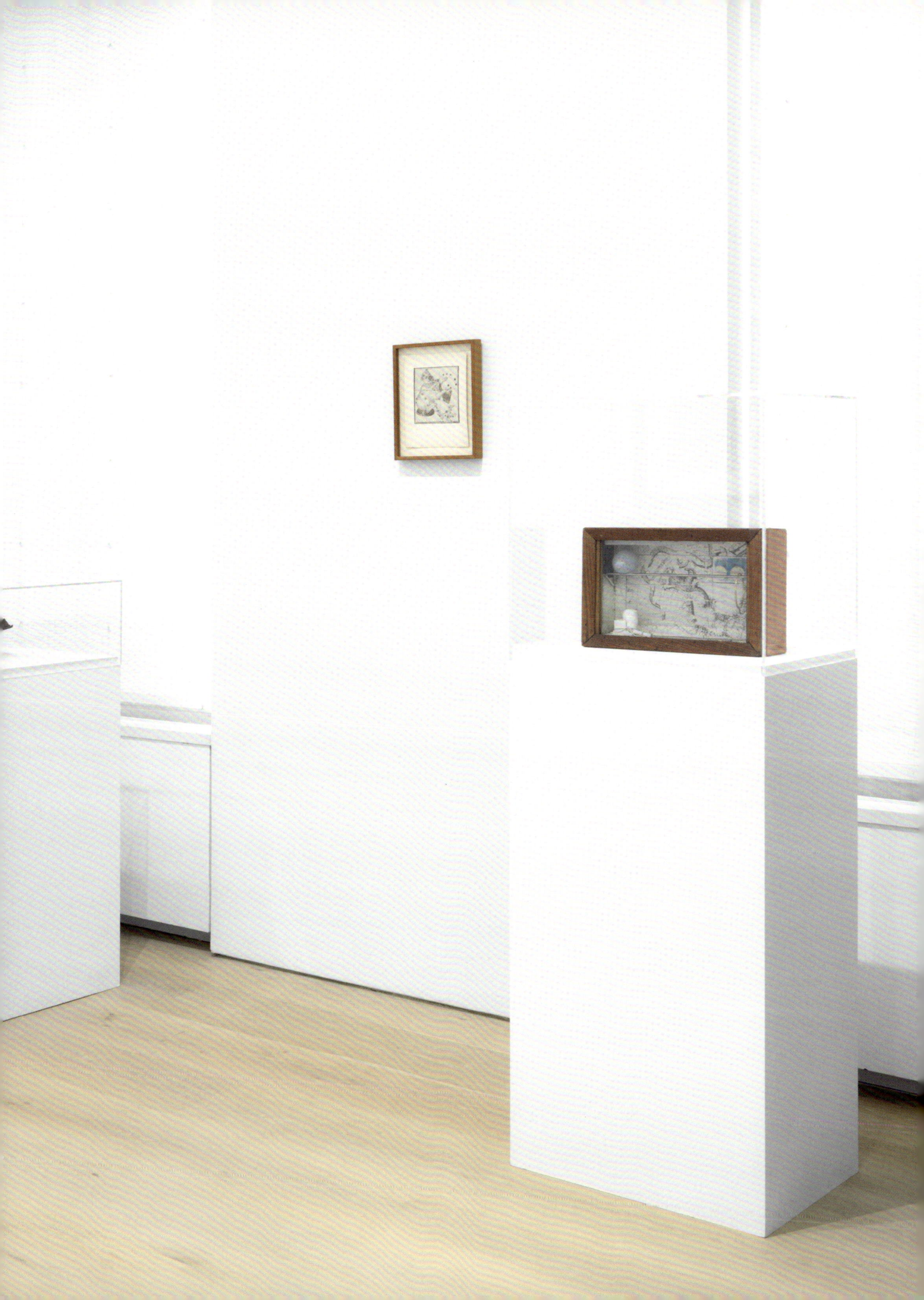

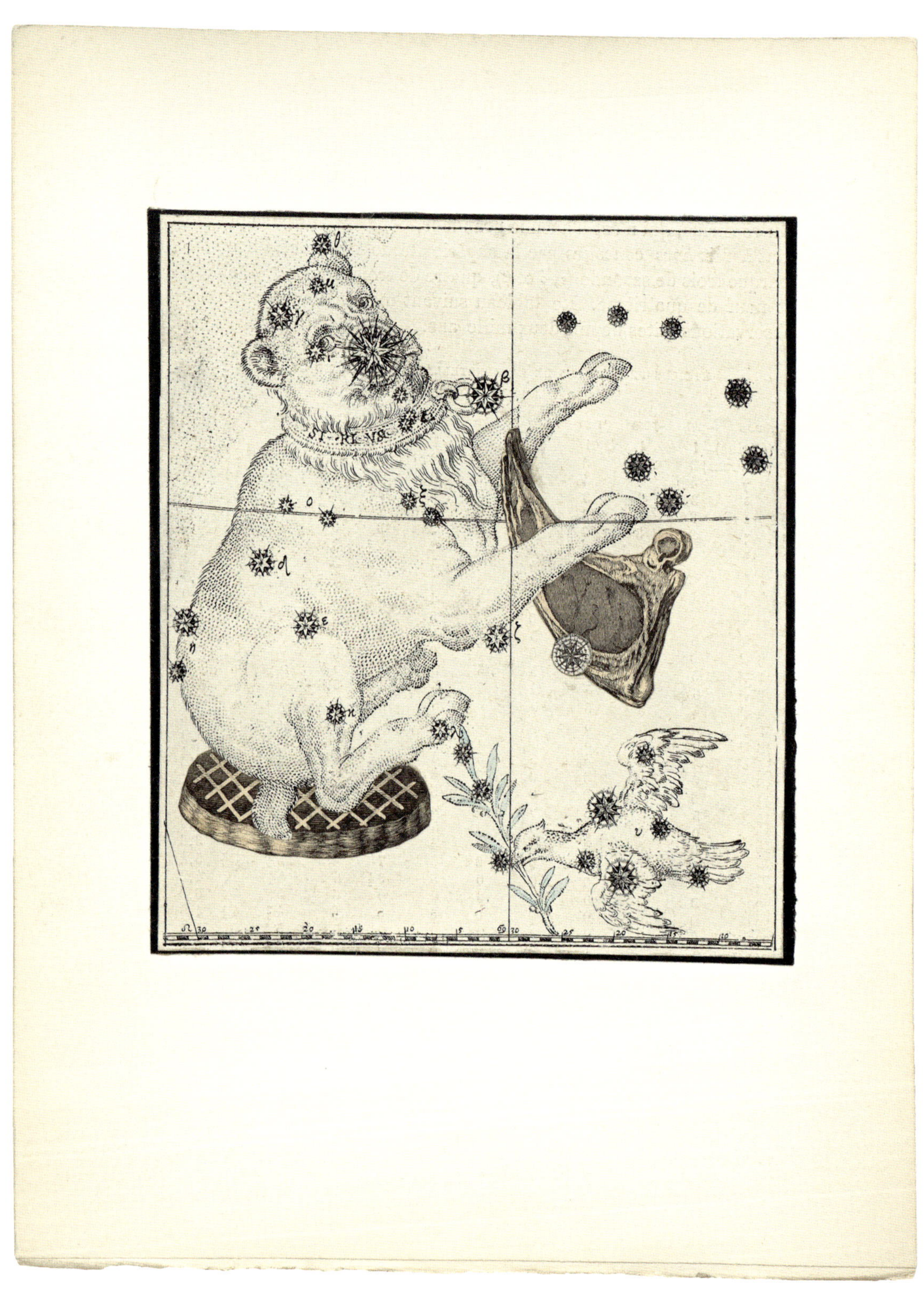

Joseph Cornell
Untitled (Le Grand Chien), c. 1930
Mixed media on paper
9 ⅜ × 7 inches | 23.8 × 17.8 cm

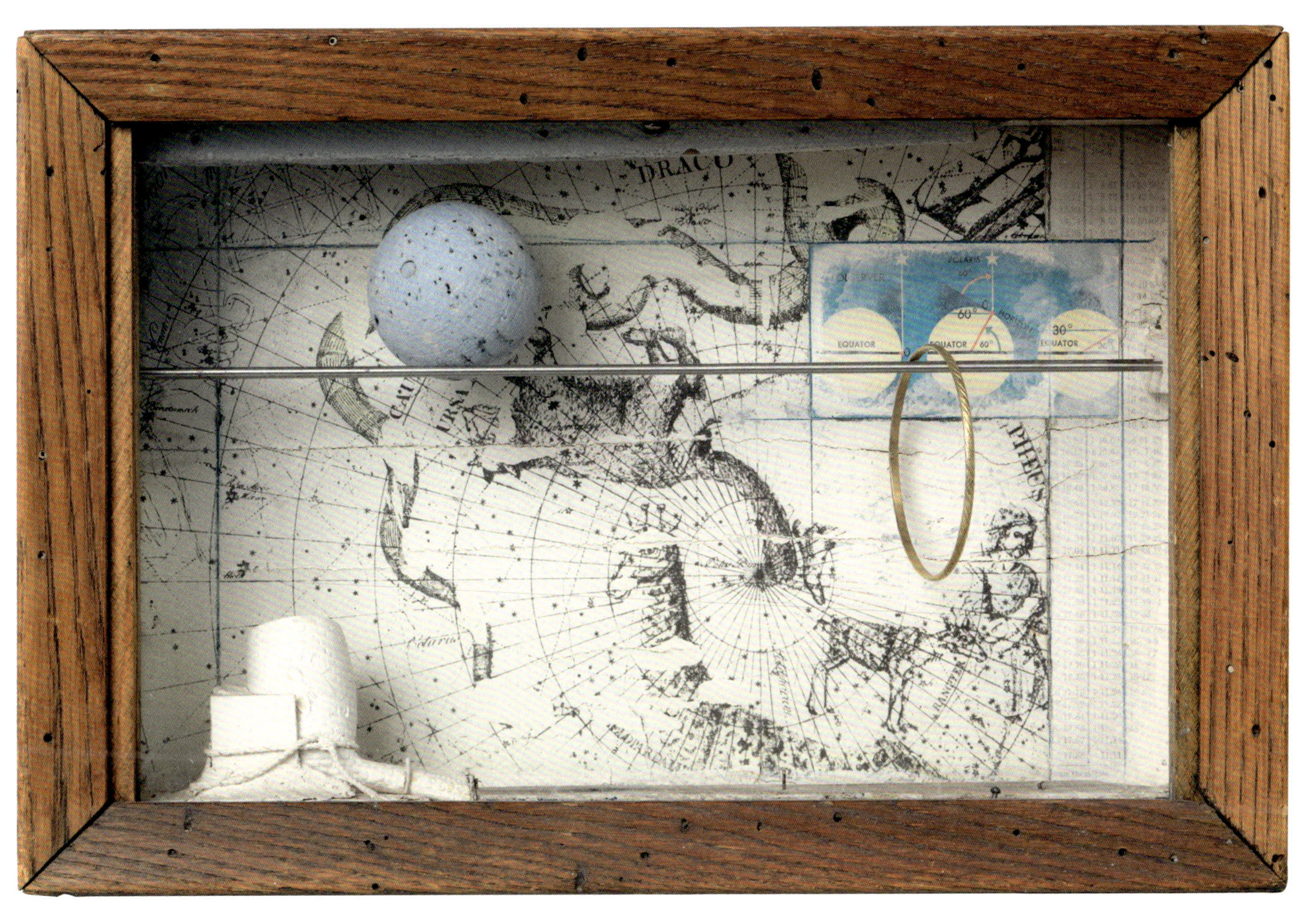

Joseph Cornell
Untitled, 1956–1958
Mixed media in wood box
9 ½ × 14 ¼ × 4 inches | 24.1 × 36.2 × 10.2 cm

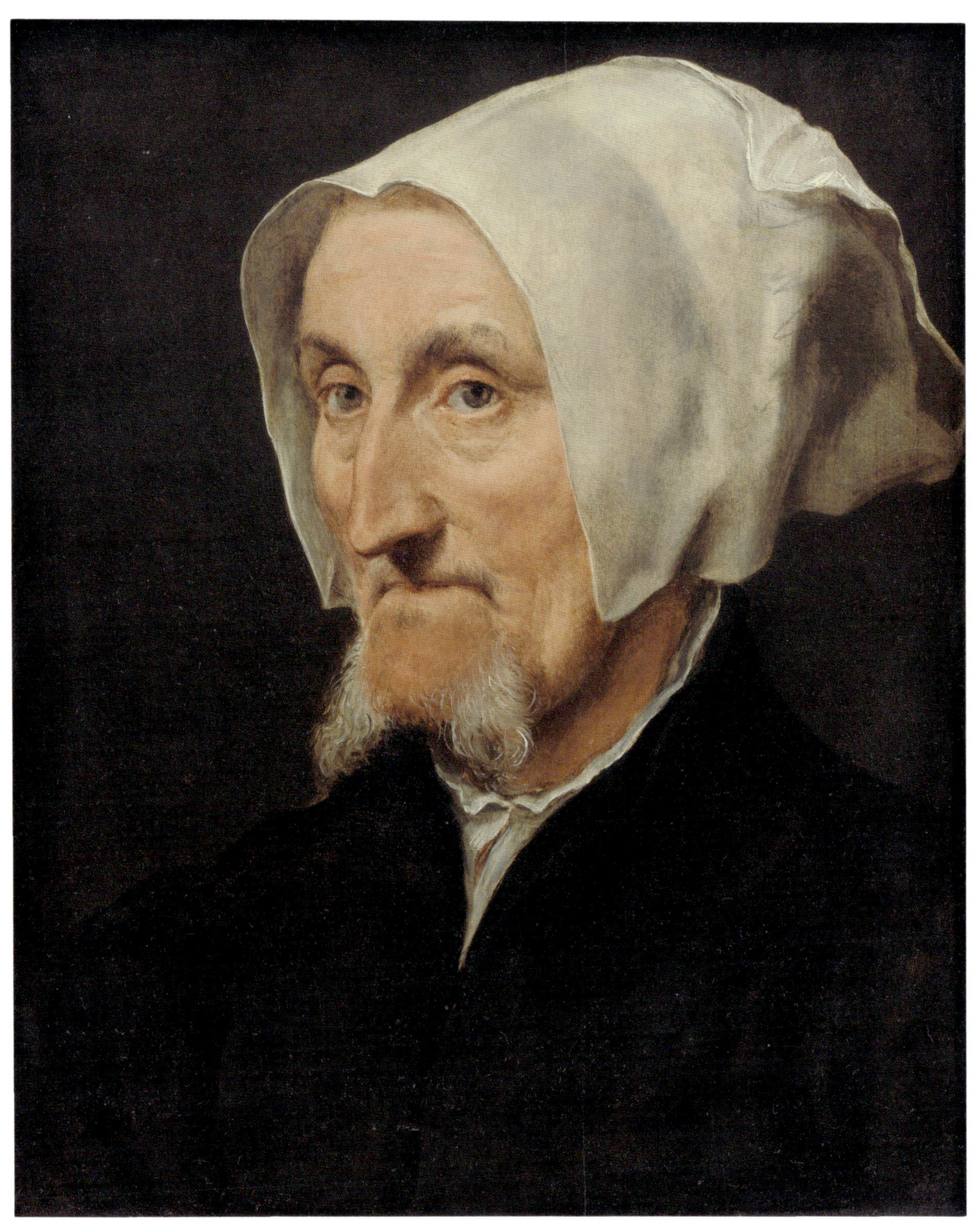

Willem Key
A Portrait of Margret Halseber of Basel –
The Lady with Two Beards, c. 1550
Oil on panel
12 ½ × 10 ¼ inches | 31.8 × 26 cm

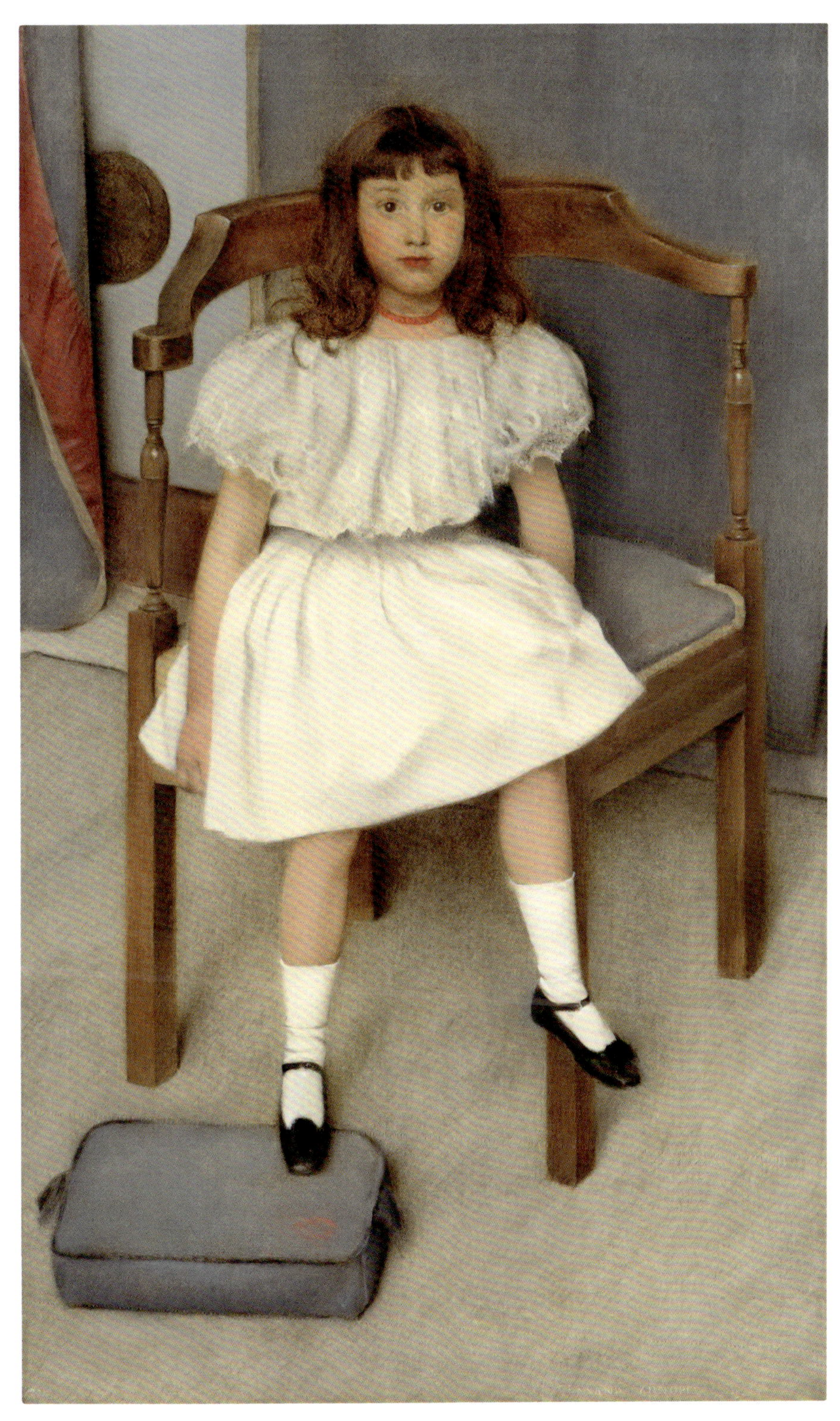

Fernand Khnopff
*Portrait of Comte Roger van der
Straeten-Ponthoz*, 1894
Oil on canvas
31 ½ × 19 ¼ inches | 80 × 48.9 cm

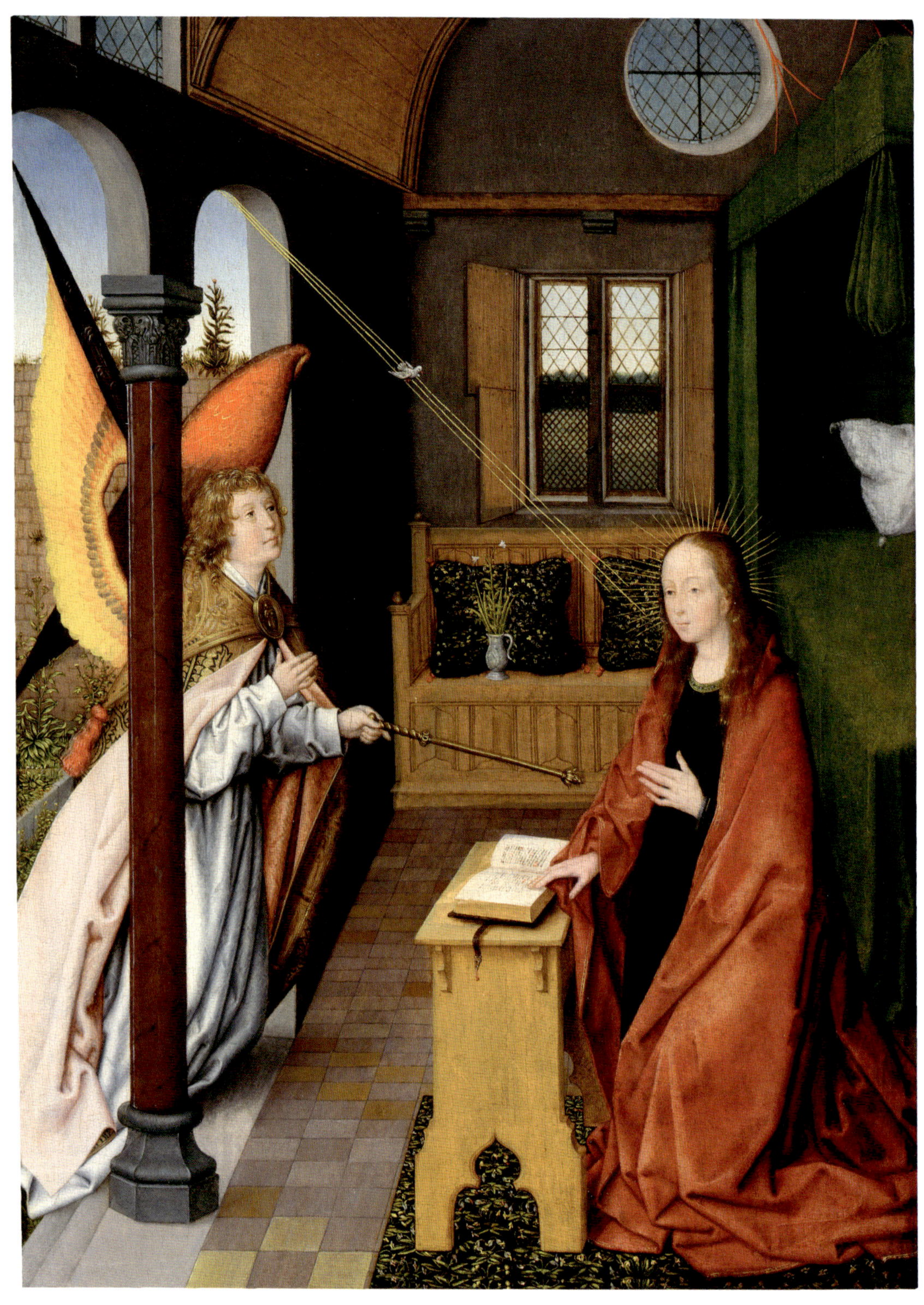

Jan Provost
Annunciation, c. 1485
Oil on panel
20 ½ × 15 inches | 52.1 × 38.1 cm

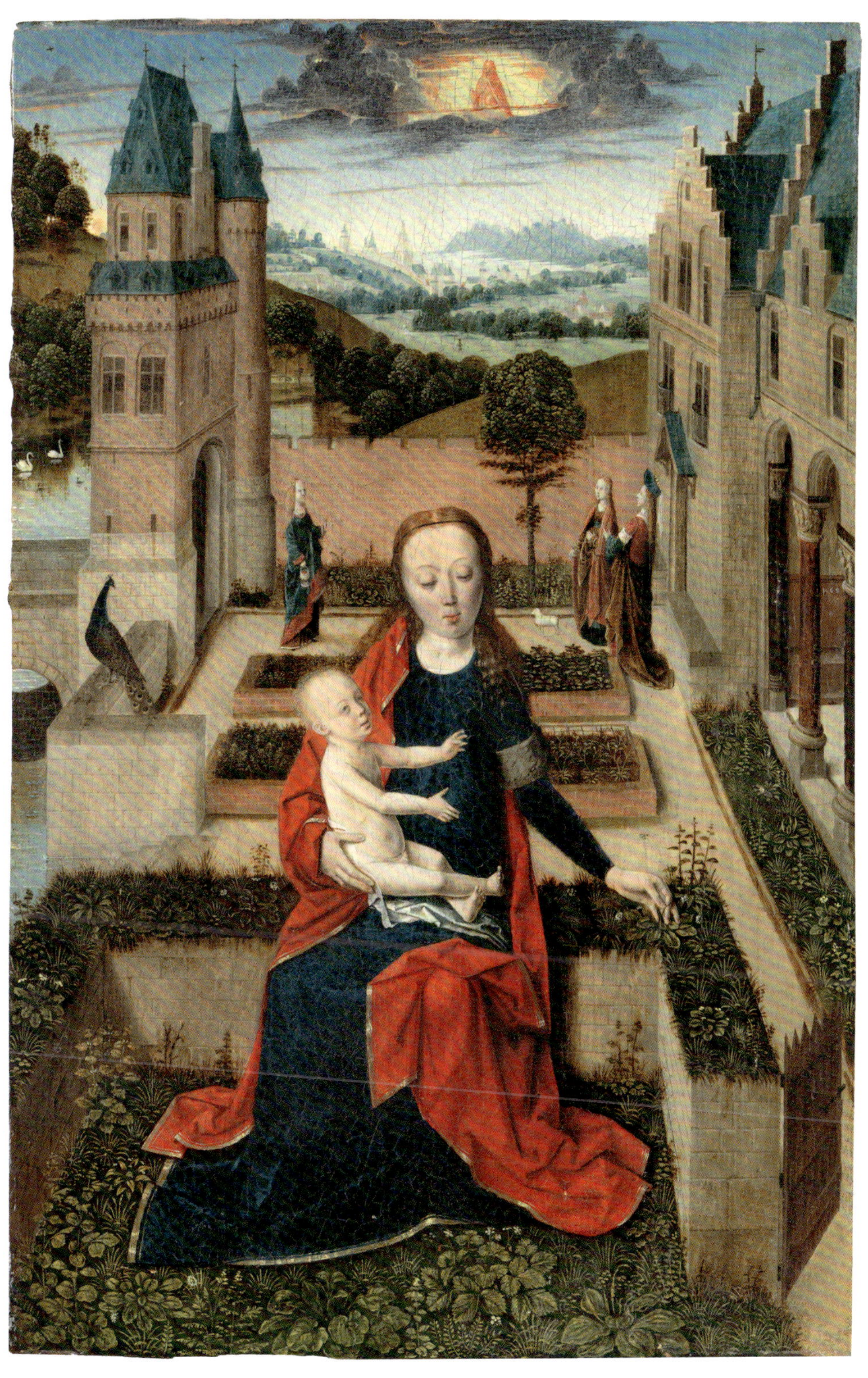

Master of the Tiburtine Sibyl
Virgin and Child with Saints Agnes, Dorothea,
and Barbara in a Courtyard Garden Beyond,
and an Extensive Landscape at Sunset, 1468
Oil on panel
13 ⅝ × 9 inches | 34.6 × 22.9 cm

Hans Memling
Tondo with the Virgin
Suckling the Child, c. 1487–1490
Oil on panel
Diameter: 7 inches | 17.9 cm

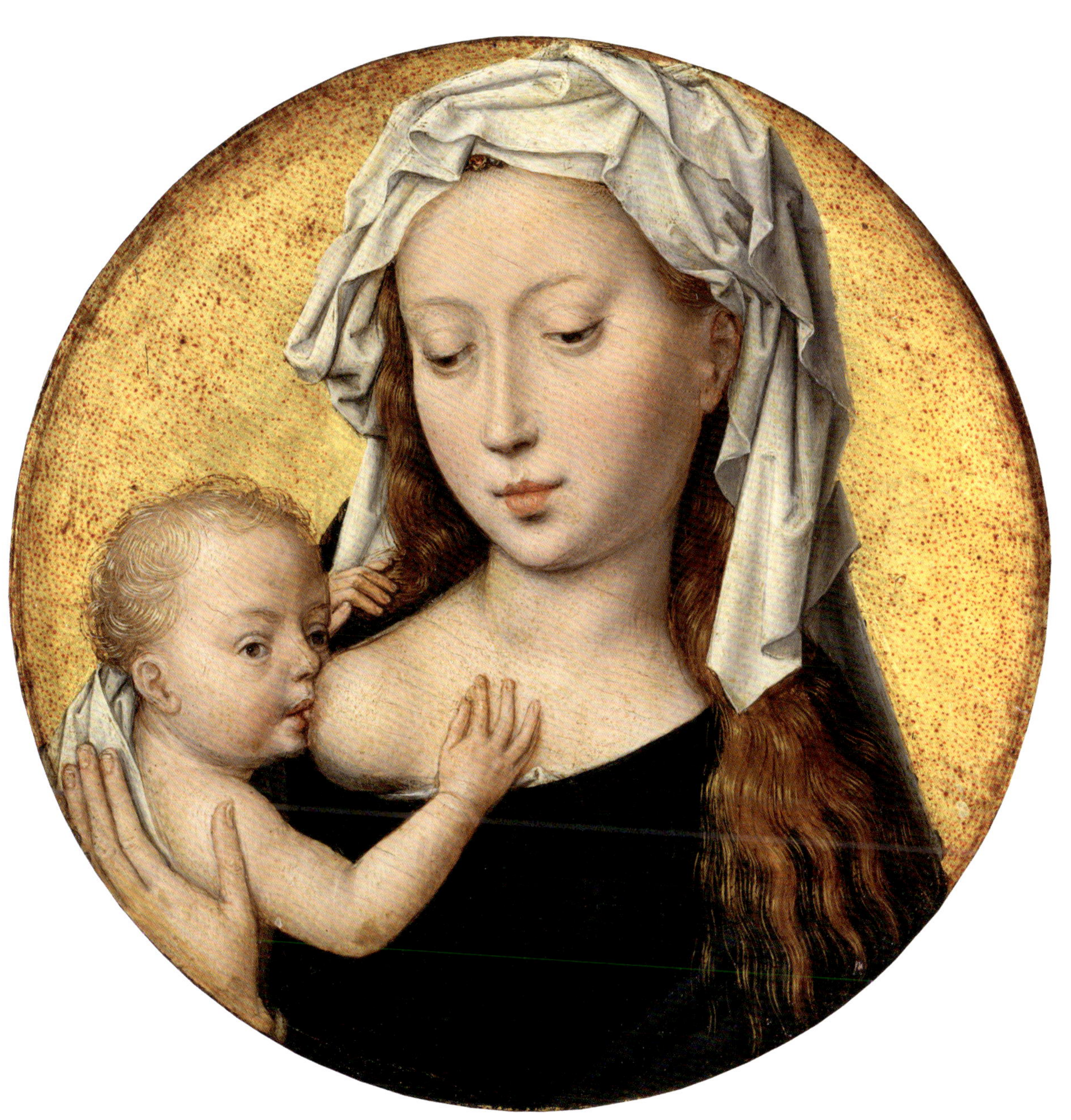

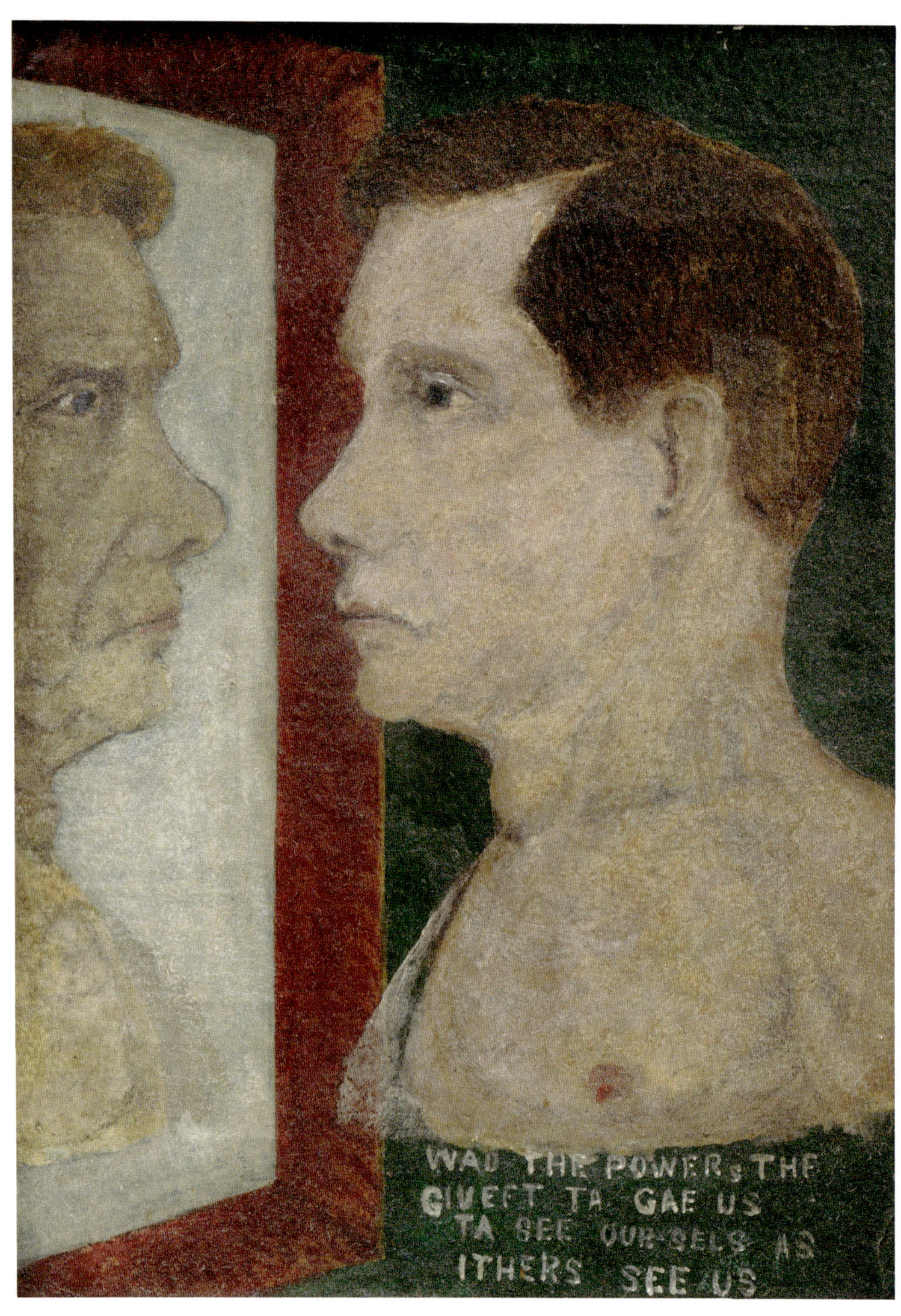

John Kane
Seen in the Mirror (Before and After), c. 1928
Oil on canvas
7 ¾ × 5 ⅝ inches | 19.7 × 14.3 cm

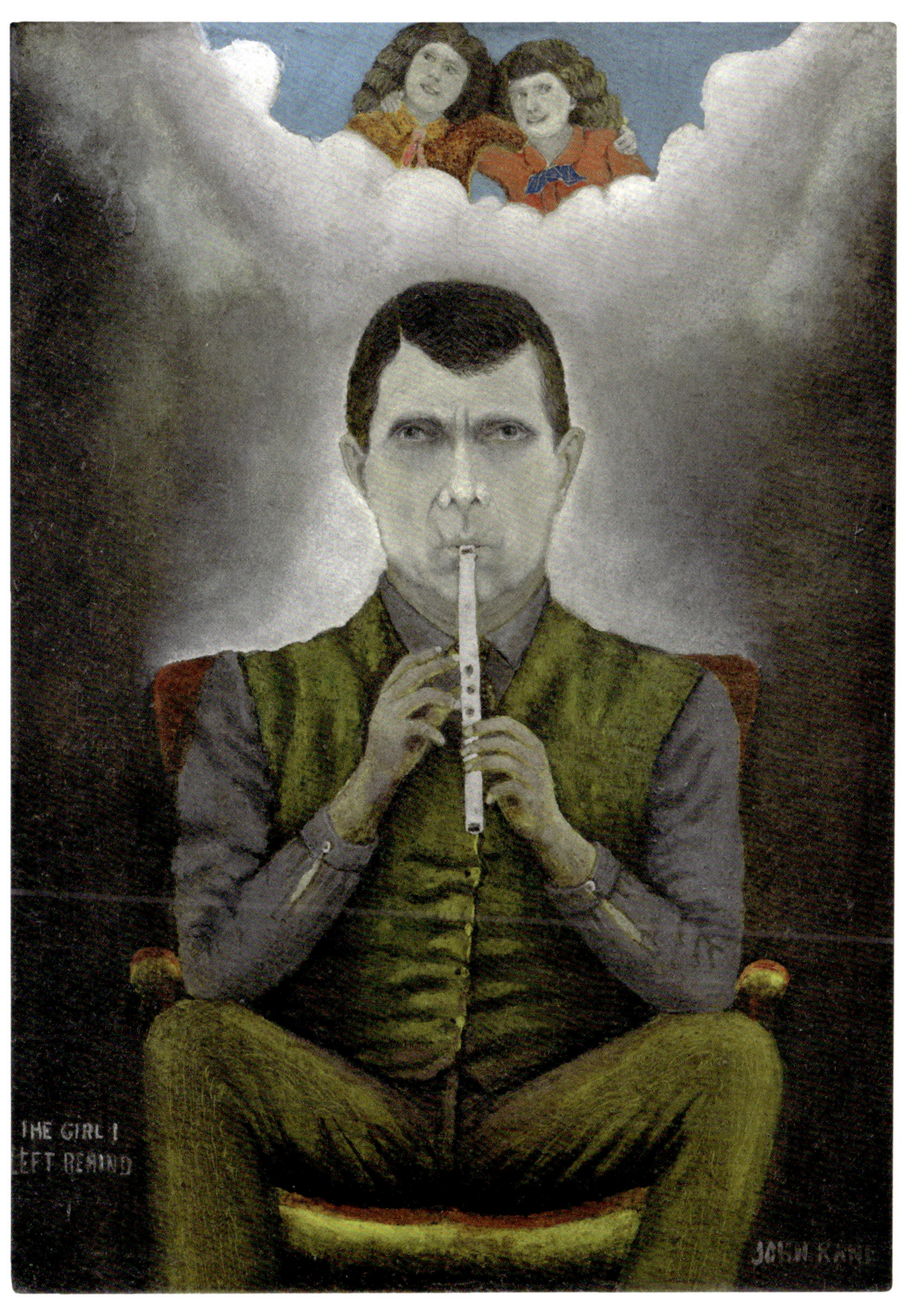

John Kane
The Girl I Left Behind, 1920
Oil on board
15 ⅜ x 11 inches | 39 × 27.9 cm

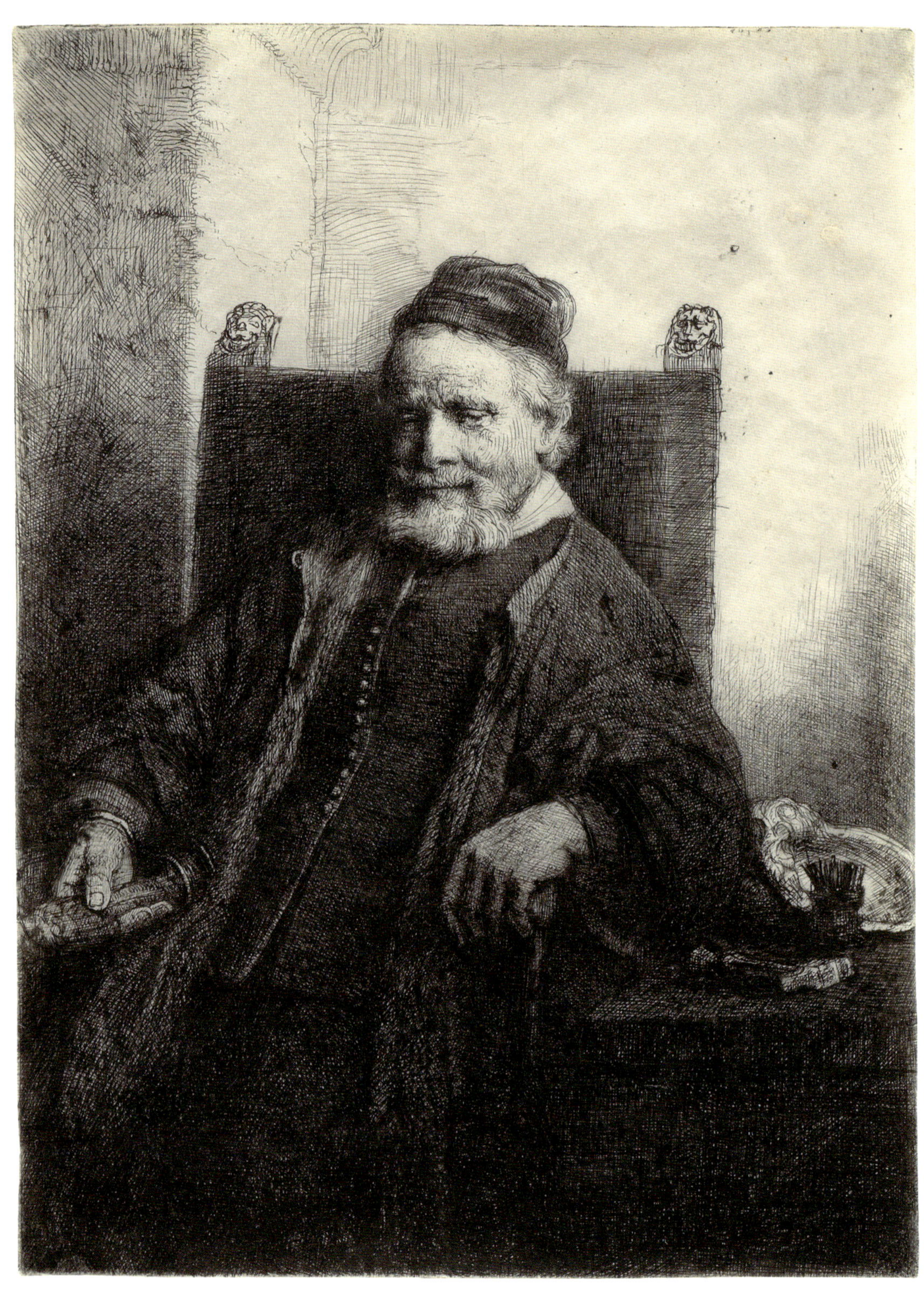

Rembrandt van Rijn
Jan Lutma, Goldsmith, 1656
Etching and drypoint on thin chine
7 ⅝ × 5 ¾ inches | 19.4 × 14.6 cm

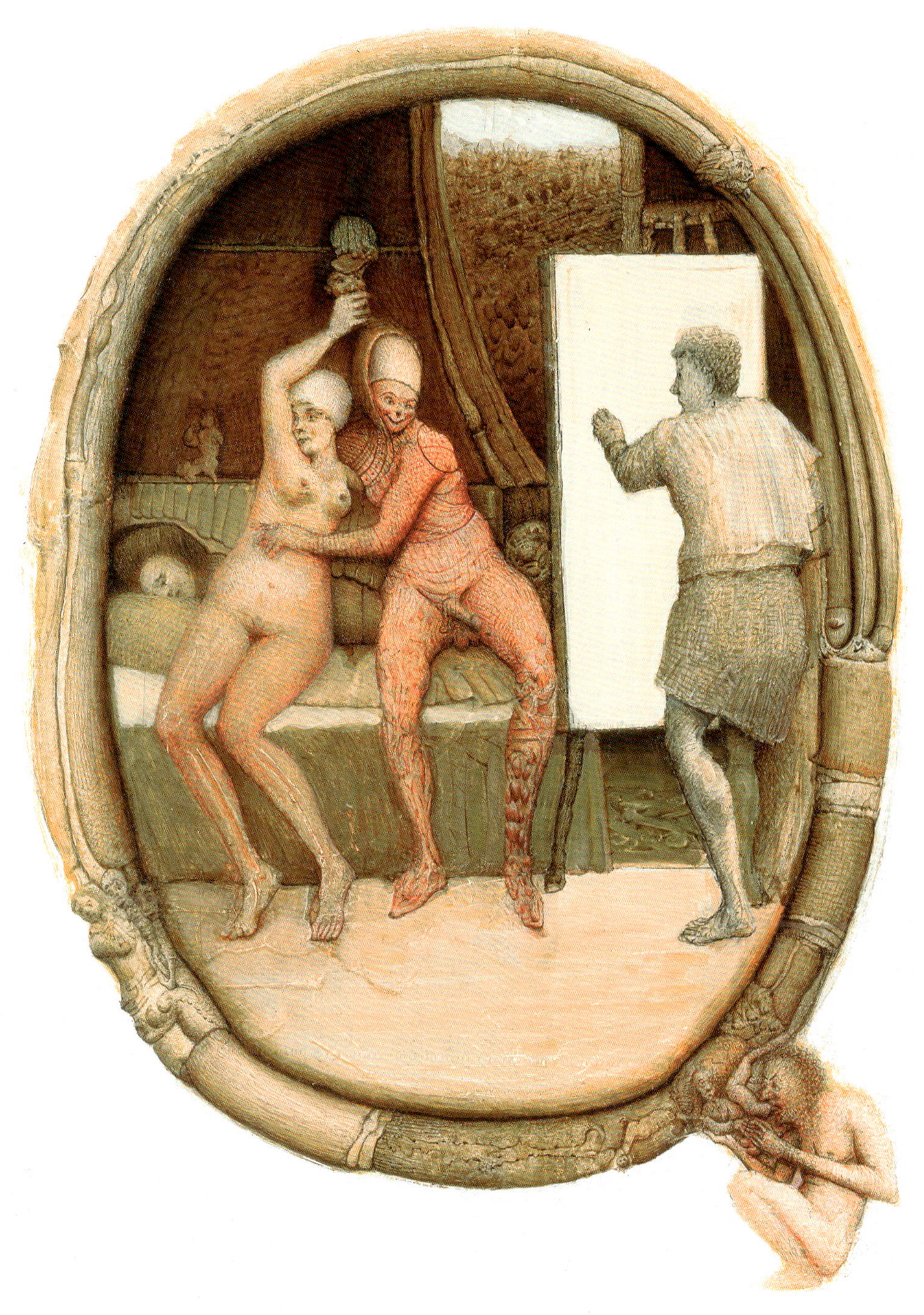

Gregory Gillespie
Painter in the Bedroom, 1995
Oil on board
39 ¾ × 32 ¾ inches | 101 × 83.2 cm

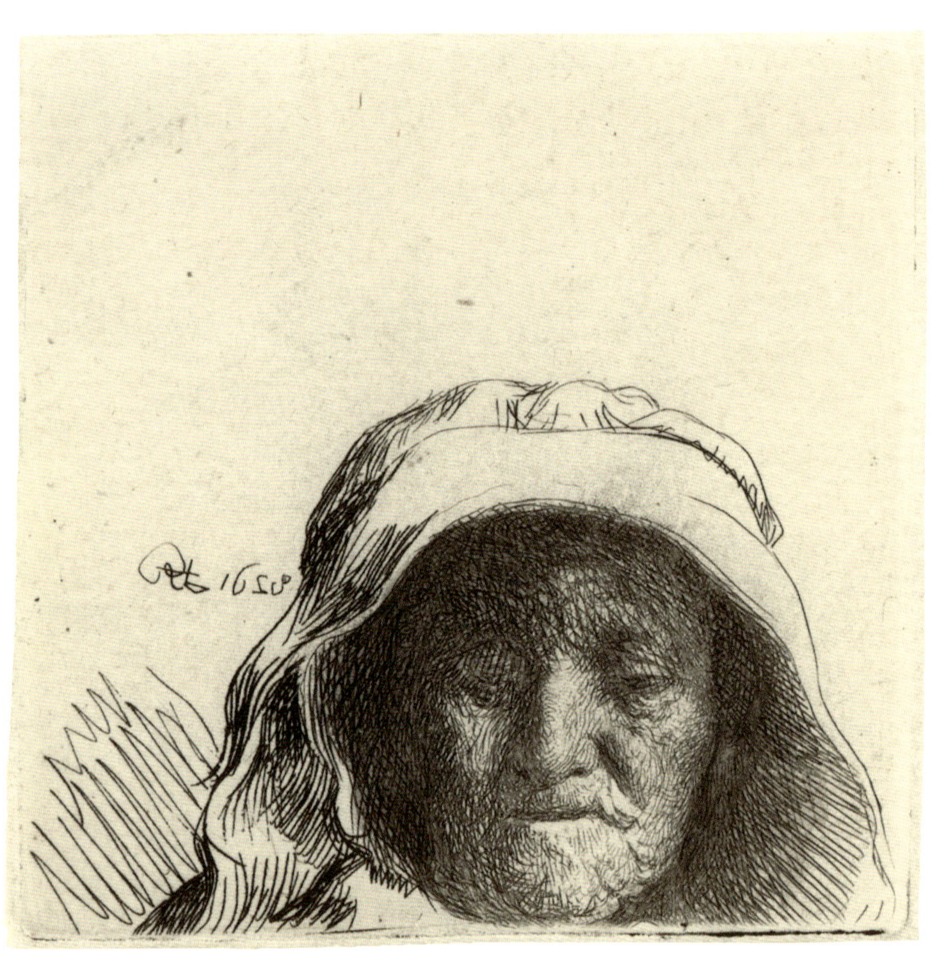

Rembrandt van Rijn
The Artist's Mother: Head Only, Full Face, 1628
Etching
2 ½ × 2 ½ inches | 6.3 × 6.3 cm

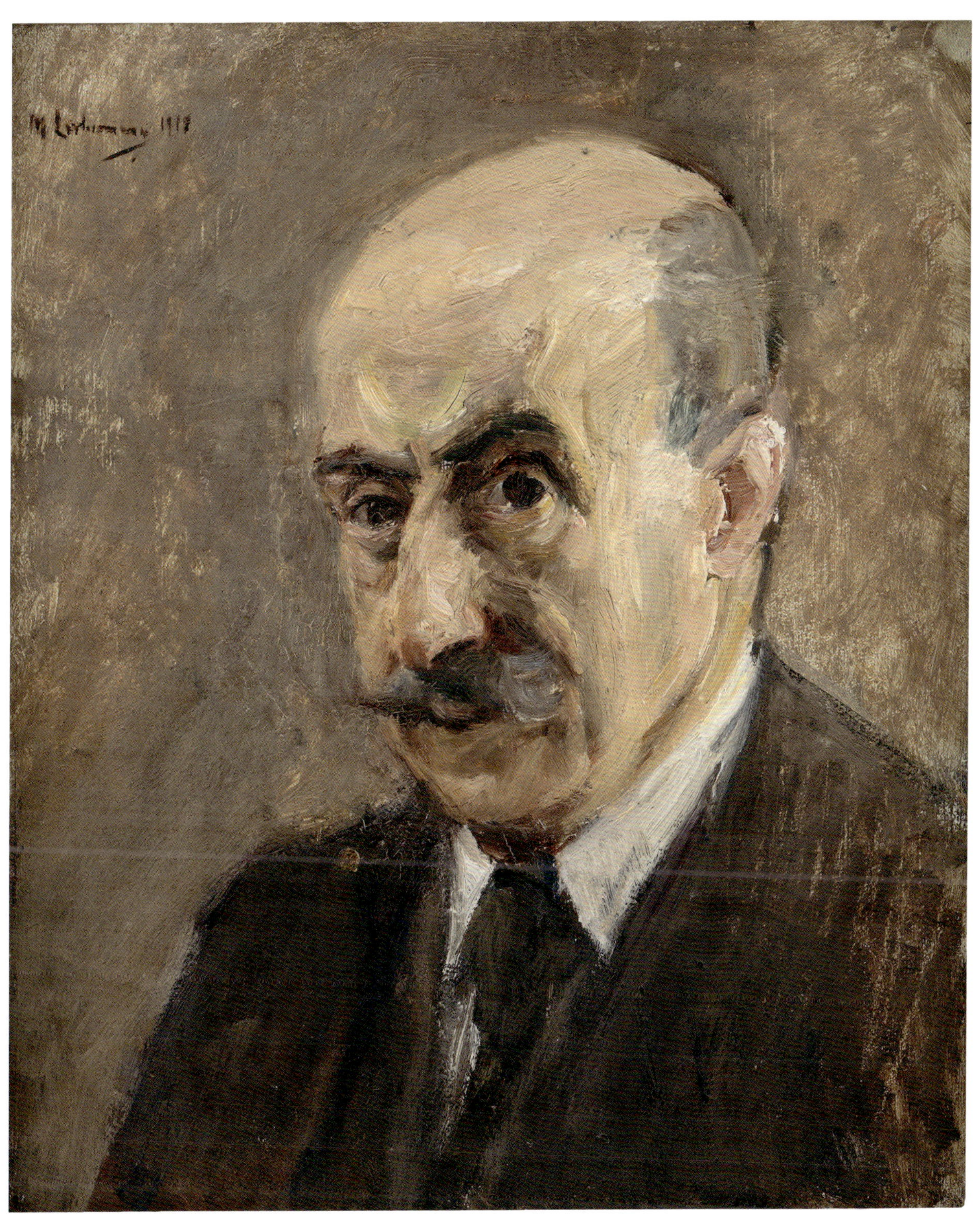

Max Liebermann
Self-Portrait, 1911
Oil on panel
14 ⅝ × 12 ⅛ inches | 37.1 × 30.8 cm

Master of the Virgo inter Virgines
The Resurrection of Christ, c. 1483–1498
Oil on panel
34 ¾ × 20 inches | 88.3 × 50.8 cm

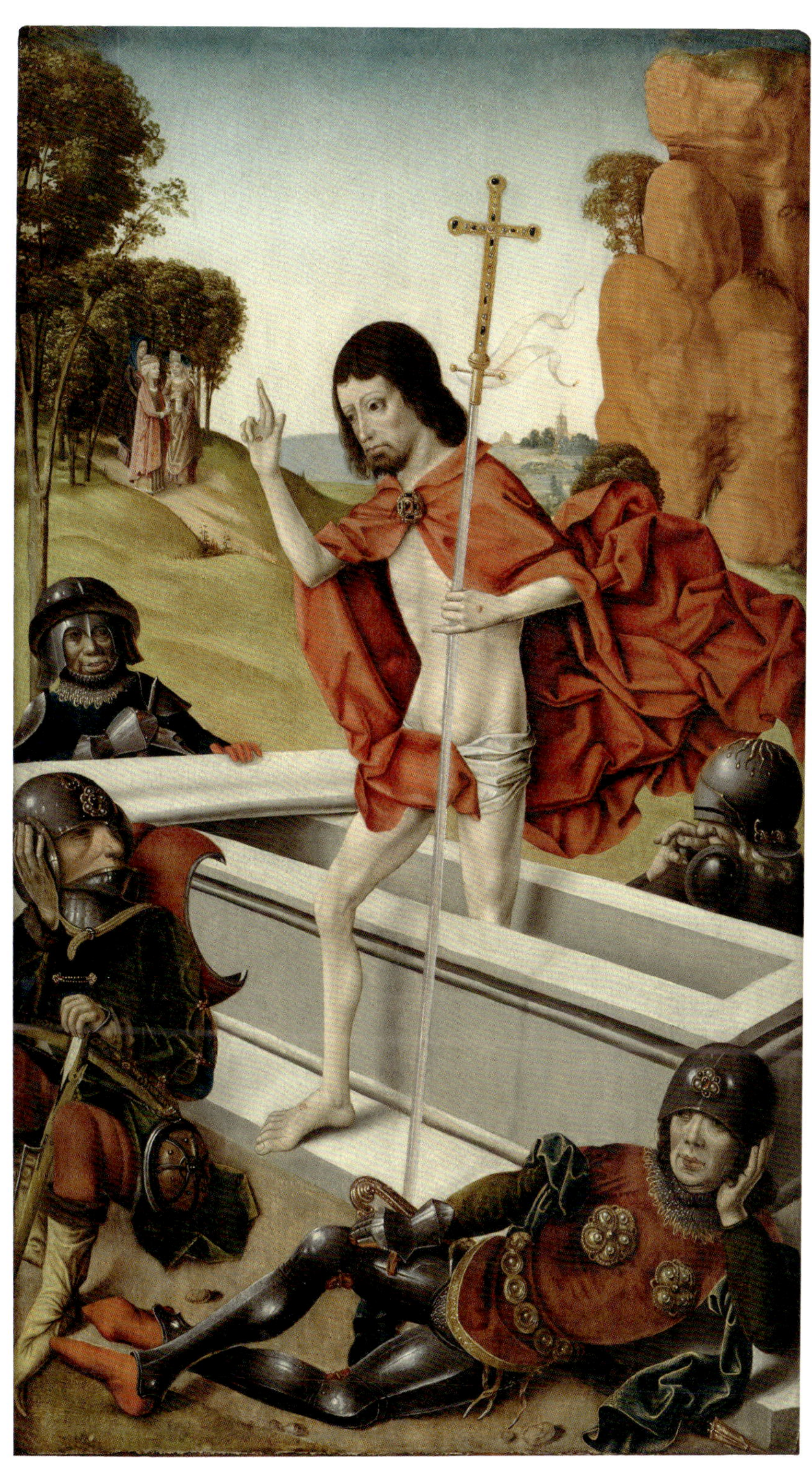

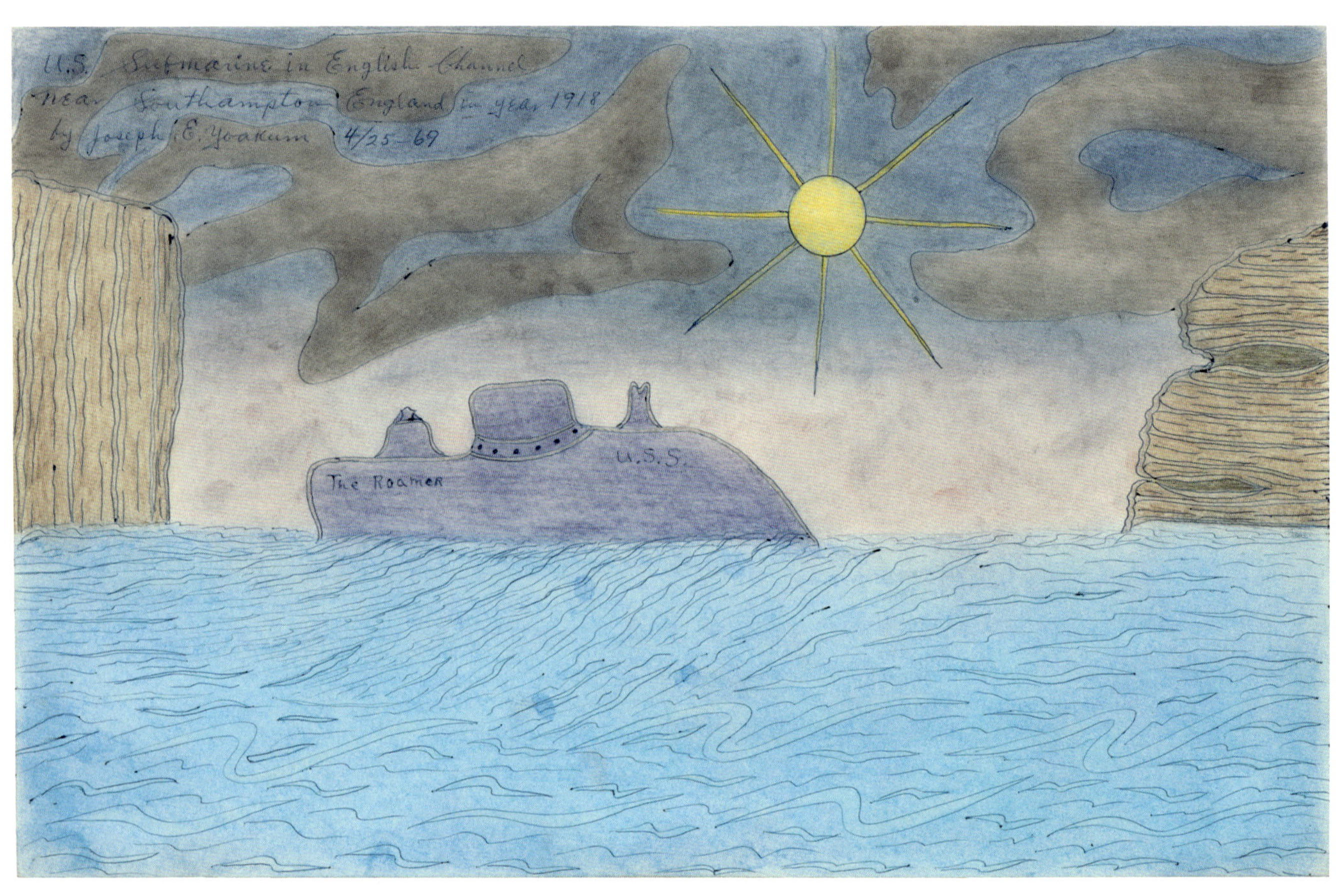

Joseph Yoakum
U.S. Submarine in English Channel near
Southampton, England, in Year 1918, 1969
Pen and colored pencil on paper
12 × 19 inches | 30.5 × 48.3 cm

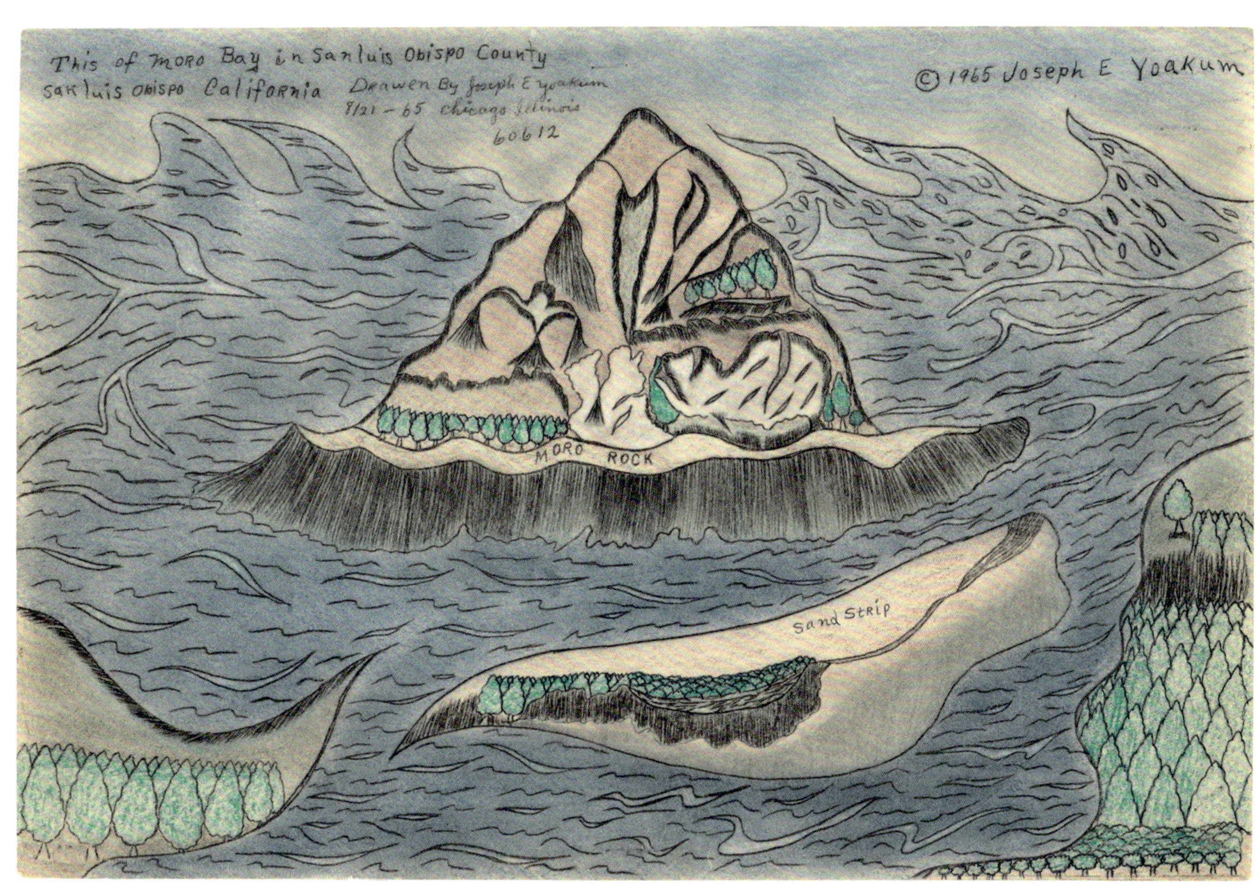

Joseph Yoakum
This of Moro Bay in San Luis Obispo County,
San Luis Obispo, California, 1965
Colored pencil, watercolor, and pen on paper
12 × 18 inches | 30.5 × 45.7 cm

Sol LeWitt
LEFT TOP: Black Horizontal,
LEFT BOTTOM: Yellow Vertical,
RIGHT TOP: Red Vertical,
RIGHT BOTTOM: Blue Horizontal, 1972
Ink on paper
14 ⅛ × 14 ⅛ inches | 35.9 × 35.9 cm

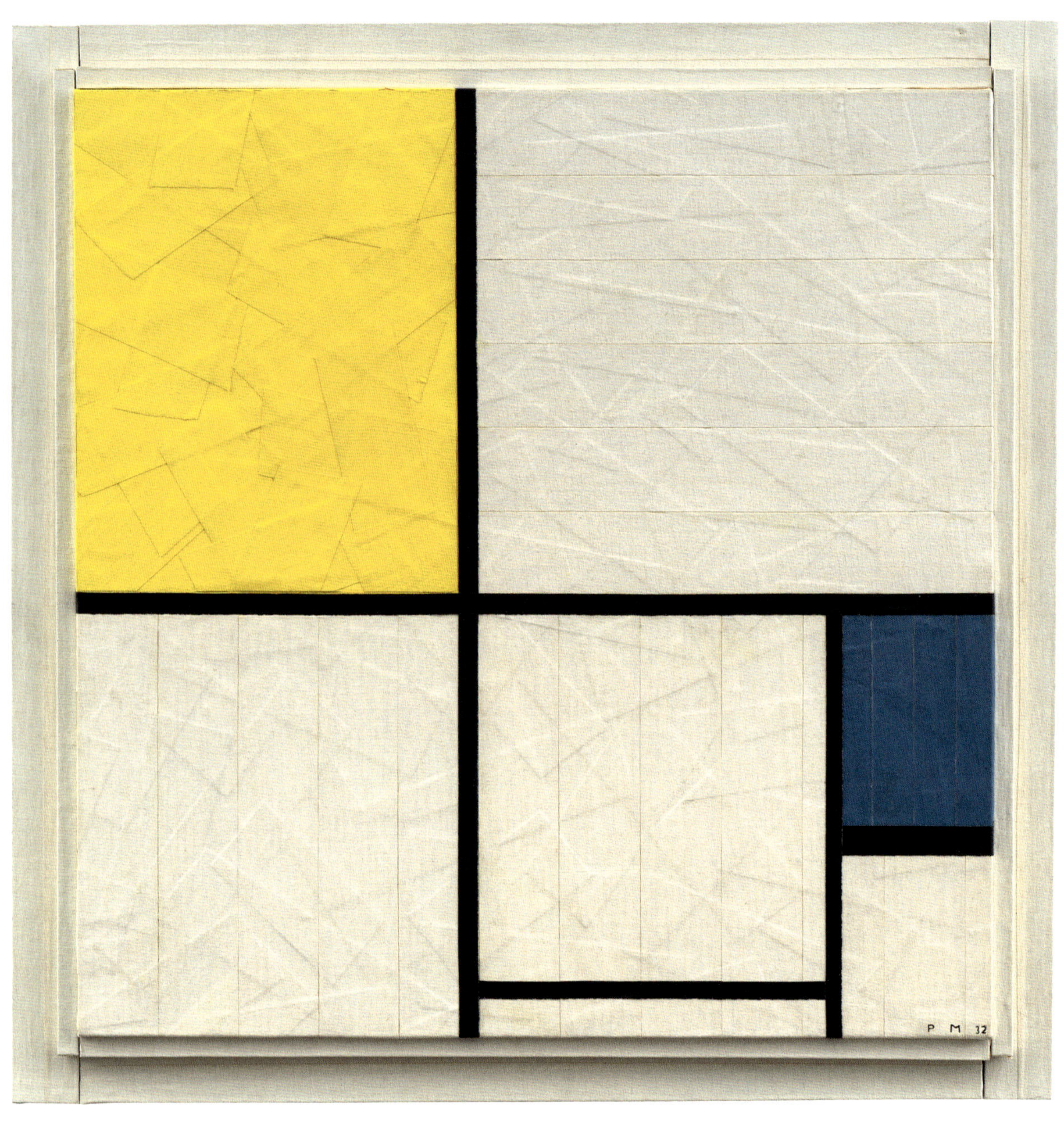

Tom Sachs
134 Composition with Yellow and Blue, 1996
Gaffer tape on plywood
25 × 25 inches | 63.5 × 63.5 cm

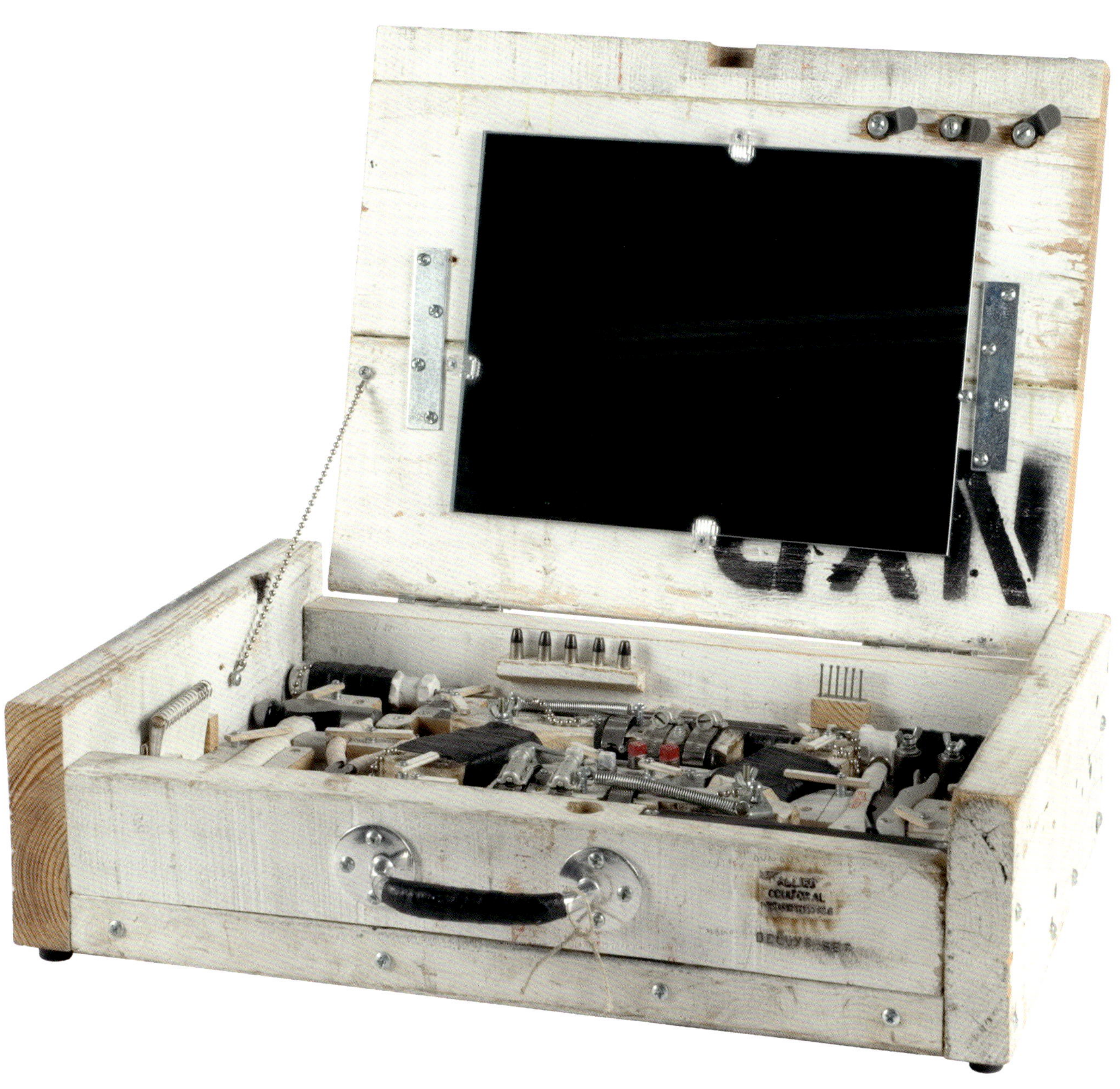

Tom Sachs
Dundus, 1998
Two working zip guns, Sharpie, paint, and mixed media
with wood box made from police barricade
Open: 20 ⅛ × 24 ¼ × 24 ⅞ inches | 51.1 × 61.5 × 63.1 cm

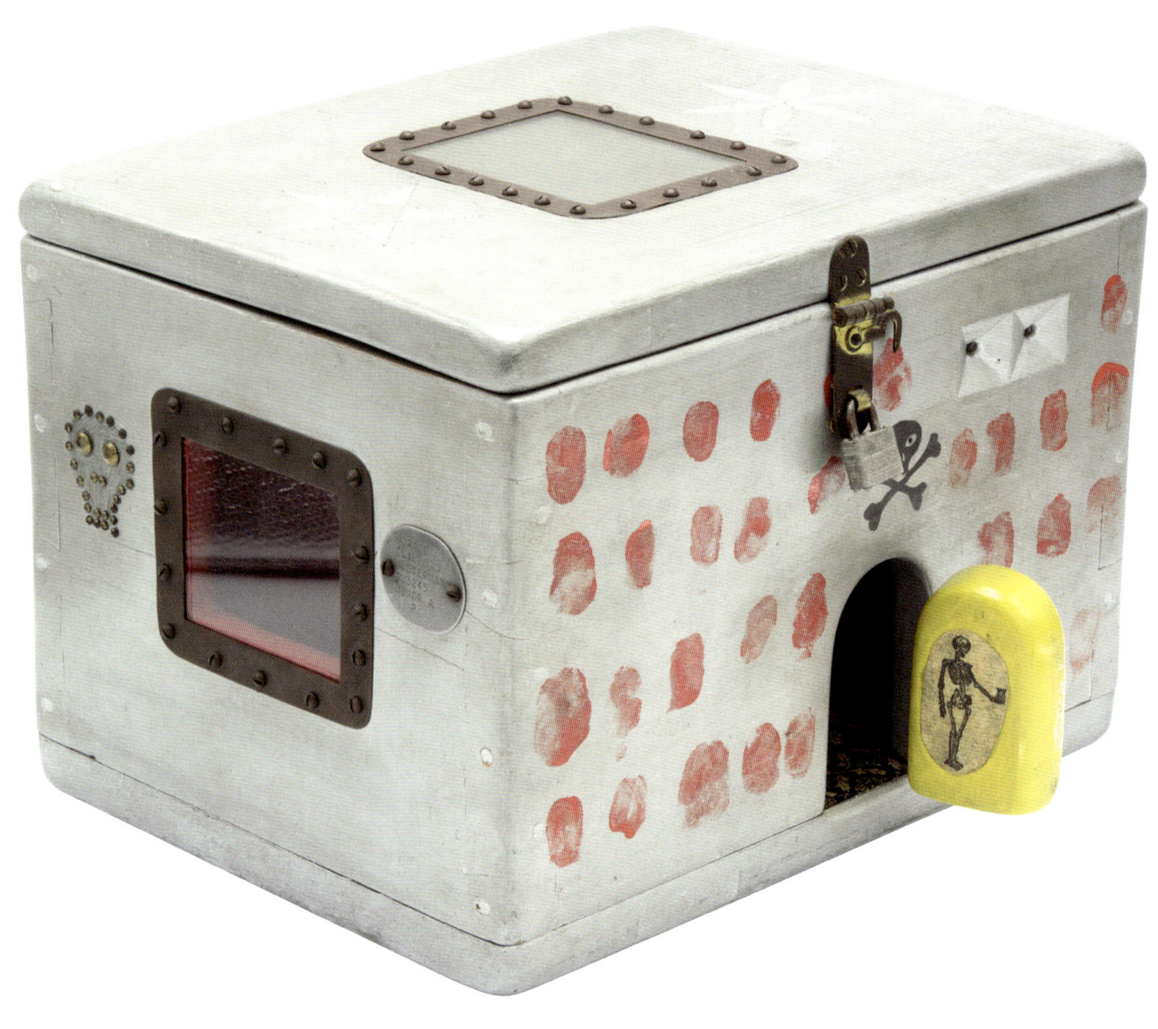

H. C. Westermann
Essentially This Is a Very Unusual Physician, 1957
Mixed media
8 ½ × 12 × 9 ¼ inches | 21.6 × 30.5 × 23.5 cm

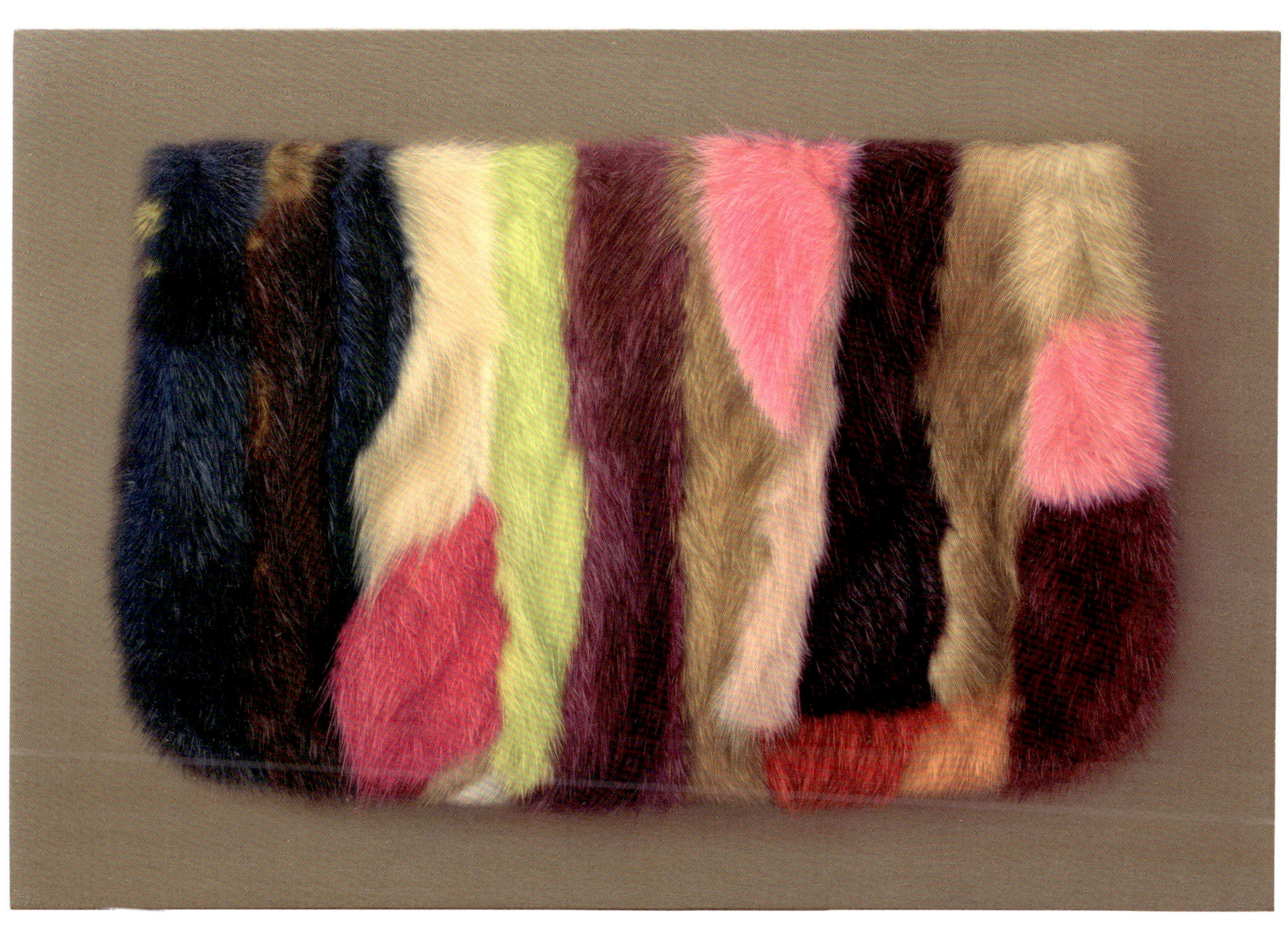

Victoria Gitman
Untitled, 2014
Oil on board
7 × 10 ⅜ inches | 17.8 × 26.4 cm

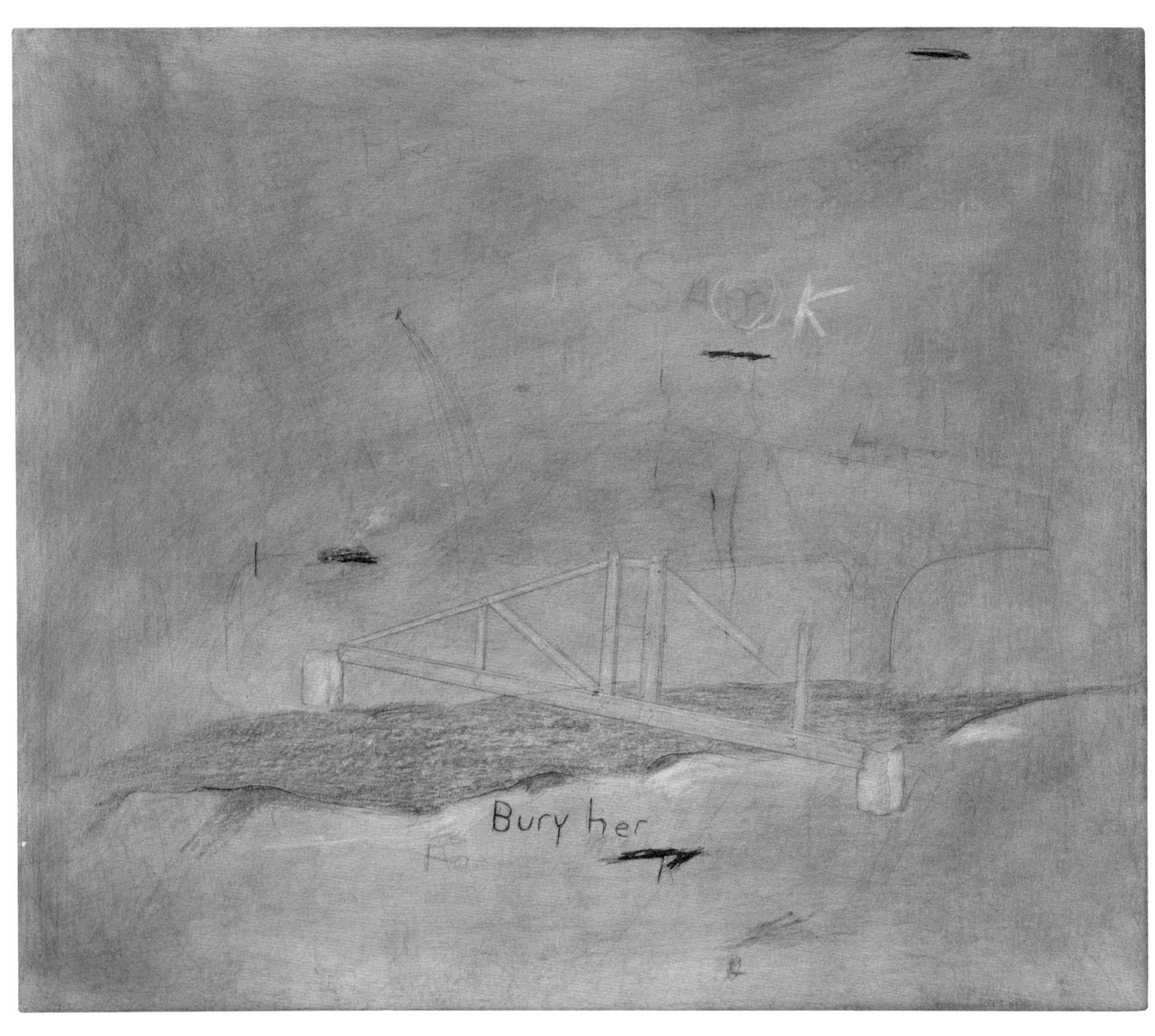

Wes Mills
Some Water under the Bridge, 1992
Graphite and powdered pigment on board
12 ½ × 15 inches | 31.8 × 38.1 cm

162

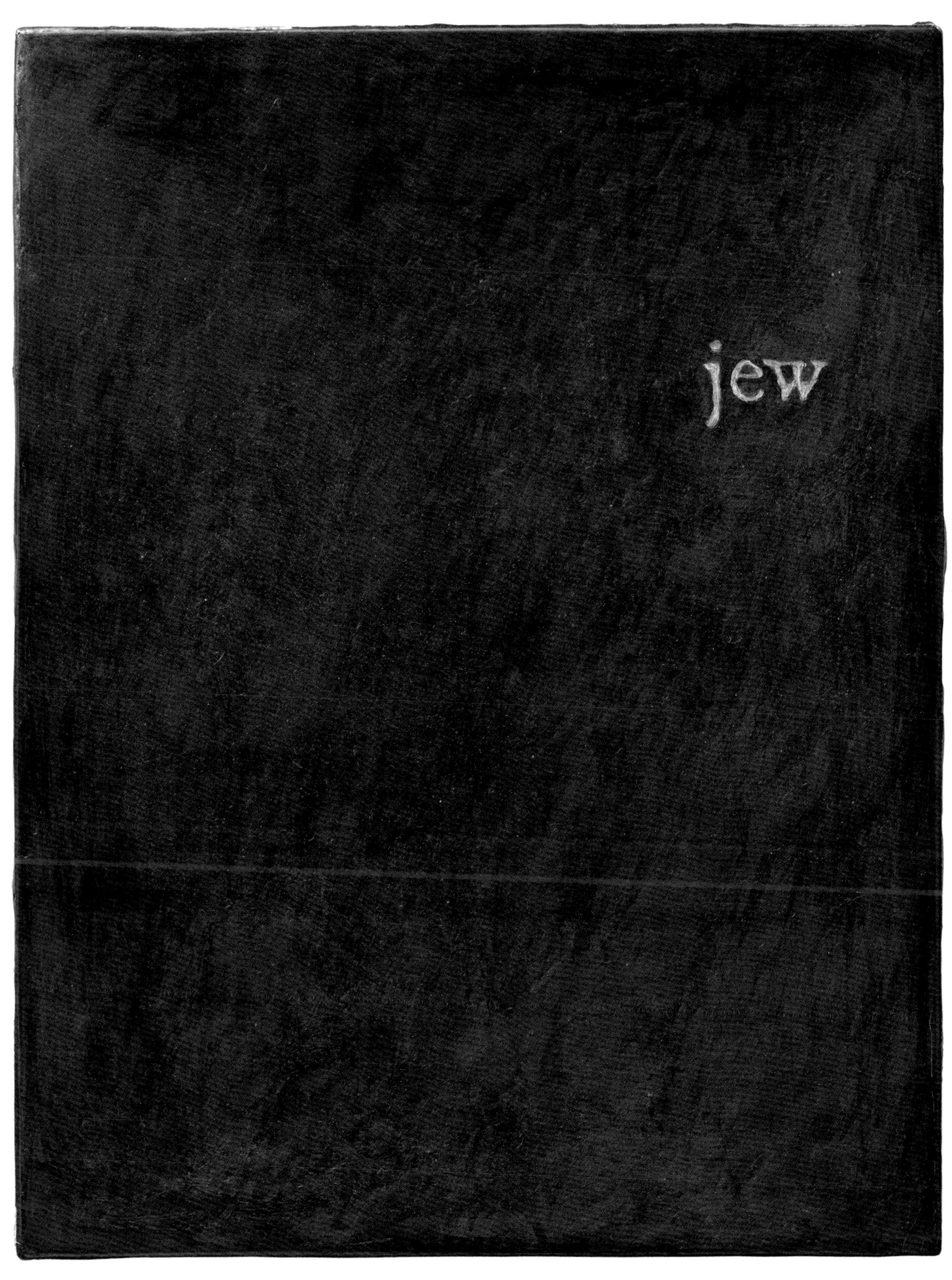

William Anastasi
Untitled, 1996
Graphite, India ink, and gesso on linen
10 ½ × 8 ¼ inches | 26.7 × 21 cm

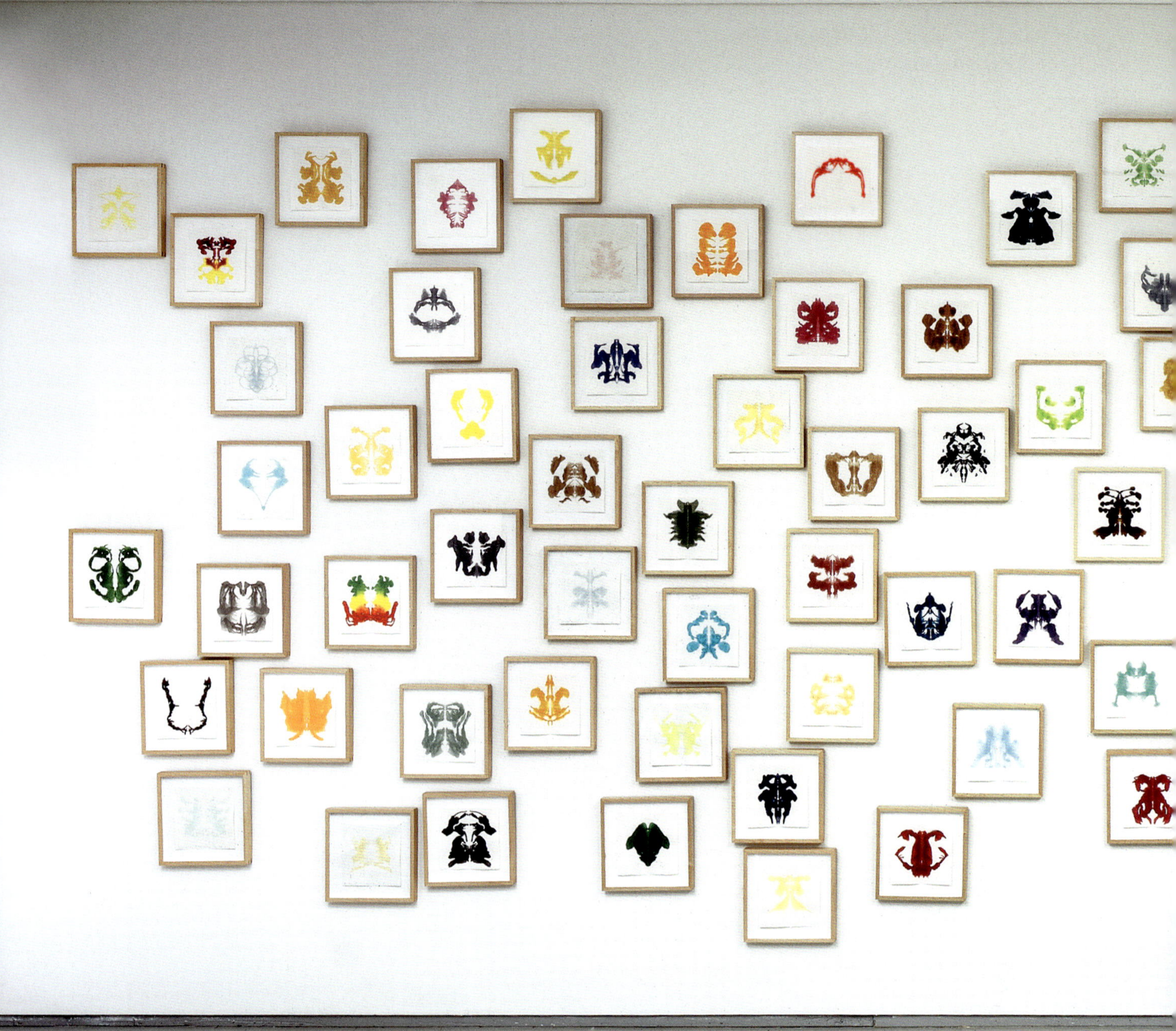

Spencer Finch
102 Colors from My Dreams (Version I), 2000–2002
Ink and graphite on paper, in 102 parts
Each: 9 × 9 inches | 22.9 × 22.9 cm

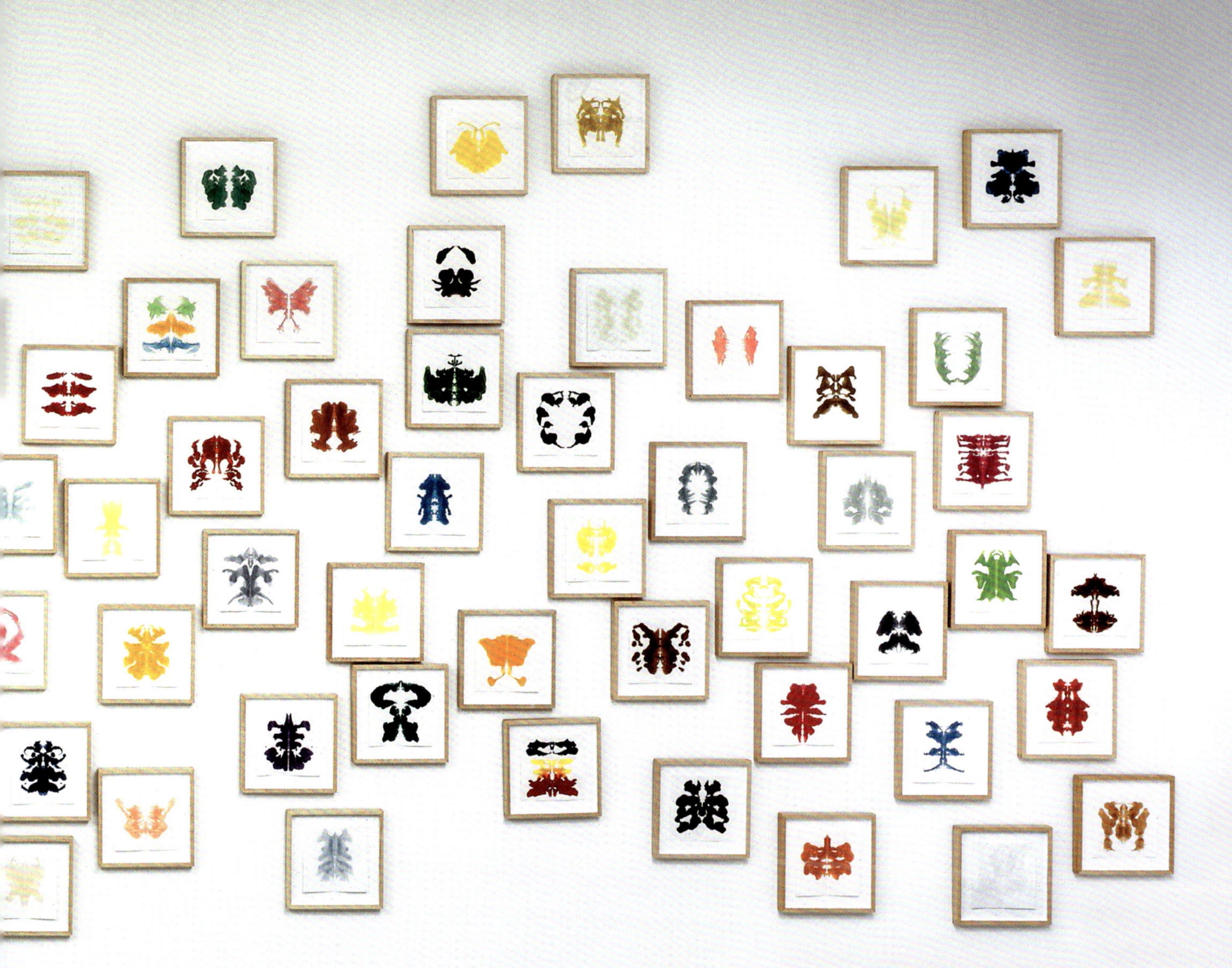

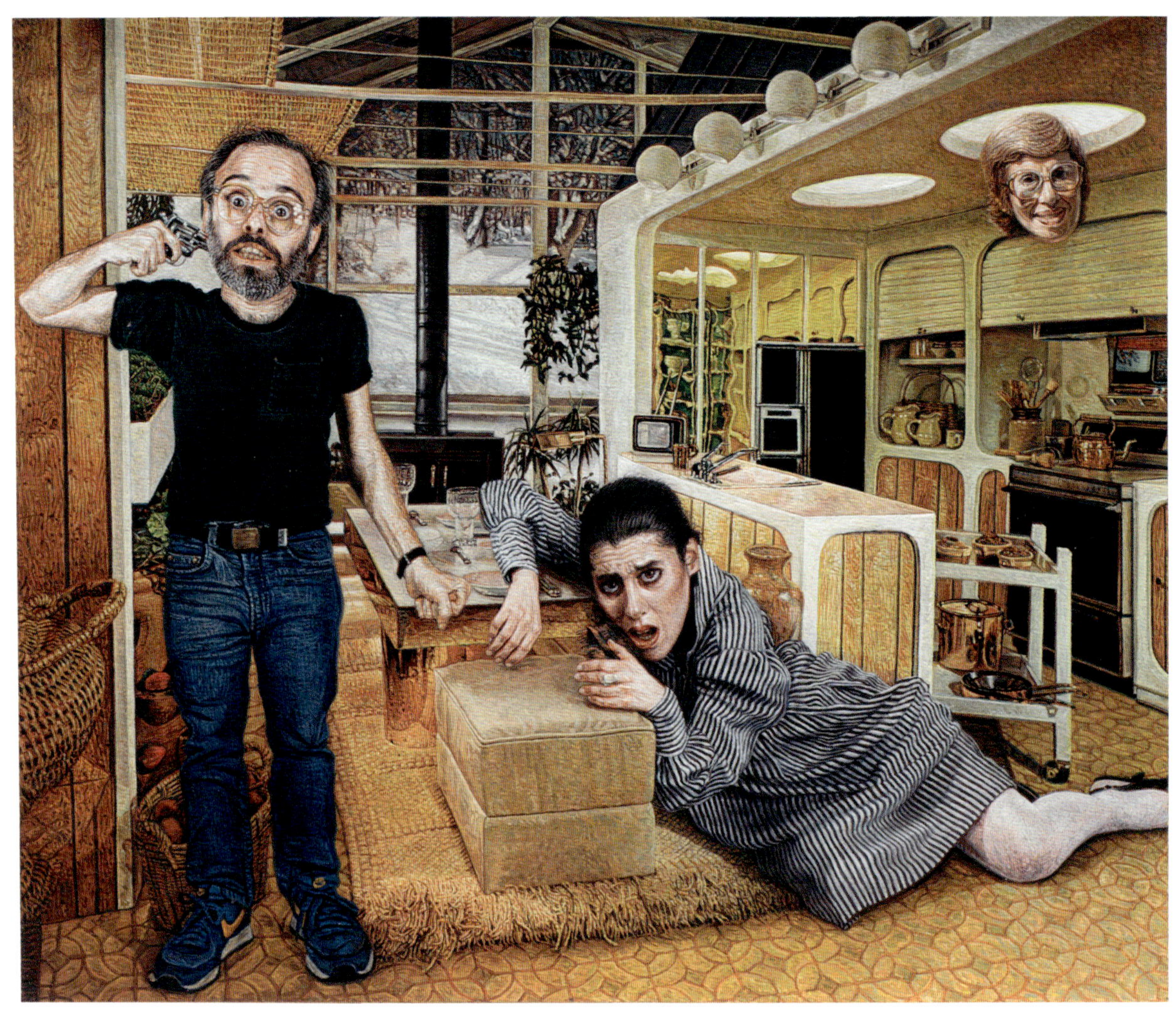

Mark Greenwold
A Family Tragedy, 1984–1985
Gouache on paper
6 ¼ × 7 ½ inches | 15.9 × 19.1 cm

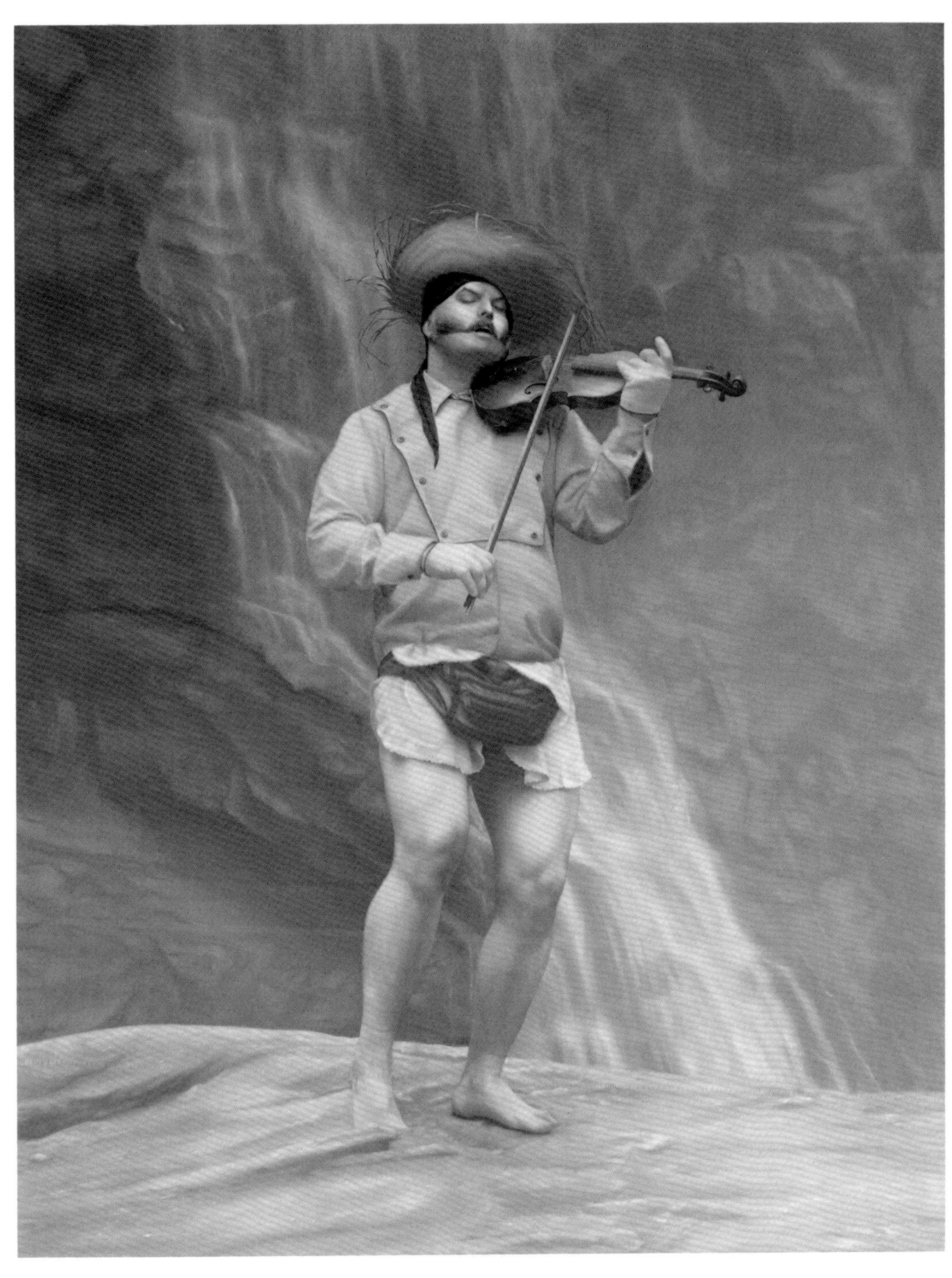

Andrew Sendor
From the Documentary "The Tchaikovsky Effect on
Fenomeno at the Geirangerfjorden, Norway," 2014
Oil on panel
45 × 34 inches | 114.3 × 86.4 cm

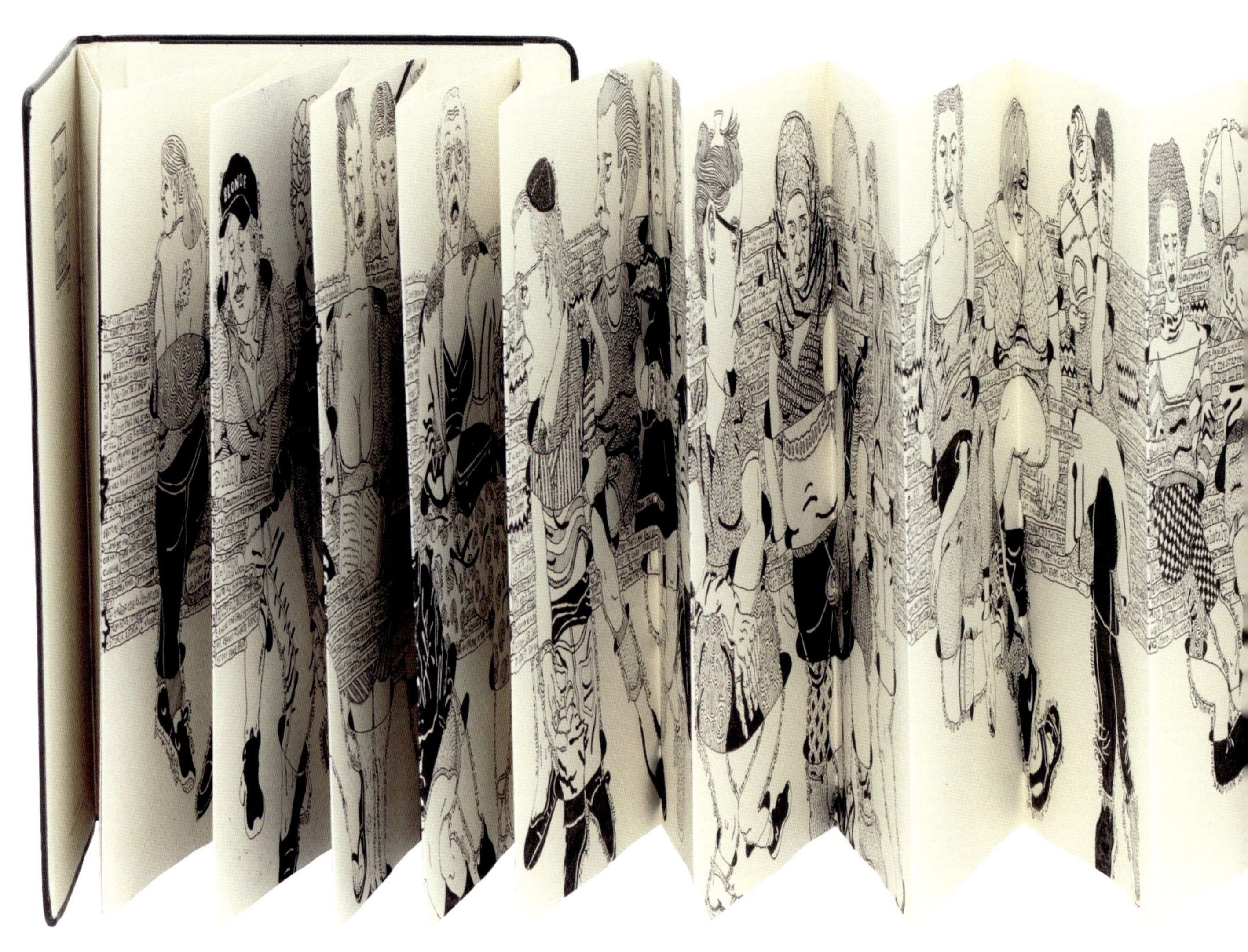

Martin Wilner
Journal of Evidence Weekly,
Volume 178 (4/30/18–10/12/18), 2018
Pen and ink on leporello book
Overall: 8 ¼ × 125 inches | 21 × 317.5 cm

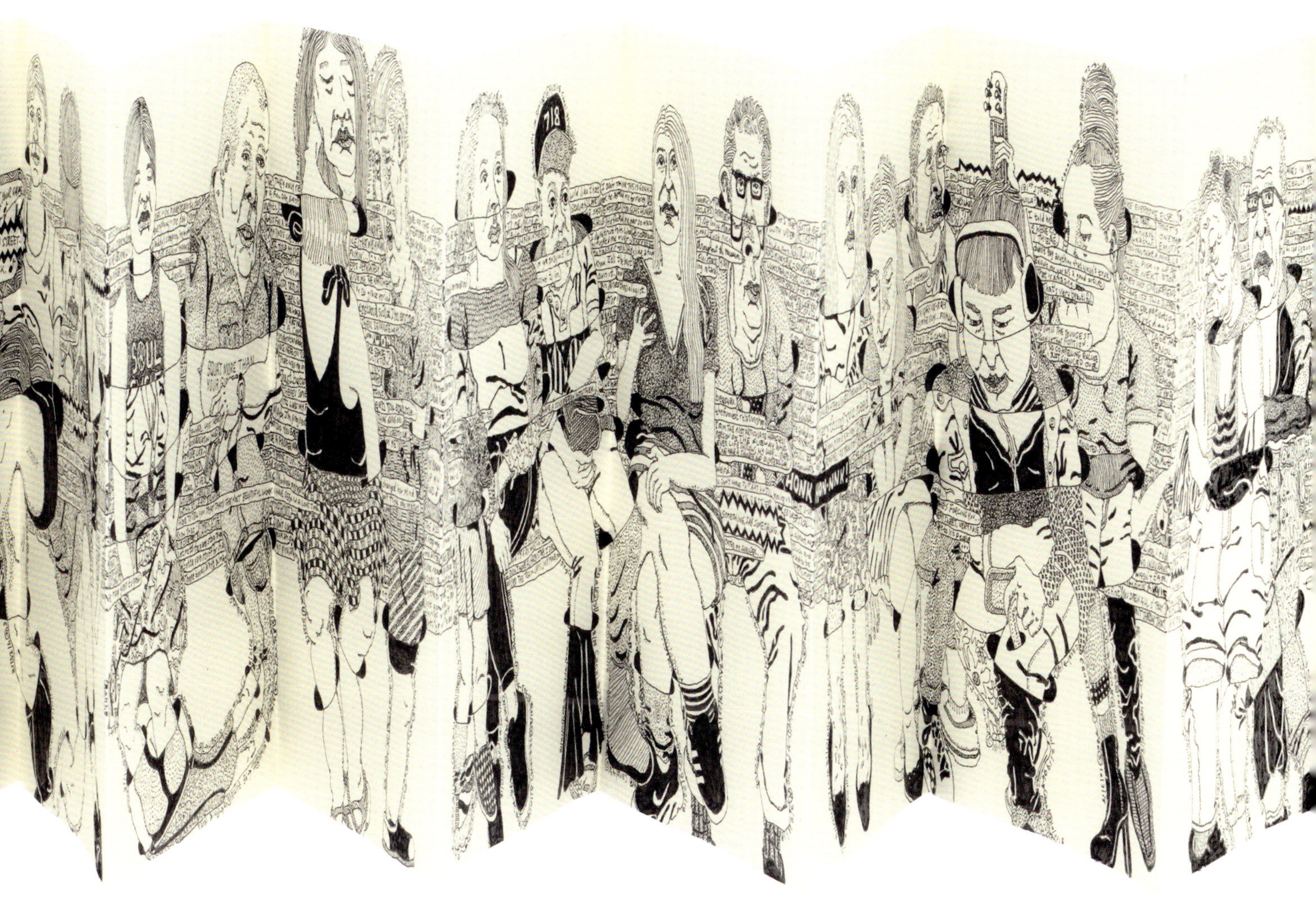

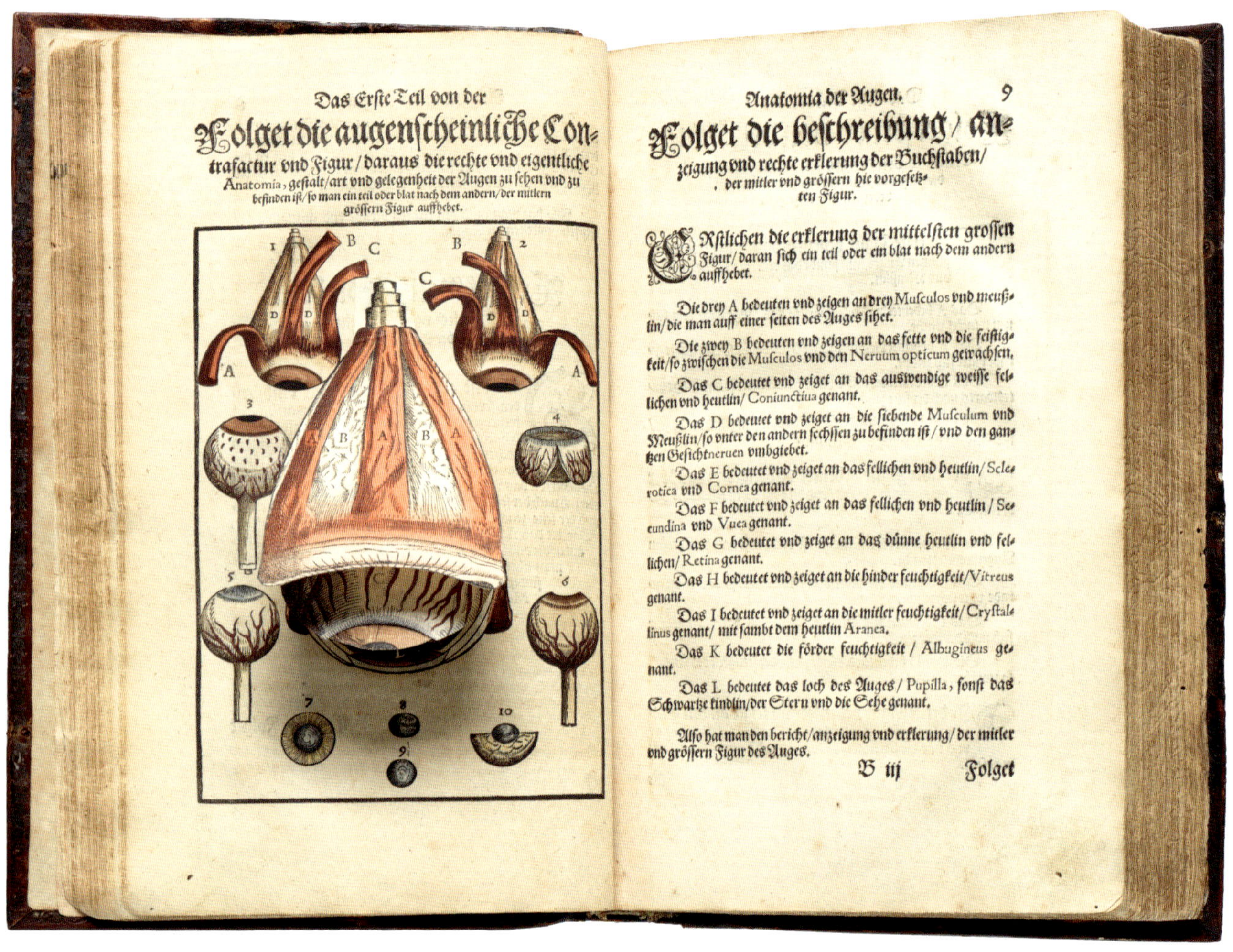

Georg Bartisch
Οφθαλμοδουλεια (*Ophthalmoduleia:*
Das ist Augendienst), 1583
Book
12 ⅝ × 8 ½ inches | 32.1 × 21.6 cm

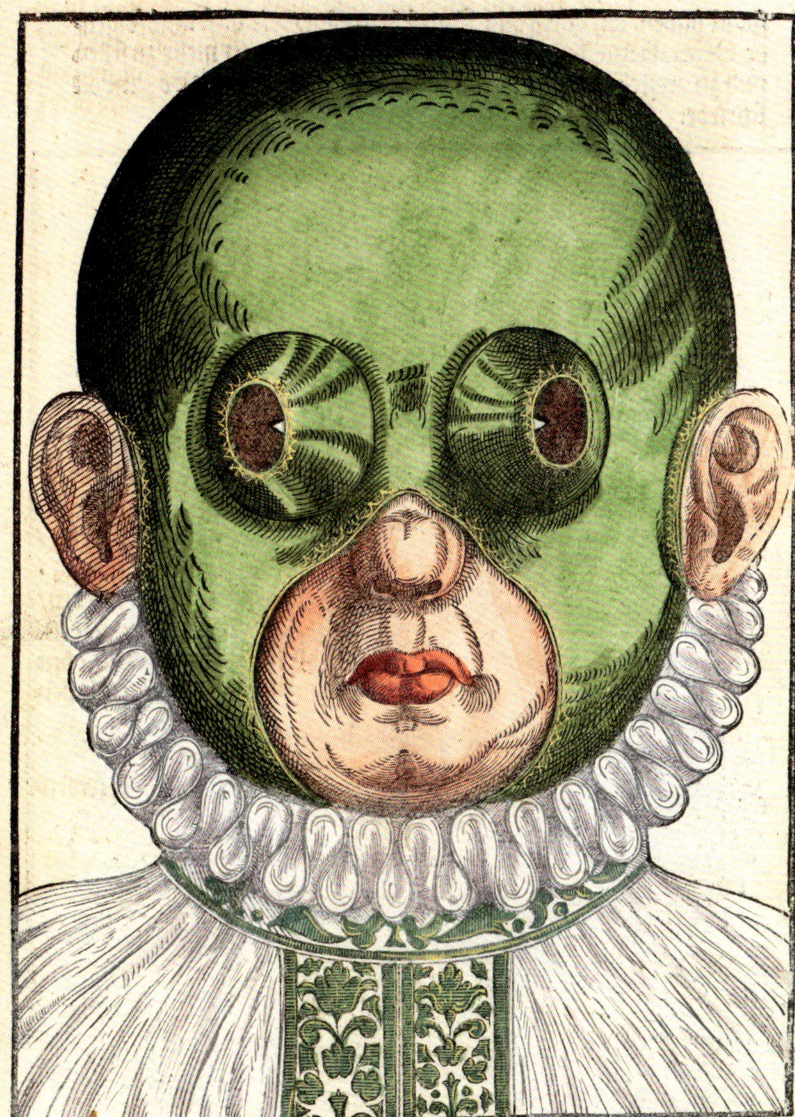

Verwendet aber ein Kind die Augen auswarts gegen den
Ohren oder Schläffen / so mus man dem Kinde auch eine sonder-
liche Kappe oder Kugel machen / dieser gestalt / das sie fornen lang
hienaus gehe / als ein Sturmhut / die sol dafornen eine lengliche
C iiij   spalte

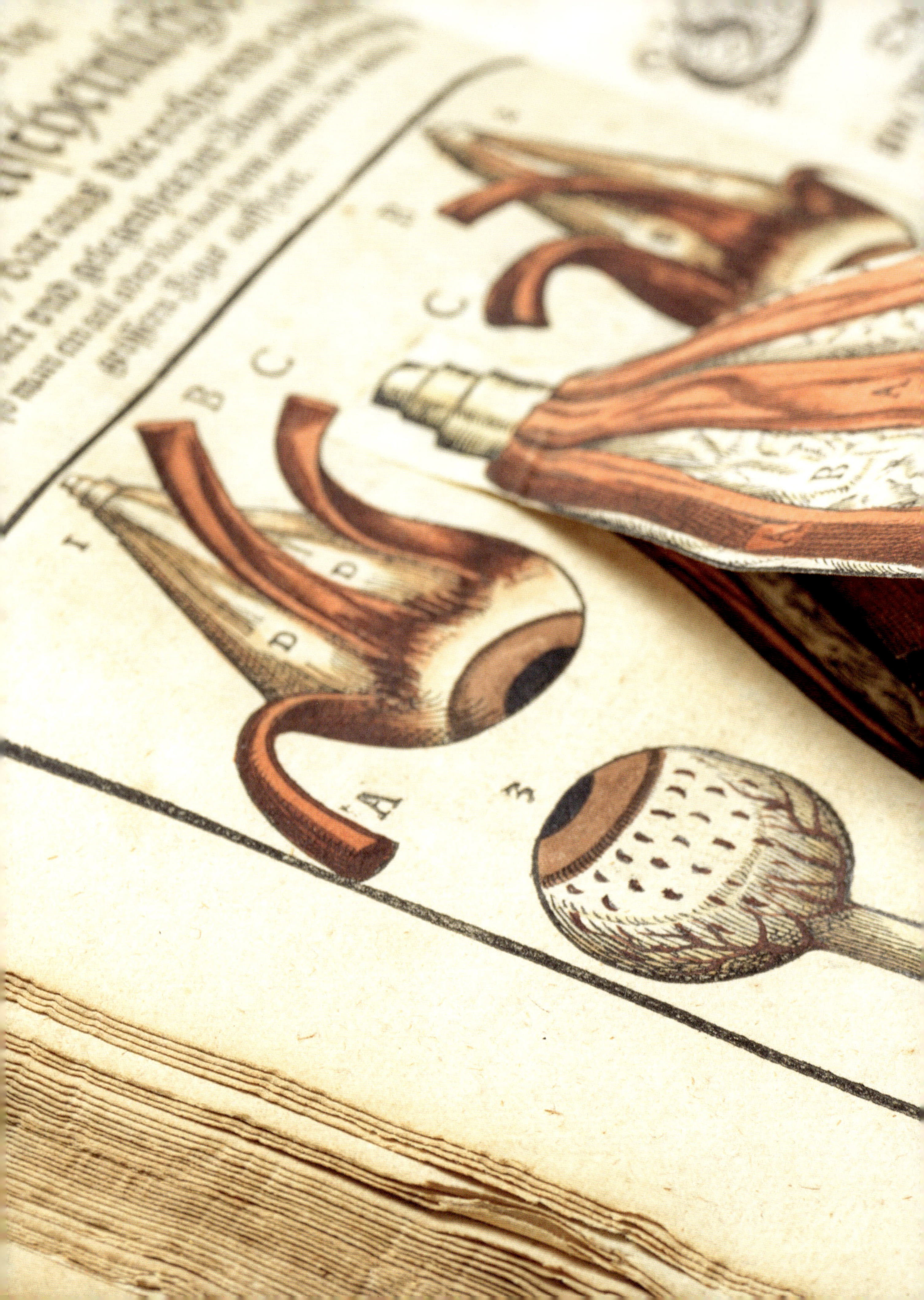
B
C
C
D
D
A
I

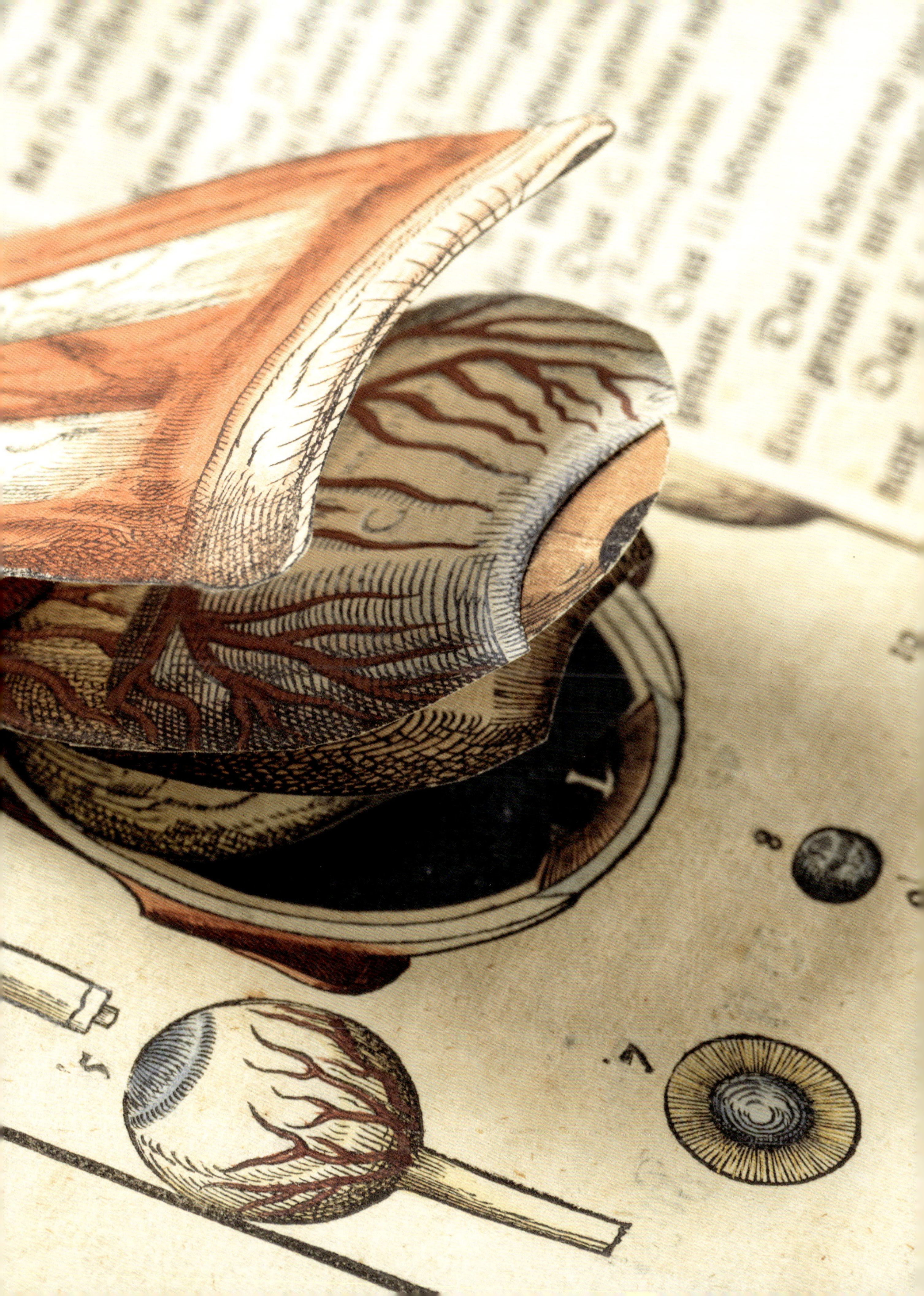
L
8
7

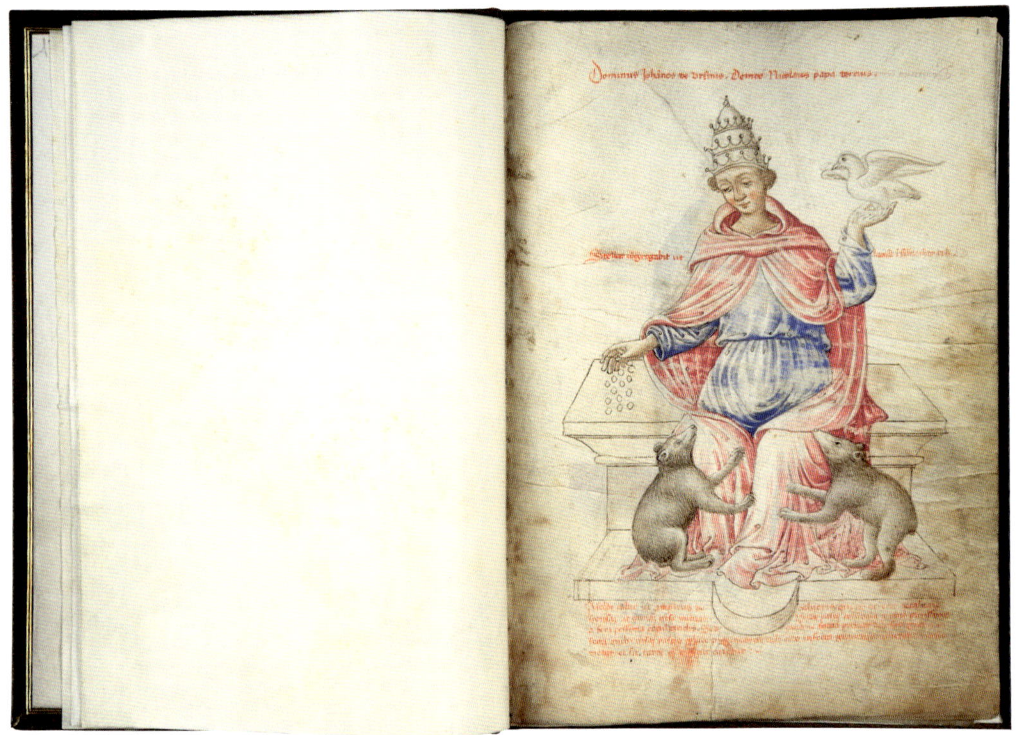

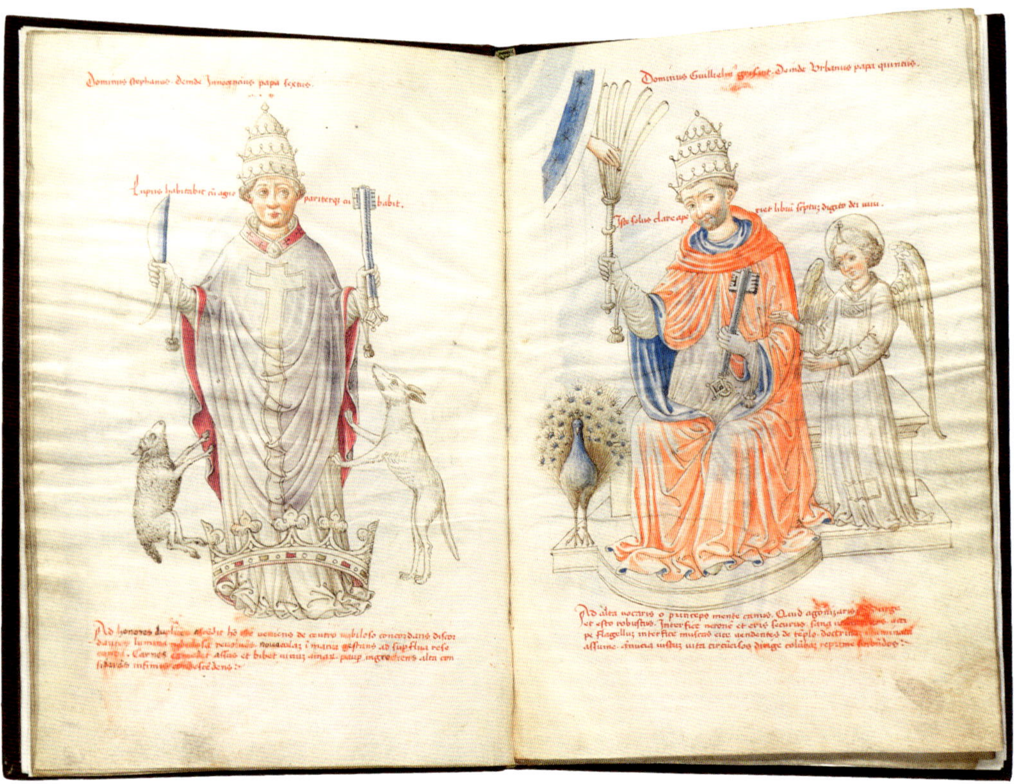

Pseudo-Joachim di Fiore
*Vaticinia sive prophetiae et imagines
summorum pontificum,* 1447–1464
Illuminated manuscript on vellum
9 ⅝ × 6 ⅞ inches | 24.4 × 17.5 cm

Dominus Petrus Rogerij dictus Clemens papa sextus

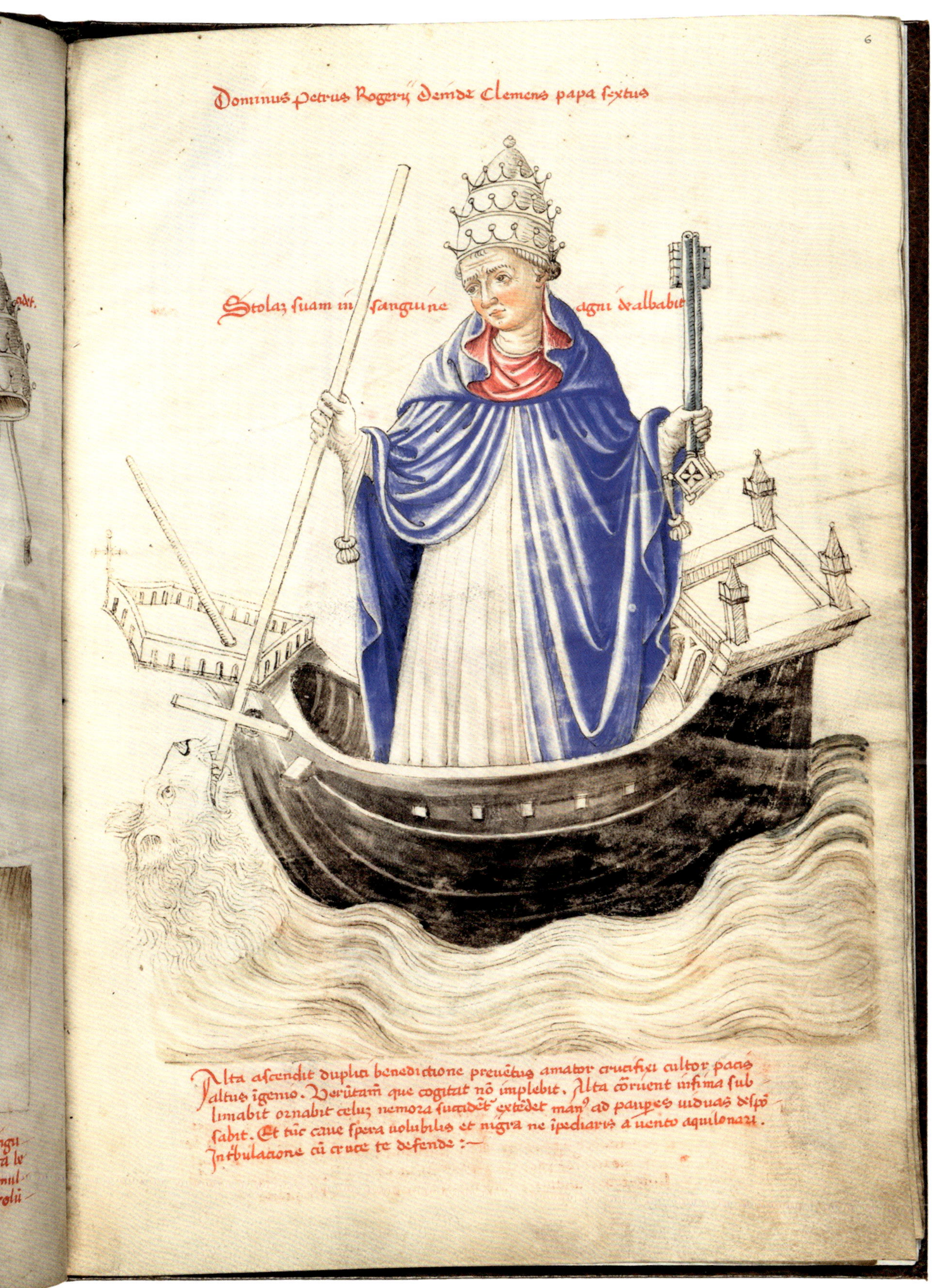

Alta ascendit duplici benedictione preuentus amator crucifixi cultor pacis
saltus ingenio. Veritatem que cogitat non implebit. Alta corruent infima sub
limabit ornabit celum nemora succidet extendet manum ad pauperes uiduas dispo
sabit. Et tunc caue spera uolubilis et nigra ne ipediaris a uento aquilonari.
In tribulatione cum cruce te defende :—

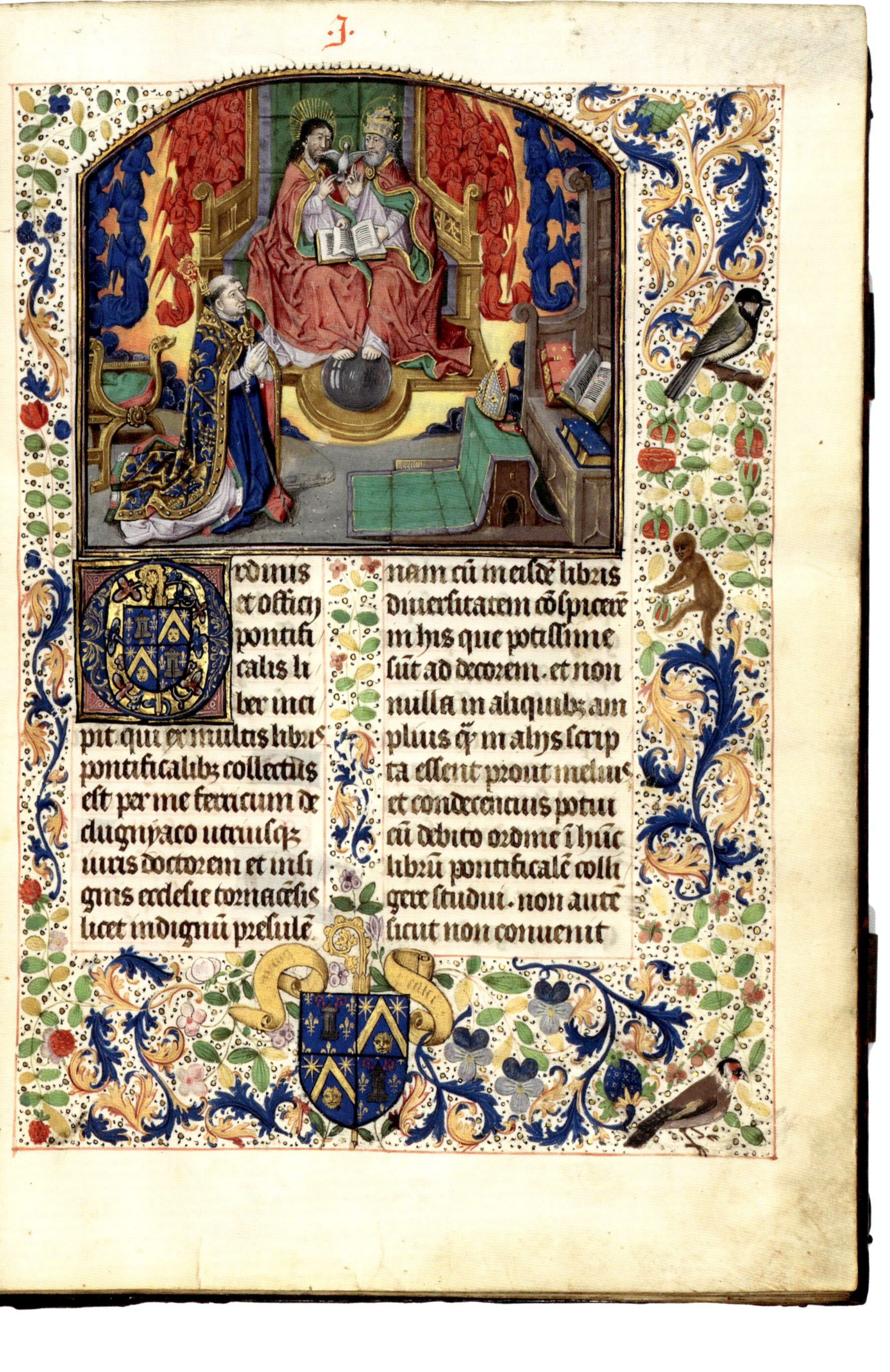

rdinis et officij pontificalis liber incipit qui ex multis libris pontificalibz collectus est per me fredericum de dugnyaco utriusqz iuris doctorem et insignis ecclesie tornacensis licet indignum presule

nam cum in eisde libris diuersitatem cospicere in his que potissime sut ad decorem. et non nulla in aliquibz amplius qz in alijs scripta essent prout melius et condecencius potui cum debito ordine i hunc libru pontificale colligere studui. non aute sicut non conuenit

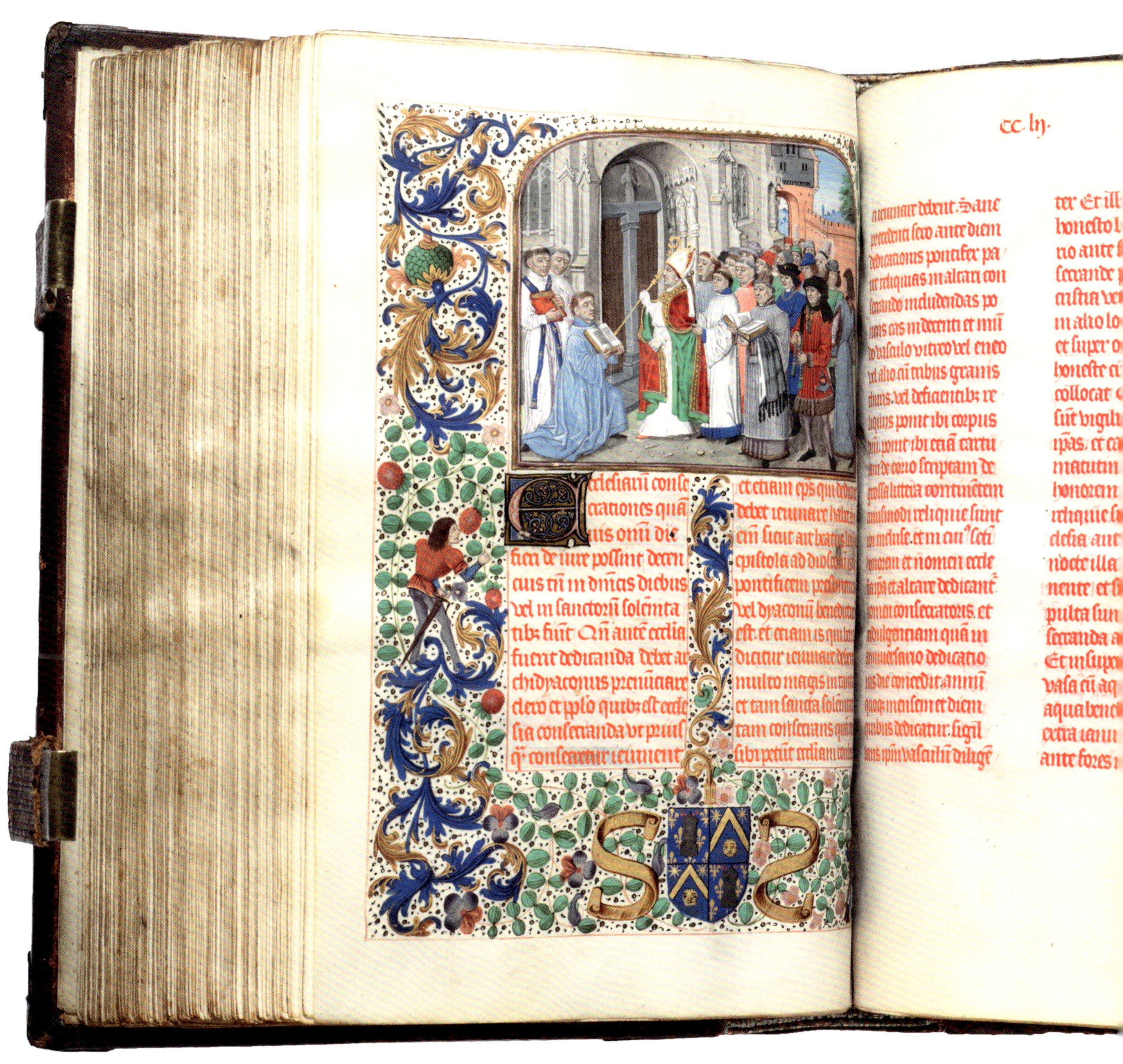

Loyset Liédet and Lieven van Lathem
The Pontifical of Ferry de Clugny,
Bishop of Tournai, 1475–1476
Illuminated manuscript on vellum
12 × 8 ⅞ inches | 30.5 × 22.5 cm

tia minori ipfi d e, per VIII . tertij Euclid . Et hæc quidem per
eccentri eccentrum fic demonftrantur . Per epicyclij quoq; epi
cyclum hoc modo. Sit mundo ac foli homocentrus a b, & a cb
diameter, in qua fumma abfis contingat. Et facto in a centro
epicyclus defcribatur d e, ac rurfus in d centro epicylium f g, in
quo terra uerfetur, omnia'q; in eodem plano zodiaci . Sitq; epicycli primi motus in fuccedetia , ac annuus ferè, fe cundi quoque hoc e d, fimiliter annuus, fed in præcedentia, ambo rumq; ad a c lineam pa res fint reuolutiones. Rurfus centrum terræ ex fin præcedentia a dat partim per ipfi d. Ex hoc manifeftum ef quòd cum terra fuer in f maximum effic Solis apogeum, in g m nimum in medijs au tem circumferentijs ip

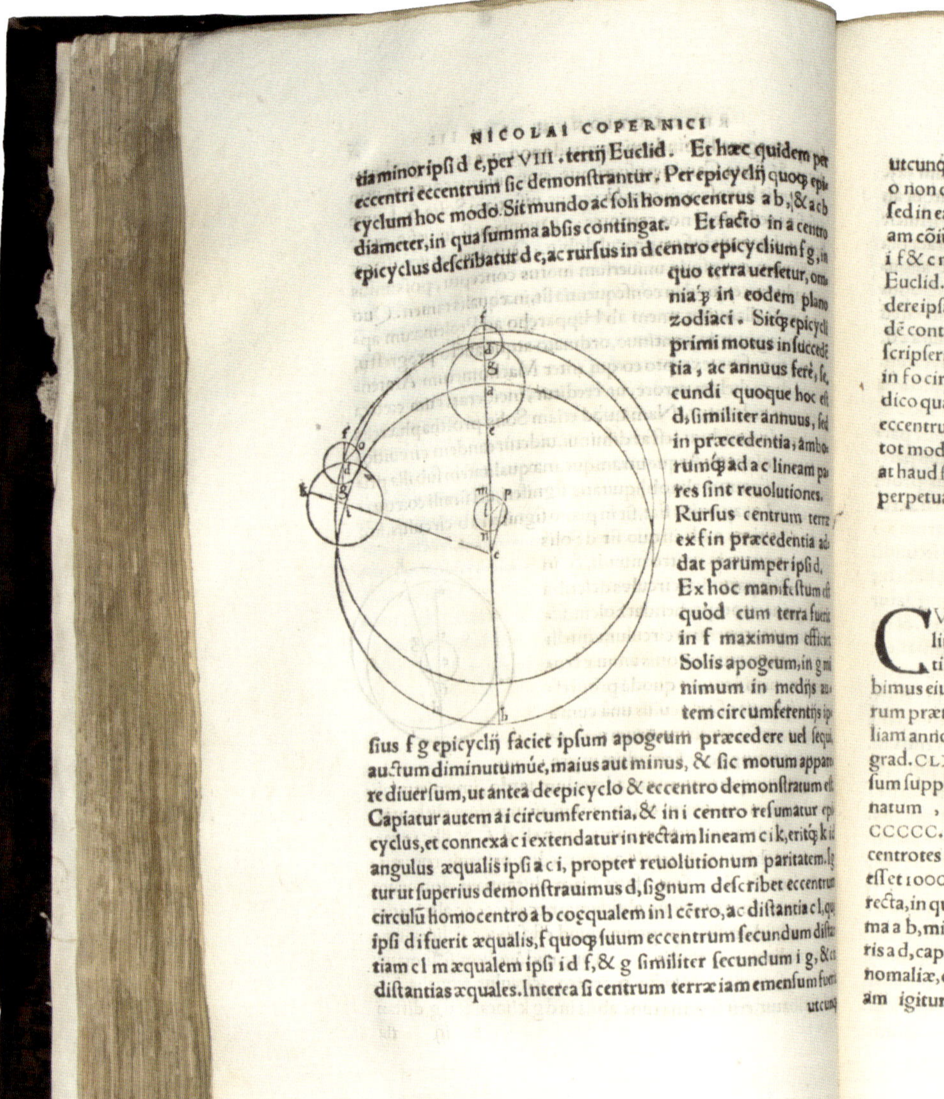

fius f g epicyclij faciet ipfum apogeum præcedere uel fequ
auctum diminutumue, maius aut minus, & fic motum appa
re diuerfum, ut antea de epicyclo & eccentro demonftratum ef
Capiatur autem a i circumferentia, & in i centro refumatur ep
cyclus, et connexa c i extendatur in rectam lineam c i k, eritq; i
angulus æqualis ipfi a c i, propter reuolutionum paritatem. Ig
tur ut fuperius demonftrauimus d, fignum defcribet eccentr
circulù homocentro a b coæqualem in l cêtro, ac diftantia c l, qu
ipfi d i fuerit æqualis, f quoq; fuum eccentrum fecundum diftan
tiam c l m æqualem ipfi id f, & g fimiliter fecundum i g, & c
diftantias æquales. Interea fi centrum terræ iam emenfum fuer
utcunq

utcunq; f o circumferentiam fecundi ac fui epicyclij, iam ipfum
o non defcribet eccentrum, cui centrum in a c linea contingat,
fed in ea quæ ipfi d o parallelus fuerit, qualis eft l p. Quod fic eti
am coïugantur o i, & c p, erüt & ipfæ æquales, minores aüt ipfis
i f & c m, & angulus d i o angulo l c p æqualis, per VIII . primi
Euclid. & pro tanto uidebitur Solis apogeum in c p linea præce
dere ipfam a Hinc etiam manifeftu eft, per eccentr epicyclum i
dê contingere. Quoniam in præexiftente folo eccentro, quem de
fcripferit d epicyclium circa l centrum, centrum terræ uoluatur
in f o circumferentia prædictis conditionibus, hoc eft, plus mo
dico quàm fuerit annua reuolutio. Superinducet enim alterum
eccentrum priori circa p centrü, accidentq; prorfus eadem. Cüq;
tot modi ad eundem numerum fefe conferant, quis locum habe
at haud facile dixerim, nifi quòd illa numerorum ac apparentiü
perpetua confonantia credere cogit eorum effe aliquem.

Quanta fit fecunda Solaris inæqualitatis
differentia.   Cap.   XXI.

CVm igitur iam uifum fuerit, quòd ifta fecunda inæqua
litas primam ac fimplicem illam anomaliam obliquita
tis figniferi, uel eius fimilitudinem fequatur, certas habe
bimus eius differentias, fi non obftiterit error aliquis obferuato
rum præteritorum. Habebimus enim ipfam fimplicem anoma
liam anno Chrifti M.CCCCC.XV. fecundum numerationem
grad. CLXV. fcrup. XXXIX. ferè, et eius principium facta retror
fum fupputatione fexaginta quatuor ferè annis ante Chriftum
natum , à quo tempore ad nos ufque colliguntur anni M.
CCCCC.LXXX. illius autem principij inuenta eft à nobis ec
centrotes maxima partium 417 . quarum quæ ex centro orbis
effet 10000. noftra uero ut oftenfum eft 323 . Sit iam a b linea
recta, in qua b fuerit Sol & mundi centrum. Eccentrotes maxi
ma a b, minima b d, defcriptiq; parui circuli, cuius dimetiens fue
ris a d, capiatur a c circumferentia pro modo primæ fimplicis a
nomaliæ, quæ erat partium CLXV. fcrup. XXXIX. Quoni
am igitur data eft a b partium 417 . quæ in principio fimpli
cis anô

An vierdē tag sprach got. Es sollē liechter in dē firmamēt des himels werdē vn̄ dē tag vn̄ die nacht teilē. vn̄ zu zaichen. vnd zeiten vnd tagē vnd iarē sein. das sie scheinen in dē firmament des himels vn̄ erlewchten die erdē. vnd es ist also geschehen. vn̄ got hat gemacht zway grosse liecht. ein grössers liecht vorzesen dē tag. vn̄ ein kleiners liecht vorzesein d naht. vn̄ die stern zetailen das liecht. vn̄ die finsternuß. Moyses gedenckt erstlich d him̄ lischen ding die got gesetzt hat in dē firmament zescheinē an dē himel. vn̄ zeerlewchtē die erdē. als die sunnē. dē mōd vnd die stern. mit dē d oberteil d werlt geziert wirdt. wie die erde mit dē dingē die in ir werdē. dan̄ nach dē er vō d natur des firmaments geredt het. so gepürt ime nachuolgēd von dē werckē des gestirns vnd vō irem ampt zesagē mit erklerung. zu welcherlay vbun̄z vnd geprauch sie gestifft vnd zu was würckung sie vō got gesand seyn. Der himlischem leiplichen ding sind zwu offenbar wurckung in die werlt. nemlich die bewegnus vn̄ die erlewchtūg. So sind d bewegnus zwu. Eine d gātzē werlt do mit d himel vn̄ die spera des lufts vn̄ feürs in. xxiiij. stūdē durch den gantzen krais d werlt mit volkōnem vmblawff bewegt werdē. Die ander bewegnus ist des gestirns. vn̄ ist aigen. vilfeltig vnd mācherlay. vnder den selbē ist die bewegnus d sunnē die fürnamst. dan̄ die sun̄ vmblawfft in xij. monaten dē zirckel aller zaichē. die sun̄ macht dē tag. so macht d lawff d sunnen durch dē selbē zirckel ein iar. Die andern bewegnussen des gestirns werdē in mancherlay zwischēfallēder zeit verbracht. Darūmb garschickerlich hat vns moyses kürtzlich diser ding aller vermanet sprechende. das die gestirn in dem firmament gesetzt sein zu ta̍ gen. iaren vnd zeitten. dar zu hat er auch gar lawter angezaigt die andern würckūg der gestirne. die ist die erlewch tūg. so er sagt das die gesetzt seyē zescheinē an̄ hymel vnd zeerlewchten die erde. darūmb zu solchen dinstperkeiten sind die leib des monds. der sunnē vnd d sternē außgetailt. vnd wiewol die sun̄ die im tag aufgeet einig allain ist ye doch ist sie ein wars liecht volkūner völligkeit. die mit fürderlichster wirm vn̄ allerclarstē schein alle ding erlewch̄ tet. dan̄ wiewol man vnzalich sterne schimern vn̄ glētzē sihet. nach dē sie aber doch mit völlige vn̄ feste liecht sind. so raichen sie kain wirm vō ime vn̄ müge auch mit irer menig die finsternus nicht vberwinden. darūmb so werdē zway fürname ding gefundē die mancherlay vnd aneinander widerwertigen gewalt habē. nēlich wirm vn̄ feüch̄ igkeit die got wunderperlich zu auffenthaltung vnd geperung aller ding erdacht hat.   Hie bey werē gar hohfra̍ ge zefiren vnd vō yder ein rechts buch zemachen wie vnd welcher maß dise gestirne in dē firmament werē. auch welche geschöpff in irem adel vnd wirde die andern vbertreffen vn̄ vō verrer art. aigenschafft. wurckung vn̄ na̍ tur des gestirns. auch vō den ihenen die sich darauß verkundung künstiger ding gepiauchen. so wil doch weder stat noch zeit gedulden lenger do von zeschreyben.

Hartmann Schedel
Das Buch der Chroniken und Geschichton, 1493
Book
18 ⅝ × 12 ⅝ inches | 47.3 × 32.1 cm

Agnes Martin
Untitled, 2003
Acrylic and graphite on canvas
60 × 60 inches | 152.4 × 152.4 cm

Mickey Cartin and David Leiber

A Conversation about Collecting Things

David Leiber I was reading Steve Holmes's essay last night, and he describes you as a boy collecting stamps and cards, and your obsession with baseball and statistics, and I feel like you're every bit as interested in sports now as you were then.

Mickey Cartin I go to MLB.com every day for about thirty minutes to make sure I'm up-to-date.

DL And you are every bit as interested in art as you are in sports. I find this notion of statistics in relation to your interest in artists and their systems of knowledge fascinating. You're drawn to statistics about sports and athletes just as you're drawn to biographical details about living artists, artists you know or not, and you enjoy that.

MC Well, it's more about their personalities than it is about their statistics. So I enjoy it but it's also a curse. I often can't go to sleep at night if I haven't gotten close to answering every question that remains in my mind from the day. I've been like that since I was a child.

DL What I also like about Steve's essay is that he talks about your endless quest for knowledge, but also your acceptance of the fact that you'll never know everything. There's the search for an encyclopedic grasp of things but then also knowing the absurdity of that, and you embrace all these contradictions in the artists you collect or in the whole idea of a collection, frankly.

MC You just said something I like, that I've accepted that I can't know everything.

DL I think you're a good reader, a good listener, you like to do homework on whatever you're interested in, though it's not even homework, it's a pleasure. But then you're also an instinctive, intuitive person. There is this notion of knowledge, research, and, at the same time, a gut feeling about things. I've known you for a long time and I always

know when you want something. If I've shown you a work, it's pretty clear you have an intuitive sense as to whether it is for you.

MC I'm mostly curious about ideas, which in the beginning often take a quite amorphous form in my head. I'm a very slow reader, so I make notes as I read, and I go back regularly and reread them.

DL Yes, we've talked about that, that you're often reading multiple texts or documents. Here's an observation about your loft and the architecture: You were very involved in the design with the architect, which leads to a more complicated question, so just bear with me.

MC Sure.

DL When I am in your loft, there is an incredible sense of horizontal lines, and a kind of linearity running between the meandering bookshelves, the curving walls, and how you also install art on the shelves, leaning the pictures. You make groups of certain artists, such as five Forrest Bess works in a line, or three Morandis in a line, and there is this sense of almost reading from left to right or right to left. Text is this beautiful notion that connects all the things you collect, the importance of the printed word, this practice of reading.

I don't know if this was intentional when you were discussing this in the design with the architect Ben van Berkel, but there is a relationship between architecture and the word that manifests itself in the way you present and live with the objects in your collection. What do you think of that?

MC I guess this makes sense to me, as you were saying it. Reading was always a struggle, as I mentioned before, and remains that way, but looking at objects and the questions that come to me immediately as I'm looking at them, and the answers that sometimes take months or years or more to land on, is really appealing to me, really exciting. I'm also interested in the work of artists whose visual interpretation of their ideas sometimes includes words, notations, or other explanations of what they are thinking when they are working, as a way of completing the work. Maybe that is some sort of vague answer to your question.

> **DL**   I think you particularly like small-scale works, where you don't have to stand across the room to take them in, but where you're putting yourself right in front of the object. The works might involve a lot of detail, too, like, as you say, small-scale text. That's not to say that a Morandi, from across the room, wouldn't reveal its structure, but you do gravitate toward smaller-scale objects.

MC   Morandi's pictures, small, yes, are complete by themselves, but I don't remember ever seeing one where there was a written word, apart from the artist's signature, which is often prominent in the image. At first, Morandi's paintings are confounding. They start off with a sense of mystery. But if you see enough of them and think about them enough, you can be guided by the enigma of his biography, and then those pictures complete themselves.

And then there is an artist like Alfred Jensen. Or maybe Adolf Wölfli is one of the best examples, where there are no works without equations or sentences or even jumbled words that require more interpretation. In the case of Wölfli, on the back of each of some twenty-five hundred works, including drawings with musical notations, is dozens of lines of autobiographical text. There is evidence of some unsettling, incomplete angst that really made me curious from the beginning, and still does. I visited the Adolf Wölfli Stiftung in Bern and got to see a couple hundred of these drawings in books that he assembled himself during his lifetime. In the end, the text is often nonsensical, and the arithmetic notation does not cohere and the pictures barely do. At some point, I realized I would never really be able to figure out what was up with him, and that could have been at the point when I recognized that he might not have made sense to himself either. But what struck me was his passion and the struggle with the continuity of every day, in a small cell in a psychiatric hospital, being given paper and colored pencils, sitting there on the floor, and making these things. From the first work of his I saw, I realized there was some great challenge there that triggered my curiosity. The need to know is common to human beings. We're all curious. But for me, it's what I meant when I said it has become a curse, a kind of neurotic obsession.

> **DL**   Right. Let me read something that I think was the kernel of Steve's text that I quite like and maybe you can comment. He talks about your omnivorous curiosity and that you're not really interested in what other people think about what you're doing. He writes: "All that mattered was how each object made Cartin feel, how it moved him in some primal way, how it prompted him to think. This was a collection devoid of any intentional organizing principles. There were no art advisers, because there was nothing for them to do."

MC   Excellent.

> **DL**   No disagreement there.

MC   No.

> **DL**   So, let's talk about Hartford, where you grew up, and the impact of the Wadsworth Atheneum, which you went to as a child. It has this amazing collection. Chick Austin, the legendary director, left quite a legacy and you've talked about how he would make a trip to Europe in the late 1930s and come back with a Mondrian, a Caravaggio, a Balthus, and a de Chirico. These were all prized as exceptional

    Mickey Cartin and David Leiber

acquisitions, purchased all at the same time, and he wasn't making hierarchical distinctions between them.

MC   Well, I can stop you just for a second—if you could keep your train of thought—I don't want to forget this: they weren't all prized acquisitions.

DL   Sure, they were probably criticized.

MC   Yes, some of them. His father-in-law was the chairman of the board, which presented a number of problems for him. One of the greatest was that some of the things he brought back were seen by many at the time as laughable. He returned from one trip with both Caravaggio's *Saint Francis of Assisi in Ecstasy* and a 1935 Mondrian grid painting. No one knew what he was doing.

DL   Changing subjects, let me ask you, in your mind, is there such a thing as an ethics to collecting?

MC   There are certain behaviors you might try to abide by if you're a thoughtful person, if that's what you mean. The obvious norms are you pay your bills and you honor your obligations. Then there's greed and then there's being considerate—things I might have had some internal battles with at times—and then there's also something I try to resist, which is sitting in judgment of other peoples' behavior toward other human beings. On the other hand, there is great fun in disagreeing with people over aesthetic matters.

DL   I ask because collectors can be kind, considerate, thoughtful people, but then there are moments when they have to be opportunistic and pounce, and you do that, like the best of them.

MC   I often find some kind of great, penetrating excitement when I see something for the first time, and I want to hold on to that feeling by acquiring the work that ignited it. So when you say "pounce," it's more that I've already looked

and I already know what I want. And in almost every case, the things I've been excited by are still around me.

DL   Some of the most interesting works for you are also among the first works you bought. The John Kane self-portrait, *Seen in the Mirror* [p. 146], was the first artwork that you bought some forty years ago. It is, in a way, one of the most significant purchases you've made, and not only because it was the first.

MC   Kane was a romantic, down-and-out kind of character. I didn't know him; he died in the mid-1930s. He was a professional but unsuccessful fighter, a committed loser. He worked on railroads, in steel mills, and in coal mines. He lost a leg in a train accident in 1891 and then began painting. I still feel the same way about him and his work that I did nearly forty years ago. Some collectors may be dismissive of their early interest in art, and there's nothing wrong with that. They evolve and maybe they go on to do other things that are still exciting to them, which in the end is what this is mostly about, right? Like, what switches you on? When you look at something, you either don't get it and walk right by it, or you stop and you think about it. You might become sort of struck or bowled over by it. That's not unusual. Isn't that the way it is?

DL   People evolve, definitely. But it seems like we're dodging something talking about collecting at this scale if we don't also talk about money. It's not like the old days, like when the Vogels were able to collect on a librarian's or civil servant's salary, paying off the artists on a monthly basis over many years.

MC   Yeah, Herb Vogel was a postal clerk, and I think Dorothy was a librarian.

DL   Exactly. I love going to the National Gallery, in DC, and seeing their names up on the wall, along with the Havemeyers and the Mellons and some of the other barons.

MC   Well said. By the way, if it weren't for the Havemeyers there would never have been Jack Tilton.

> **DL**   When the Vogels started collecting, they took the bus everywhere—they would never take a taxi or go out to dinner. They would make their five-dollar-a-month payment to Frank Stella. It's an amazing story that doesn't exist anymore.

MC   Yes. And I can stop you for one second: they had excellent art consultants.

> **DL**   The artists!

MC   Like Sol LeWitt and Mel Bochner.

> **DL**   It's exemplary. In your case, obviously you started collecting when you had a little bit of means. I hate to use the expression "disposable income" . . .

MC   I didn't have any disposable income. When I bought that first painting, I paid it off over eighteen months. I didn't buy it from a dealer but from a friend who lived in Hartford.

> **DL**   Okay. Were there periods when you felt that it was really a stretch but you still pushed yourself to buy something? Or maybe there was a moment when you sold your business and there were suddenly more possibilities to collect different things and to collect more in-depth. Were there defining moments, as there always are?

MC   Well, I was very curious about Jackson Pollock, mostly about his biography, and before I had even bought my first picture, the Kane self-portrait, I went to visit Pollock's studio in— what's that neighborhood of East Hampton?

> **DL**   Springs?

MC   Right. He was a fascinating character. I just didn't understand the drip paintings, but I admired him quite a bit as a true eccentric, a kind of barroom brawler. I never once thought about buying one of his paintings, though, because by the time I figured out who he was, I realized I'd never be able to afford one.

> **DL**   Let's say we're talking about an artist, living or deceased, who is a new discovery to you. You strike me as someone who would prefer that no one else was interested in the work, so that you could have the best possible choice, without competition from other collectors. Whereas some collectors might be eager to know how much interest or competition there is from other collectors and where they stand. Maybe I'm wrong, but something I've noticed about you is that you would much rather buy the work you want regardless of who else is interested.

MC   I think that's true. There is always plenty of art if you're curious. In my experience, if you keep looking, it won't be long before you find the next thing that you can't get out of your head.

> **DL**   Right.

MC   It is also true that I don't really care if other people are interested in the work if I've already convinced myself of it. This could sound cynical, but I don't think I've ever really cared. I have had fun raising questions about why people find an interest in something that I just can't comprehend. And then, on occasion, I have changed my mind about some of those artists. But for the most part, for better or worse, the way I feel in the first half hour or so of seeing a work is how I feel throughout the following decades.

> **DL**   Yes. And when something doesn't work out or if you need to wait—or if a work is not available, like when you first visited Sidney Janis and wanted to buy a Morris Hirshfield—it takes patience. The virtue of

patience is that there is this sense of kismet, that things will work out, and maybe an opportunity presents itself later, and it's actually a better opportunity. I think that's probably true in many cases for you and why you probably don't have any regrets about things you didn't buy—

MC   I have regrets about things that I was very attracted to but that I couldn't afford, simple as that. But this wasn't my whole life. I had other things going on that took up a lot of my time and resources. I did spend a lot of time at it, though. I took a trip to New York every week for many years. So it was important to me.

> **DL**   Right. That's when we met. I remember it well—it was sometime in the '90s. You came into Sperone Westwater and you were looking at a Guillermo Kuitca. Or maybe we met through Tom Sachs. . . .

MC   I remember coming to see you the first time we met, and it was about Kuitca.

> **DL**   And you were with James Rondeau.

MC   That's right, I was. He is brilliant. He was still in graduate school at Williams College then, working in Hartford at the Wadsworth a few days a week.

> **DL**   And when you moved to New York, which was in the early 2000s, I think that was also more or less the time you started to really go to the TEFAF art fair in Maastricht. You got almost more excited about that fair than Art Basel.

MC   Who wouldn't?

> **DL**   Why did a fair like Maastricht interest you more than Art Basel?

MC   I would say mainly because I was learning about things that I didn't know existed and was

finding things I didn't think I could actually see at a fair. I was seeing things for the first time, such as early editions of books I had some vague previous knowledge of. I didn't know you could actually look at an early Albrecht Dürer book on perspective, for instance. Also there were paintings that fit the same description, names I'd read in art history books or seen in a museum, but at TEFAF they were for sale. I met some really interesting people there whom I connected with and whom I learned a lot from, just by going to visit them at the fair or in their homes or whatever. It was a remarkable, eye-opening experience.

> **DL**   I touched on the bookshelves and the architecture earlier in reference to the loft, but obviously the library is so important to you. You like having reference books around that you can dip in and out of.

MC   It's essential to me.

> **DL**   There are handmade books; there are books from the earliest period of printing, in the late fifteenth century; there are catalogues raisonnés; there are artists' books, such as the Alighiero Boetti or Sol LeWitt books. Then you also have collections of collectors' inventories, for example, which you're drawn to. I noticed you have a set of books from J. P. Morgan, one of a handful of copies of his own library inventory.

MC   I have a set of his collection catalogues of his bronzes, tapestries, paintings, and books. I think he spent an inconceivable amount of money to produce limited-edition sets of these catalogues so that he could make an impression on the other rich guys he was competing with, including Henry Clay Frick, Andrew Mellon, and Joseph Widener. Self-published collection catalogues interest me for a couple of reasons. One is that they show the unstoppable egos of these people in really graphic ways, which I find kind of exciting, if not also offensive, and the other is that they were really quite serious about this stuff. They weren't casual in any way about collecting.

DL How did the loft come to be?

MC I was working with the architect Ben van Berkel on a project in Hartford that never got off the ground. We became friends, and one day when we were flying from Amsterdam to New York, he said, "Why don't you build an apartment in New York? I'll work on it with you." It really excited me. He took out a notebook and made some sketches, which I still have, and that was the beginning of this project. It is a place that continues to inspire me. The library itself started out with a collection of art history reference books, and then it was really on a dare, which I proposed to myself, that I started learning about and buying other books, especially early printed books and manuscripts, because I didn't know anything about these things. The first illuminated manuscript I bought was commissioned by Ferry de Clugny in 1475, found its way to the library of Pope Sixtus IV, and then it was in the first group of books to enter the Apostolic Library at the Vatican in the sixteenth century. I don't know how I had the nerve to do it. The fact I could put this on my own library shelves—it was fascinating to me and still is.

DL When most people say they have a library, it's very focused. They might have just catalogues raisonnés or catalogues from gallery or museum shows of a particular artist. But yours has grown to include all kinds of illuminated manuscripts or other books that are filled with paintings, like the Augsburg *Book of Miracles* [pp. 106–107]. So I'm sure the presence of the library, even if you're not looking at these books all the time, is inspiring. I know for me, books can have unexpected value at certain moments—they can really move you forward as a collector and give you ideas. It's this very alive thing.

MC Well, it is. I've thought about this in the past—I don't know if we've ever talked about

this—but without printed materials about art, I have a feeling that people's interest wouldn't be as widespread as it is today.

DL For you, you're talking about?

MC Yes, but I'm thinking in general.

DL In our digital world, people think that the book has been replaced by digital culture, but I would say it has only made the printed word stronger, the library stronger, the neighborhood bookshop more interesting. There has been pushback. Look at the popularity of artists' books and book fairs, what Printed Matter has been doing. I learned from my brother Steven that a library is also a metaphor for a collector or for having a collection. It's not that you look at everything every day, or that you need to have everything around you all the time. But just knowing that you have a particular book, that you can reference it, that you can open it up and connect with it, is a very good feeling.

MC Yes! It's like a fascination. Right in front of me on my shelf right now are three Bob Dylan biographies next to one on Sigmund Freud, which is next to one on Joseph Duveen, one on Joe DiMaggio, and one on Kurt Cobain. Then, there's Ed Ruscha's *Stains* [pp. 94–95].

DL Exactly, and you bought a Boetti book from me, and the Ruscha from Steven.

MC Yes, and Steven was the rarest of unusual and rare birds. Is that a good way of saying that?

DL Tell me something more, we'll close with Steven. I love hearing about him.

MC Well, I remember we had a really nice dinner once in Venice and the thing that attracted me most to him was his irrepressible passion. If you asked him a question that he didn't want

 Mickey Cartin and David Leiber

to answer, he would just dismiss it. Am I right about that?

DL   Absolutely.

MC   Or, if you struck a chord, he could go on in whispers and a sort of change of cadence. He was just so expressive and had such passion, so that's what I meant about how rare he was. It was always clear to me that he wasn't dealing in artist ephemera and books for the money.

DL   Indeed. Very nice.

MC   So now when we finish this conversation, I'm going to spend a couple of hours rummaging through the library again.

Great care has been taken to credit all images and artworks correctly. In cases of errors or omissions, please contact the publisher so that corrections can be made in future editions.

Photography

Cover, pp. 27, 28–29, 30–31, 32–33, 34–35, 36–37, 38–39, 40–41, 42–43, 44–45, 54, 55, 66, 67, 68, 69, 71, 75, 77, 78, 79, 82, 83, 89, 90, 91, 102, 103, 109, 111, 114, 115, 117, 121, 123, 125, 126–127, 130, 131, 135, 138, 141, 146, 147, 148, 151, 153, 154, 155, 157, 158, 161, 162, 163, 166, 167: Maris Hutchinson

pp. 8–9, 47, 50, 51, 52, 53, 56–57, 63, 64–65, 70, 72–73, 74, 80, 84, 85, 86–87, 92–93, 94, 95, 98–99, 100, 101, 104–105, 112, 120, 124, 134, 136–137, 140, 168–169, 171, 174 (top), 175, 176: Kerry McFate

pp. 16–17, 97, 106, 107, 108, 119, 128, 129, 132, 142, 145, 159, 160, 164–165, 178: Courtesy Cartin Collection

p. 49: Dan Bradica

pp. 81, 113, 118, 122, 139, 150: Stephen Arnold

p. 88: © 2023 Museum of Fine Arts, Boston

p. 143: © Christie's Images Limited, 2023

p. 149: Courtesy Forum Gallery

pp. 170, 172–173, 174 (bottom), 177: Allison Chipak

p. 179: Courtesy Dr. Jörn Günther Rare Books, Basel

p. 181: Kerry McFate, courtesy Pace Gallery

Artworks

pp. 49, 50, 51: © 2023 The Josef and Anni Albers Foundation/Artists Rights Society (ARS), New York

p. 52: © 2023 Artists Rights Society (ARS), New York/ADAGP, Paris

pp. 54, 55: © Estate of Myron Stout. Courtesy Washburn Gallery

pp. 59–61: © One Million Years Foundation

p. 63: © Charles LeDray

p. 66: © Joe Coleman

p. 69: © 2023 Artists Rights Society (ARS), New York/SIAE, Rome

p. 70: © Cecilia Edefalk. Courtesy the artist and Gladstone Gallery

p. 71: © Robert Crumb, 1966

p. 77: © Henry Koerner Estate

pp. 78, 79: © The Estate of Algernon Cecil Newton RA

p. 83: © Lucas Arruda

p. 88: © Martin Puryear, courtesy Matthew Marks Gallery

p. 89: © Estate of Martín Ramírez

pp. 90, 91: © 2023 Artists Rights Society (ARS), New York/SIAE, Rome

pp. 94–95: © Ed Ruscha

p. 97: © Estate of Jean-Michel Basquiat. Licensed by Artestar, New York

p. 102: © 2023 Robert and Gail Rentzer for Estate of Morris Hirshfield/Licensed by VAGA at Artists Rights Society (ARS), New York

p. 103: © 2023 Artists Rights Society (ARS), New York

p. 111: © 2023 Tony Fitzpatrick

p. 112: © 2023 Artists Rights Society (ARS), New York/VG Bild-Kunst, Bonn

p. 114: © 2023 Estate of Paul Laffoley/Artists Rights Society (ARS), New York

p. 117: © 2023 Artists Rights Society (ARS), New York/ADAGP, Paris

p. 119: The Estate of Wallace Berman and Kohn Gallery, Los Angeles

pp. 124, 125: Courtesy Albert York Estate, Davis & Langdale Company

pp. 126–127: © 2023 Estate of Alfred Jensen/Artists Rights Society (ARS), New York

p. 128: © Fred Tomaselli 2023. Courtesy the artist and James Cohan, New York

p. 129: © Walton Ford. Courtesy the artist and Gagosian

p. 134: © Francis Alÿs

pp. 138, 139: © 2023 The Joseph and Robert Cornell Memorial Foundation/Licensed by VAGA at Artists Rights Society (ARS), New York

pp. 146, 147: © Estate of John Kane. Courtesy Galerie St. Etienne, New York

p. 149: © 2023 The Gregory Gillespie Trust

p. 157: © 2023 The LeWitt Estate/Artists Rights Society (ARS), New York

pp. 158, 159: © Tom Sachs

p. 160: © 2023 Dumbarton Arts, LLC/Licensed by VAGA at Artists Rights Society (ARS), New York

p. 161: Courtesy the artist and Garth Greenan Gallery, New York

p. 162: © 1992 Wes Mills

p. 163: Courtesy the artist and Sandra Gering Inc.

pp. 164–165: Courtesy the artist

p. 166: Courtesy the artist and Garth Greenan Gallery, New York

p. 167: © Andrew Sendor. Courtesy the artist and Sperone Westwater, New York

pp. 168–169: © Martin Wilner. Courtesy the artist and Hales, London and New York

p. 181: © Agnes Martin Foundation, New York/Artists Rights Society (ARS), New York

Published by David Zwirner Books
on the occasion of

**Seen in the Mirror: Things from
the Cartin Collection**
David Zwirner, 537 West 20th Street,
New York
November 4–December 18, 2021

Curated by Steven Holmes
and David Leiber

David Zwirner Books
520 West 20th Street
New York, New York 100011
+1 212 727 2070
davidzwirnerbooks.com

Editors: Elizabeth Gordon,
Steven Holmes
Editorial Coordinator: Jessica Palinski
Proofreader: Anna Drozda

Design: Practise (James Goggin)
Photography coordination:
Allison Chipak, Virginia Stroh
Production: Luke Chase, Jules Thomson
Color separations: VeronaLibri, Verona
Printer: VeronaLibri, Verona

Type: LL Geigy (Robert Huber,
Lineto, 2023)
Paper: Périgord, 170 gsm

Publication © 2023 David Zwirner
Books and the Cartin Collection

"An Intensity of Vision" © 2023
   Luke Syson
"Ceci n'est pas une collection"
   © 2023 Steven Holmes
"A Conversation about Collecting
   Things" © 2023 Mickey Cartin
   and David Leiber

Artwork and photography credits can
be found on page 191.

This publication does not include
reproductions of all works exhibited at
David Zwirner, New York, and works
on pages 49, 59–61, 70, 88, 97, 108,
111, 114, 119, 126–127, 128, 129, 132, 133,
142, 143, 145, 149, 159, 160, 161, 162,
163, 164–165, 166, 178, 179, and 181 were
not included in the exhibition.

Works on pages 50, 54, 55, 59–61, 63,
66, 71, 77, 83, 88, 90, 97, 108, 109, 112,
124, 125, 132, 133, 134, 139, 142, 143, 145,
154, 155, 157, 158, 178, 179, and 181 are
no longer part of the Cartin Collection.

All rights reserved. No part of this book
may be reproduced or transmitted in
any form or by any means, electronic or
mechanical, including photographing,
recording, or information storage
and retrieval, without prior permission
in writing from the publisher.

ISBN 978-1-64423-109-8

Library of Congress Control Number:
2023901465

Printed in Italy

Front and back cover, pp. 8–9, 16–17,
27–45: Views of the Cartin residence,
New York, 2021–2022

pp. 47, 56–57, 72–73, 86–87, 92–93,
98–99, 136–137: Installation views,
*Seen in the Mirror: Things from
the Cartin Collection*, David Zwirner,
New York, 2021

Steven Holmes is the curator of
the Cartin Collection.

David Leiber is a partner at David Zwirner.

Luke Syson is the director and
Marlay curator of the Fitzwilliam Museum,
Cambridge, England.